The
Mac Xcode™ 2
Book

The
Mac Xcode™ 2
Book

Michael E. Cohen and Dennis R. Cohen
Andy Ihnatko, Series Author

WILEY

Wiley Publishing, Inc.

The Mac Xcode™ 2 Book

Published by
Wiley Publishing, Inc.
111 River Street
Hoboken, NJ 07030-5774
www.wiley.com

Copyright © 2005 by Wiley Publishing, Inc., Indianapolis, Indiana
Published simultaneously in Canada

Library of Congress Control Number: 2005924604

ISBN-13: 978-0-7645-8411-4

ISBN-10: 0-7645-8411-1

Manufactured in the United States of America

10 9 8 7 6 5 4 3 2 1

1K/QX/QW/QV/IN

For general information on our other products and services please contact our Customer Care Department within the U.S. at 800-762-2974, outside the U.S. at 317-572-3993 or fax 317-572-4002.

For technical support please visit www.wiley.com/techsupport.

Wiley also publishes its books in a variety of electronic formats. Some content that appears in print may not be available in electronic books.

Trademarks: Wiley and the Wiley logo are trademarks or registered trademarks of John Wiley & Sons, Inc. and/or its affiliates in the United States and other countries, and may not be used without written permission. Mac Xcode is a trademark of Apple Computer, Inc. All other trademarks are the property of their respective owners. Wiley Publishing, Inc. is not associated with any product or vendor mentioned in this book.

For Lisa

— Michael Cohen

For Spenser, Michael, and the rest of the clan.

— Dennis Cohen

Credits

Acquisitions Editor
Michael Roney

Project Editor
Sarah Hellert

Technical Editor
Brad Black

Copy Editor
Kim Heusel

Editorial Manager
Robyn B. Siesky

Vice President & Executive Group Publisher
Richard Swadley

Vice President and Publisher
Barry Pruett

Project Coordinator
Maridee V. Ennis

Graphics and Production Specialists
Carrie A. Foster
Lauren Goddard
Denny Hager
Jennifer Heleine
Heather Pope
Amanda Spagnuolo

Quality Control Technicians
Susan Moritz
Joe Niesen
Dwight Ramsey

Proofreader
Laura L. Bowman

Indexer
Rebecca R. Plunkett

Cover Image
Anthony Bunyan

Foreword

I suppose that the first thing you ought to know about Xcode is that it's a work of pure evil, conceived and built with just one goal in mind: Bringing an end to my entire way of life and nudging me ever closer to that day when I'm in a line of work that centers around the question of whether a basket of fries is done yet.

There was once a time when a software developer could stride this landscape like a modern-day Colossus. Macintosh developers, in particular. If practically nobody amongst the general population knew how to write a working program, folks who could write *Macintosh* software were even rarer. You'd be more likely to encounter a good left-handed relief pitcher or a bass player who doesn't need to hold down a day job.

It was all just so gloriously complicated. First, you needed to know Pascal, a language that few people used. Then, you needed to learn how to write event-oriented code, and then onward to probing the arcana of the Macintosh toolbox. And then you were home-free; you just needed to find a way to buy about $1200 worth of development tools and documentation while still keeping the wolves and the student-loan officers from your door. And did I mention that in the *very* early days, you couldn't even *write* Mac software on an actual Mac? You needed to buy a Lisa, the Mac's predecessor.

All in all, this system was hugely successful, from my selfish point of view: Very few people decided to learn how to write Mac apps.

Oh, it was a golden age, my friends; as Mac developers, we had it all! Arrogance! We knew so much more than everyone else! Money! As contractors, we could charge a premium for our all-too-rare skills! Adulation! Mac users were so desperate for new software that we could release an app that did nothing more than display the correct time in the typeface of the user's choice, and we would be hailed like Apollo astronauts fresh from splashdown!

Software development was already getting too easy by the time that Xcode came along. It's just one of the final nails in our coffin. Now, any software developer can transition to Mac development fairly easily. Creating an app is largely a matter of filling in the blanks; Xcode does most of the heavy lifting for you, and you can create some relatively muscular apps by just filling in a few blanks with Cocoa. And you're free to use whatever language you like. If you want to write an entire suite of Microsoft Office–compatible apps using nothing but AppleScript, Xcode won't judge you; it'll just help you as much as it possibly can to achieve your (truly demented) dreams.

Foreword

So now that Xcode delivers a wedgie to those of us who don't want more people to write Mac software, Apple upgrades the experience to super atomic status by (a) giving it away for free, and (b) making it as egalitarian as a "real" software-development system can be. You can write a kick-butt image-editing app in Xcode from the ground up with the full intention of taking Photoshop down a peg or two. But if you're a network administrator who's spent the past five years building a collection of perl and python scripts that automate many of your routine daily tasks, Xcode can fulfill the simple goal of staple-gunning a user interface to your scripts. In short order, Xcode can take these command-line tools that only you, personally, can understand and operate and morph them into polished, professional, easy-to-operate utilities that thousands of users will happily pay you $40 for. And at its heart, this new app is still using your original script code.

And speaking of script code, is it *really* fair of Apple to give end-users such a clearly marked and gradual path towards becoming developers? The line between the two has definitely been smudged. Xcode loves AppleScript as much as users do — or should, in a perfect world — and moving from a scripter to an application developer is now just a question of increasing your knowledge and experience bit by bit, with very real rewards at every step of the way. You start by giving your script a real user interface and before long, you're adding features that you could never pull off in AppleScript's script editor alone.

This foreword is a bit curmudgeonly and for that, I apologize. I meant to get you all revved up about Xcode. That's easy. Five years ago, I wrote applications using three or four different development systems, depending on the scale and the nature of what I was trying to build. Nowadays, whether I'm banging something out in an hour or a year, Xcode is the only icon I need to click.

I suppose I should be happy that Xcode is doing wonderful things for the Mac OS. I am. Really. Xcode is helping non-programmers become programmers, non-Mac programmers get excited about adding Mac development to their box of skills, and it's helping existing Mac programmers produce better work faster and more often.

These are all good things. I shall no doubt have plenty of time to contemplate all this as I wait for the next basket of fries to be ready to pull out of the machine.

Andy Ihnatko
Series Author
Somewhere in Massachusetts

Preface

Here's where we explain why we wrote this book.

Money had something to do with it. Come on, would you devote the several months it takes to research, write, and illustrate a book like this for nothing? (Oh, you would? Well, our publisher would *love* you!)

But — and you really have to trust us on this — money wasn't the only reason we wrote this book (if you saw our contract, you'd *totally* know that money wasn't the only reason). The subject matter hooked us, too.

What most people don't seem to know (and, if they ever did know, they quickly filed the information in the part of the brain that's most like the back of our sock drawer) is that every copy of Mac OS X comes with a complete, incredibly powerful and mature set of software development goodies known as Xcode. Xcode has compilers. It has editors. And design tools. Examples. Documentation. Code libraries up the wazoo. It's the sort of software development setup that would ordinarily cost a developer hundreds and hundreds of dollars. And it all comes as a free bonus when you buy a new Mac or a copy of Mac OS X.

Oh, sure, the vast majority of Mac users don't ever need to know about Xcode. If most Mac owners never did anything with the Developer CD that comes with Mac OS X other than use it as a shiny coaster, they'd still have a rich, wonderful, and productive relationship with their Macs.

But what we're honestly surprised by is how many of our more techno-geeky friends and associates — and we mean "geeky" in the best and most complimentary sense here — responded "X-what?" when we told them we were writing a book about Xcode. Until we told them a little more about it. And then their eyes lit up and they said, "Cool."

We know there are a lot of people out there who dabble in code but who aren't professional software engineers. Some people code simply for fun, as a hobby. For them, Xcode is hobbyist heaven. Then there are those people who have to sling a bit of code now and then as part of their jobs, even though they're not really programmers. For them, Xcode is a convenient and surprisingly easy-to-use way to crank out the occasional tool or utility. Then there are the students who are just getting into the black art that's been euphemistically (mis?)named Computer Science. For them, Xcode is like having a 24-hour technology lab living on their laptops.

Preface

And then there are the professional software engineers. Xcode is for them, too, and in spades. Because, although it is approachable and usable by even the most dewy-eyed novice, Xcode is no compromised, feature-poor, dumbed-down toy version of a programming environment. It's the real deal, built upon the work of literally thousands of programmers over the course of several decades and sporting the latest refinements in software development methodology. It's the same set of tools that Apple uses to build Mac OS X, and you have to admit that that's a pretty sophisticated and demanding bit of coding.

And, like we said, Xcode 2 comes free in every package of Tiger.

If you have never written, read, or looked at a line of code, you might still find some value in this book, and you might even end up wanting to learn how to code — but this book is *not* meant to teach you programming, nor does it even attempt to do so: You're going to have to pick that skill up some other way. But if you *do* know something about programming, and you happen to have a Mac (or can lay your hands on one), this book shows you how to take full advantage of Apple's Xcode software development environment.

Although we've worked as professional software engineers in the past, we haven't done so in years, and, frankly, we've never missed it all that much — hobbyist programming, working on what we want to work on rather than what a Dilbertian pointy-haired boss mandates is much more satisfying. However, after spending the last few months putting Xcode through its paces, we've started having these little fantasies again about writing the totally killer app and attaining geek glory.

It's a sweet dream. We thought we'd share it with you.

Elements Used in this Book

So, how to get you started? First, let's introduce you to the unique structure of the book that you hold in your hands. There are a couple of book elements that you need to know about.

Sidebars

You'll notice these sidebars scattered here and there throughout the pages of the book. Sidebars are where we take the opportunity to digress or illuminate. We share information that might enhance your understanding of the topic at hand, that add new perspective, or that we just plain find interesting.

Ideally, the effect of these sidebars will be like the "commentary track" you'd find on a good DVD of a great movie. Possibly it's like having some idiot in the audience yelling at the screen while you're trying to enjoy *Vertigo*. Hard to tell. Our hopes are high, and frankly, you might as well just grin and bear it because there really isn't much you can do about it at this point.

A BOOK YOU SHOULD BUY AFTER BUYING THIS ONE

Actually, Andy got the idea from Martin Gardner's *The Annotated Alice,* in which the complete text of Lewis Carroll's classic is accompanied by sidebars that explain just exactly what the guy was talking about. You know, on the off-chance that you're not aware that mercurous nitrate was a key chemical used in the manufacture of felt, and hatmakers often suffered from mercury poisoning and exhibited psychotic behavior.

The book's still in print and led to a whole line of "annotated" classics (in fact, Michael helped design and program the first electronic edition of *The Annotated Alice*). Definitely worth a look.

Though we suppose you *could* just put this book back on the shelf and spend the dough on Roger Ebert's *Movie Yearbook* instead. Hmm. That honestly never occurred to us. Well, okay, the man has a Pulitzer and everything, but did he ever teach you how to build a word processor without writing a single line of code? Just don't do anything rash; that's all we ask.

Notes

And then there are those comments that we inserted because we're undisciplined and uncontrollable — and we need to comment on the discussion at hand. Right now. With sidebars, there's sort of an implied warranty. If you read the sidebar, you'll probably learn something useful, but not essential. But Notes are mostly here because we have a hard time controlling our impulses. All we can promise is that each note certainly seemed like a good idea at the time, and our hearts were in the right place, absolutely.

 Note

See, as a writer, you soon learn that the most difficult part of the job is figuring out just how much caffeine you need to drink before sitting down at the keyboard, and how often you need to redose over the course of the day. Some people need the assistance of university medical facilities and complex nuclear imaging devices to monitor the serotonin levels of their brains. All *we* have to do is read back the stuff we've written over the past hour or so. With our medical plans, it's a real time- and money-saver.

Tips

These little extras might make your life easier or get the job done quicker.

Tip

If you never pay attention to a single one of the tips in this book, you won't miss anything essential. But if you do pay attention to our tips, you'll never have a bad hair day, you'll always get the table you want in restaurants, you'll amaze your friends, you'll confound your enemies, and you'll walk with a spring in your step and with a song in your heart. Just like us.

Book Organization

Part I: The IDE of the Tiger

This part introduces you to the Xcode environment, starting you off with a quick tutorial in which you build a complete application, and then takes you on a tour of the Xcode programming environment and the programming project templates it has to offer.

Part II: Code Mountain

Here's where we cover the compilers included with Xcode, and where we go over the features and capabilities of that fundamental tool with which every programmer spends endless hours: the program editor. We describe Xcode's built-in set of reference works and search facilities, too.

Part III: Drag-and-Drop Dead Gorgeous

Apple's Interface Builder application and Xcode's class and data modeling tools are the subject of this part. Once you get a look at these, you'll wonder how you programmed without them.

Part IV: If You Build It, It May Run

Xcode supports a variety of programming languages and code libraries, and this is the part you'll consult when you need to know the details of how to take full advantage your favorite language (whether AppleScript, Java, or even Objective-C++) in the Xcode environment.

Part V: Of Cat Herding and Flea Baths: Debugging, Optimizing, and Version Control

This part describes the sophisticated professional-quality tools Xcode provides for debugging programs, for fine-tuning their operation, and for sharing the development effort among team members. Though this part is not just for the pros, they'll find much of interest to them here.

Part VI: Appendixes

We wrap things up by describing some of the software development kits Apple provides with Xcode, and show how to convert projects from other development environments to Xcode.

Acknowledgments

Michael Cohen

Lots of people to thank. First, Dennis, of course, who lured me from literary studies into programming in the first place, and then a couple of decades later enticed me into this whole book-writing enterprise. Deep thanks goes to Bruce Kijewski for the timely loan of a fabulous aluminum 17-inch PowerBook G4 when my Tigerized iBook took an unscheduled maintenance break — this book would have fallen far behind schedule without his generous aid. Special thanks to Jason Hoffman of TextDrive, Inc., whose timely help in setting up a Subversion repository made Chapter 18 more than just a theoretical discussion. And, of course, I second Dennis's thank-you to our editors and Andy, who encouraged us to go as crazy as we needed to go. Finally, I simply can't thank the Digital Medievalist enough for her daily support and finely tuned critical eye — without her, this author would have given up somewhere around Chapter 2.

Dennis Cohen

The first individual I want to thank is my exceedingly clever younger brother and coauthor, Michael — he provided the foundation, structure, glue, and a lot of the other materials that made this work possible. I'd also like to thank our editors, who assisted us in getting this job done without ever frustrating our efforts — they were always supportive, which is rarer than you might think. Finally, I'd like to thank Andy Ihnatko for coming up with a series approach where we didn't have to be stultifying when covering technical material — in fact, we were told to "keep it lively," which made writing this book a lot more fun.

About the Authors

Michael Cohen (left) has been committing digital crimes against the state of the art since the days of punch cards. At various times a teacher, a programmer, a multimedia designer, a Webmaster, and a writer, Michael has employed various Apple computers (from a][+ to a Lisa to at least five different Macs) in the course of making his living for over a quarter of a century... one reason, surely, that he still retains his youthful demeanor and infectious grin. He lives with his wife, the Digital Medievalist, in Santa Monica, California, within walking distance of a fine Apple Store, where some of his other books reportedly have been seen on sale.

Dennis Cohen (right, laughing behind Michael's back) started programming with toggle switches, paper tape, punch cards, and teletype terminals about the time Voyager started its journey to Jupiter and beyond (he was working at the Jet Propulsion Laboratory's Deep Space Network at the time). He got started with Apple products with the Apple /// and, after a short stint with the Lisa, moved to the Macintosh when it was released — his dual G5 is his 12th Mac (four of them are still in use). He's authored or coauthored more than a dozen books, has contributed to almost 20 others, and been the technical editor on almost 200 titles. Dennis lives in Sunnyvale, California, with his Boston Terrier, Spenser (who knows which key to hit to make the CD tray open).

Andy Ihnatko describes himself as "The world's 42nd most-beloved industry personality," because "it's vaguely-credible but utterly impossible to prove or disprove, and thus precisely the sort of tagline I was looking for." An unabashed geek ("The bashings ended when I left high school for Rensselaer Polytechnic, thank God"), Andy's been writing about tech since 1989. In the past, he's written for every single magazine or Web site with the word "Mac" in it, highlighted by ten years as the *MacUser* and then the *Macworld* back-page opinion columnist. He's currently the *Chicago Sun-Times* technology columnist. Andy lives in Boston with his two goldfish, Click and Drag.

Contents

Contents

Contents

PART I

The IDE of the Tiger

"Hello, World!" Version 48,345,093.1

In This Chapter

You *Have* Installed Xcode, Haven't You? • The Project Assistant Has a Nice Bow Tie!
Getting in Your Face • Hooking Up • A Little Typecasting
Do You Feel Lucky? Well Do You? • The Lessons of Hello, World!

Greetings, programmer!

In this chapter, you will take your first steps on the long, event-filled journey into the world of Macintosh OS X software development — unless, of course, you've already done some Macintosh OS X software development, in which case these won't be your first steps now, will they? If so, think of this chapter as an encore telecast. (Yes, we're mixing metaphors; we can do that because we have recently renewed our poetic licenses.)

The Mac has had a long and often deserved reputation for being a difficult platform for which to develop. At different times, the difficulties have been due to different things. For instance, the first Macs were difficult to program simply because the Mac didn't *have* any tools that let programmers program for it: You needed an Apple Lisa (raise your hands if you remember those... okay, put them down; it's not like we can see you out there) wired up to a Mac and running a Macintosh development kit. Then, of course, there was the matter of the Macintosh toolbox, those sets of specialized routines and functions built into the early Mac ROMs, which programmers had to learn to understand and use, and which were documented in a heap of very heavy and continually updated loose-leaf binders. Wrapping one's head around those was not a project for a rainy afternoon.

But, some 20 years into the Macintosh era, things have gotten better... not that you don't need to learn a bunch of stuff (hey, if programming were easy, everyone would be doing it), but the programming environment is cheap (free, in fact, which is at the lower limit of cheap), and the documentation, instead of bowing your bookshelves, is now at your fingertips as you code. And, of course, the tools are a lot — and we mean, a *whole* lot — better.

Apple collectively calls these tools *Xcode*. And with them, we're going to write yet another version of that staple of introductory programming classes, the "Hello, World!" application. In the process, you'll get a quick preview of the power and, dare we say it, utter coolness of twenty-first-century Mac programming. So let's get ready to rumble...

YOU *HAVE* INSTALLED XCODE, HAVEN'T YOU?

Yes, Apple really does provide this wonderful Xcode tool chest free of charge (well, free if you don't count the fact that you have to have Tiger to make use of it and Tiger isn't exactly free). Unlike most of the other really cool toys Apple includes with Tiger, such as iTunes and iChat, Xcode doesn't get installed automatically — you have to do that yourself. So, slip your Tiger DVD back into your Mac and look for a folder named Xcode — you'll probably have to scroll down to find it.

1. **Open the Xcode folder and double-click the Xcode.mpkg file to present the very familiar Installer dialog (shown in Figure 1-1).**

2. **Click Continue to see the Software License Agreement.** Click Continue again and agree to the license agreement (after reading every last clause and condition and consulting with the friendly legal adviser that you have on retainer for just such occasions... or not), and then click Continue yet another time.

3. **Choose a destination volume, which must be a Tiger start-up volume.**

4. **Click Continue, click Install, and then type an Administrator password as shown in Figure 1-2.** (If you're not running from an Administrator account, you'll need to enter an Administrator account's user name in the Name field.)

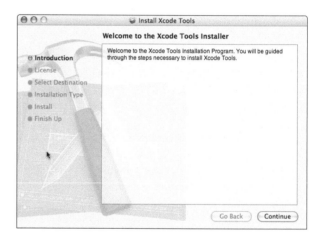

Figure 1-1
Xcode's installer looks very familiar

Figure 1-2
You need Administrator access to install Xcode

Then, sit back, listen to your iPod, and wait while the Installer creates a Developer folder at the root level of your start-up volume and fills it with all the bright and shiny Xcode goodies. When the Installer finishes its tasks, click the Close button. In the Finder, you'll see a Developer directory such as the one shown in Figure 1-3.

Figure 1-3
When all is said and done...

Now that you have Xcode installed, your creative urges are welling, but when you double-click Xcode (it's in Developer ➜ Applications), you'll find that you still need to configure Xcode, and the Xcode Assistant (see Figure 1-4) will hold your hand through the setup process (which is really quite a trick, when you stop to consider that the assistant has no hands). In other words, there are a few more steps on this meandering path.

Figure 1-4
We're installed; let's get set up

5. **Click Next.** The Assistant, as shown in Figure 1-5, asks you a couple of questions about how you want to build your projects. First, you can have Xcode place your builds' results in the project directory or in another directory you specify. Second, if your product is complex enough to build intermediate elements (subprojects, if you will), you can decide whether they should be stored where the final build goes or in another location that you specify. Of course, the explanation at the bottom of the Assistant's window told you all of this already — and if you didn't follow all of what we and the window just told you, you should probably accept the default settings; Apple (usually) chooses defaults that make sense.

Figure 1-5

Tell Xcode where you want to store the things you build

6. **Click Next.** The Assistant now inquires whether Xcode should keep track of all your open windows when you close a project or quit from Xcode so that reopening the project will reopen all your windows just as they were when you closed the project. You can see this really simple step in Figure 1-6.

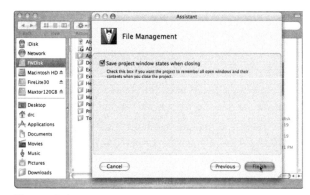

Figure 1-6

Do you like to pick up where you left off when you reopen a project?

7. **Click Finish.**

If you want to see what's new in this version of Xcode, choose Help ➜ Show Release Notes, and Xcode opens a documentation window, as shown in Figure 1-7, displaying the Release Notes for your Xcode version.

THE PROJECT ASSISTANT HAS A NICE BOW TIE!

All righty. Xcode is installed, and you've fired it up once just to make sure that it works. So let's actually do something with it. Like, say, create a new project...

▼ **Note**

Right now we're just going to blast through this whole building-a-program business step by step without (much) in-depth explanation. In later parts of the book we'll tell you more — much more — about what's going on when you perform actions like those that follow. For example, you'll see figures suspiciously similar to the ones that follow in the next chapter when we give you a slo-mo replay of the New Project Assistant. Here, however, we focus just on getting something done.

---

1. **Choose New Project from the File menu.** It's easy to find this command because it's right at the top of the File menu (see Figure 1-8). When you choose New Project, you get the New Project Assistant (see Figure 1-9), which, like most Mac OS X assistants, is represented by a headless torso wearing a bow tie. You'll see this dude a lot; even though he doesn't have a head (or other extremities), he can be quite helpful.

Xcode 2.0 Release Notes

You can always get back to this file by choosing *Show Release Notes* from the *Help* menu. Release notes for the Xcode 1.5 release can be accessed with the *Show Older Release Notes* menu item.

General Improvements

- Xcode now ships with three different user interfaces, known as *Workspaces* (which can be chosen via the *General* preferences panel). All three workspaces support all functionality of Xcode, but do so with different layouts:
  - *Default Workspace* - This layout mimics that which is found in Xcode 1.2 along with various improvements such as having attached editors to the *Build*, *Project Find*, and *SCM* windows.
  - *All-In-One Workspace* - This layout permits the user to conduct virtually all tasks within a single window.
  - *Condensed Project Workspace* - This layout is similar to that found in the *Default Workspace*, though it separates the detail view into a separate window from the project window.
- Favorites Bar
  - A "Favorites" bar has been added to the top of the Project window. This is hidden (and empty) by default and may be displayed via the View menu. This bar works much like the Safari favorites bar works. You may drag any project content (files, folders, groups, smart groups, on disk html, etc. and drop it onto the Favorites bar at any location (existing items will slide out of the way to make room). You may drag items off the Favorites bar to delete them. The purpose of the Favorites Bar is to allow rapid navigation to items you use often. For example, many of you have commented that the Smart Groups would be much more useful if they were not always scrolled out of sight. With this feature, you may drop them on the Favorites Bar to always have access to them.
  - Any item in the favorites bar may be single or double clicked just as if you were clicking it in the Groups & Files view. However, doing so will not automatically reveal the Groups & Files view. This is by design since we have more and more users who want to keep the Groups & Files view hidden. In addition, each item in the Favorites bar has the same context menu as they would have if you right clicked on them elsewhere (such as the Groups & Files view). For containers (such as groups and folders), you may hold the left mouse down on the container item to expose a popup menu which reflects the content of that container. This allows you to quickly navigate the nested content of the container. Finally, option-left-clicking on the item will allow you to rename the item in place. These items are the "real thing," so renaming them in the Favorites bar will rename them in the Groups & Files view as well (and vice-versa).
  - Current but temporary limitations of the Favorites bar : Though project content and files dragged into the Favorites bar will be remembered if you close and re-open the project, Smart Groups will not (they will

Figure 1-7
The 411 on what's new in this version of Xcode

Figure 1-8
It's easy to start a new Xcode project...

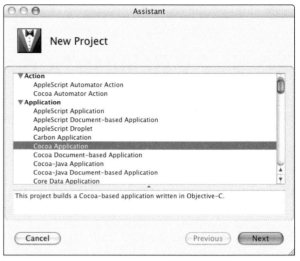

Figure 1-9
...just let the New Project Assistant do its stuff

Figure 1-10
Give the new project a name and place to live

2. **Click Cocoa Application and then click Next.** The
   Project Assistant dude is not done with you; he wants
   to know what you want to call the project and where
   you want to save it (see Figure 1-10).

3. **Type a project name in the Project Name field.** As you type, the Assistant dude fills out the second field, which is going to be the complete Unix-style path (that is, the same way you type paths in the Finder's Go to Folder dialog) to where your project is stored. If you don't mess with the second field, your project ends up in your Home directory in a folder that has the project name you typed.

4. **Click Finish.**

And lo! There's your new project, in a project window (see Figure 1-11) that's chock-full (what *is* a chock and how full

can you get one, anyway?) of all sorts of things you don't understand... yet. But you will; oh, you will! (Cue the evil laughter sound effect.)

At this very instant, you have a complete application ready to build and run if you like. Now, we're not saying you *should* build your project, but if you *did* (say, for example, by clicking that inviting Build and Go icon at the top of the project window), Xcode would compile, link, and then launch your new, utterly useless-but-very-cool-nonetheless application — which is already sophisticated enough to show you a (blank) window and a set of standard menus.

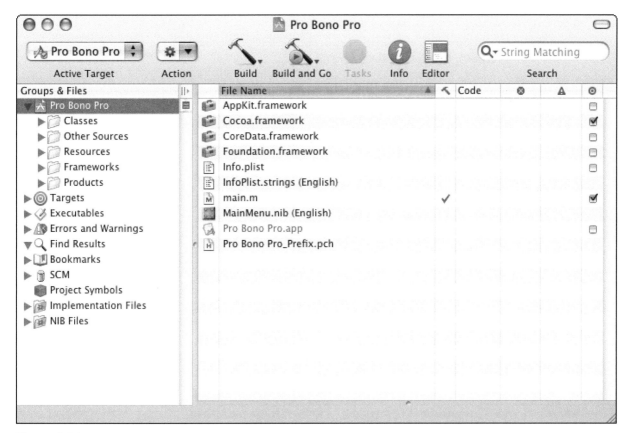

Figure 1-11
A new project, untouched by human hands

Tip

The standard menus in your application include a program menu with a Quit command — you'll probably want to use this command if you disregarded our half-hearted advice and built your project in order to see what would happen.

GETTING IN YOUR FACE

If you're like just about every other programmer we ever met, you are probably itching to write some code. We suggest, however, that you soothe your itchy patches with some Benadryl or hydrocortisone cream, because we're not going to be typing any code yet. There's a lot to get out of the way, first — for example, it wouldn't be a bad idea to decide just what it is that our program is going to do.

Because our program is the traditional Hello, World! program, it should, as all such programs do, display the message, "Hello, world!" Because it's a Mac program, it should display this message in a window, and, because Mac programs are user friendly, it should let the user click something to produce the message. In short, we need a window, a button, and a text display area.

If you build and run the project we just created, you'll discover that the default Cocoa application already provides a window. So that's one down. Next, we need to add the button and the text display area to our project's window.

You may be thinking: Aha! *Now* we're going to write some code. Nope. Still not yet. Instead, we're going to build our program's interface graphically with Xcode's Interface Builder application and let *it* do most of the coding for us. But don't worry: Eventually you'll get to type some code yourself. Honest. Maybe even a *whole line* of it...

1. **Double-click the MainMenu.nib file shown in the project window.** This file appears in the right pane of your project window (see Figure 1-11); it was generated automatically when you created the project. Double-

clicking it opens Interface Builder, the Xcode application that lets you assemble the standard elements of Mac OS X's graphical user interface by using palettes and drag-and-drop techniques. (Chapter 9 covers this mind bogglingly cool tool in greater depth.)

When Interface Builder finishes launching, you see something like Figure 1-12: a window named Window, a window named Cocoa-Menus, and a window named MainMenu.nib, all floating over your project window. The Window window is your application's main window. The Cocoa-Menus window is a palette that contains user interface elements you can add to your project; its name changes depending on the types of user interface elements displayed in it. The MainMenu.nib window shows the interface elements contained in your project; currently, it shows that your project contains a window element, a menu element, and a couple of other necessary things.

 Note

The user interface elements shown in Interface Builder are, technically, instances of classes that are predefined as part of Mac OS X's Cocoa framework. If you know something about object-oriented programming, you'll know what we're talking about; if not, you should bone up on the basic concepts a little: Mac OS X is *very* object-oriented.

2. **Click the Controls icon in the palette.** This icon, shown here, appears at the top of the interface elements palette, second from the left. When you click the icon, the palette's name changes to Cocoa-Controls, and the palette displays a set of control widgets that you can click and drag into the interface you are building.

 Tip

When you point at an element in Interface Builder's Cocoa interface elements palette, a tool tip appears that identifies the Cocoa class to which the element belongs. You may notice, for example, that many of the different-looking buttons appearing in the Cocoa-Controls palette actually belong to the NSButton class, a class that is defined in the Cocoa frameworks. Chapter 7 describes how you can consult documentation describing the frameworks and their classes at any time as you work. (Okay, that's really two tips here — we're generous.)

3. **Click and drag the button labeled Button from the top left of the Cocoa-Controls palette to the application's window and release the mouse.** This is how you add interface elements to your application (see Figure 1-13). If, at this moment, you were to save your work (and guess what? ⌘+S will do that very thing) and then build your application again, the button would appear in the application's main window exactly where you put it in Interface Builder.

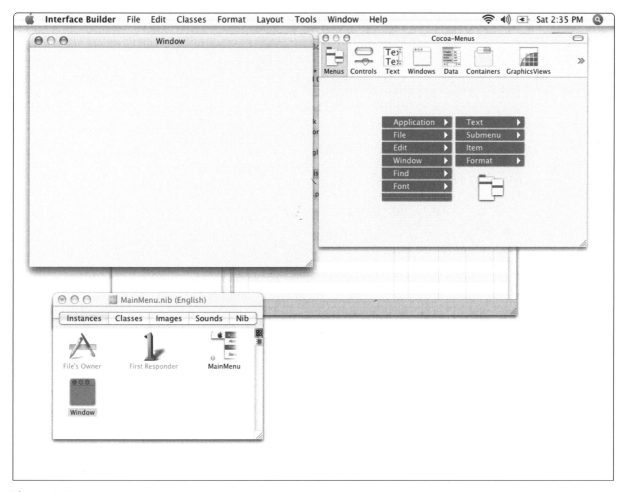

Figure 1-12
The program's user interface as seen in Interface Builder

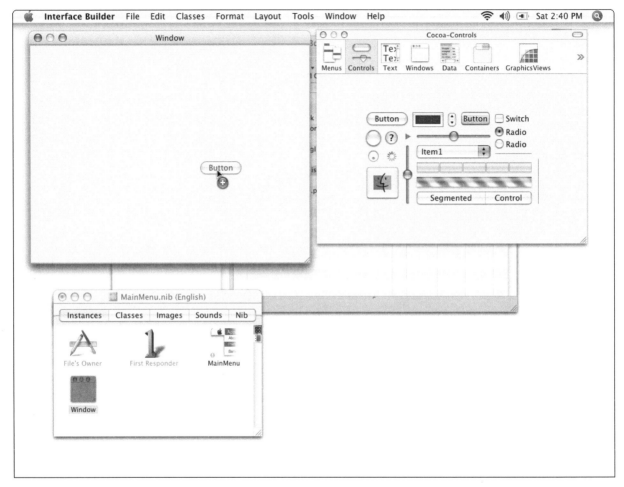

Figure 1-13
Adding an interface element to the application's main window

4. **Click and drag one of the button's handles on its left or right side to make it wider.**

5. **Double-click the button's label to select it, and then type a new label for the button.** Figure 1-14 shows you how we adjusted the button's size and location and the label we gave it; feel free to modify your button to suit your own aesthetic sensibilities — it's easy to do and fun for the whole family.

6. **Click the text icon in the palette.** This icon, shown here, appears at the top of the interface elements palette, third from the left. When you click the icon, the palette's name changes to Cocoa-Text, and the palette displays a set of text widgets, which, just like the controls, you can drag into the interface you are building.

A SMALL PACKAGE OF VALUE WILL COME TO YOU, SHORTLY

All of the button's characteristics that you have (and will) set in this tutorial are saved in the MainMenu.nib file that belongs to your project, and that file becomes part of the application's resources when you build your project. For you Mac old-timers, this arrangement is conceptually somewhat like the old resource fork of days gone by, but architecturally it's quite different. Modern Mac applications (like the one that we are making here) are usually stored in special directories, called *packages*, that just happen to *look* like files. Inside of packages live various directories and files, including the .nib files containing the application's interface elements.

You can easily see inside of packages in the Finder: Simply Control + click the file (or right-click for you multibutton mousers out there) and select Show Package Contents from the contextual menu. Like magic, a new Finder window opens and you can go traipsing through the package to your heart's content. If you find a .nib file, you can double-click it and it will open in Interface Builder — which we really must tell you is both an exceedingly exciting and a dangerously foolhardy thing to do with any application that you care about in any way. Using this trick, you can walk on the wild side, destroying various applications' interfaces with Interface Builder, just like Mac old-timers could do with ResEdit. The Old and True Rules apply: Only mess around with copies, and hack responsibly.

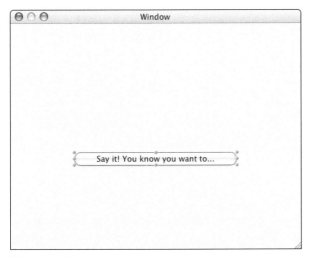

Figure 1-14
A resized and relabeled button now adorns the interface

7. **Click and drag a blank NSTextField object from the Cocoa-Text palette to the application's window and release the mouse.** This field, like the button you previously added, is now part of the application's main window (see Figure 1-15), and it is where your app is going to display its Hello, World message. (If you can't find it, the NSTextField object is the recessed-looking blank text field on the left side of the Cocoa-Text palette as shown in Figure 1-15.)

8. **Click and drag one of the field's handles on its left or right side to make it wider.** You want to make the field wide enough to display the Hello, World message. You can also click the field and drag it where you think it looks best in the window.

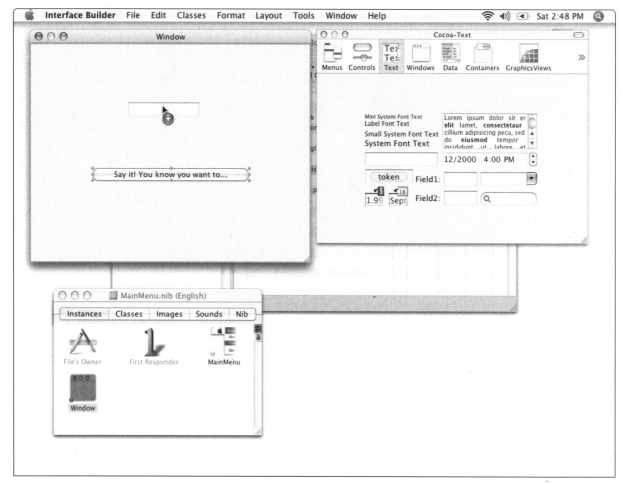

Figure 1-15
Toss in a text field to display the Hello, World message

9. **(Optional) Double-click the field to put an insertion point into it, and then type some text for the field to display.** The field in your application's main window initially will contain this text when the application runs. If you like, you can also use the Font and Text submenus in Interface Builder's Format menu to style the field's text however you want. You can see our version of the field in Figure 1-16.

10. **Save your work using either ⌘+S or Save from the File menu.**

You now have all the elements of the app's user interface in place. Were you to build and run the app right now, you'd have a fully functional nonfunctional program; that is, the button, field, and window would appear, but they wouldn't do anything very interesting. Wiring them up is our next mission.

THE N WORDS

So far, you've seen a couple of interface elements that represent certain Cocoa framework classes: The button you dragged into your window, for example, is an NSButton, and the text field you dragged is an NSTextField. So, what's up with this "NS" stuff?

Those letters are a historical holdover. The classes in the Cocoa framework were originally developed at Steve Job's previous computer company, NeXT, which Apple bought in the late 1990s. These classes, as well as much of the Cocoa framework, were part of the NeXTStep class libraries, and the NS, in case you haven't guessed by now, stands for "NeXTStep." Interface Builder itself, in fact, is a direct descendent of the interface-building tool from the NeXTStep system. One might be tempted to think that Cocoa is simply NeXTStep with a candy coating. One might be right.

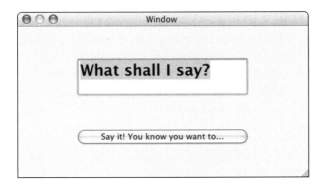

Figure 1-16
The Hello, World! app's text display field gets some style and content

HOOKING UP

Right out of the wrapper, Cocoa buttons and text fields are pretty smart: A Cocoa button "knows" when it has been clicked and can even tell another object, "Hey, I've been clicked!" and a Cocoa text field can easily be told to display any given piece of text. So here's what we have to figure out next: how to translate our button's "Hey, I've been clicked!" message into a message that tells our text field what to display. There are lots of possible answers (that's what makes programming the enjoyable, creative time-sink that it is); the approach we will take is the Model-View-Controller approach that all the best authorities in the field consider to be The Right Approach to object-oriented programming (and we're not about to argue with all the best authorities in the field without a really good reason, such as a cash payment or a free week on Maui).

This is what you need to do: Create a new type of object to control the interaction between our button and our field. This controller object will listen to the button, and, when the button tells the controller object that it's been clicked, the controller object will tell the text field what to display. Setting this sort of thing up with Interface Builder is pretty easy.

And, no, we're *still* not going to be writing any code yet, but we're getting closer.

1. **Click the Classes tab in the MainMenu.nib window. Scroll all the way to the left, and click NSObject (see Figure 1-17).** NSObject is the Cocoa class from which all other Cocoa classes descend. We want our new controller class to be a Cocoa class, so this is the perfect place to start.

▼ **Note**

The NSObject class, like other Cocoa classes, appears in gray in the MainMenu.nib window in order to indicate that it is a standard class and not one that you

THE ABCS OF MVC IN OOP

The Model-View-Controller (MVC) way of thinking about object-oriented programming (OOP) is just a way to reduce the brain-cramp that can occur when you design large, complicated programs that have a whole slew of interrelated functions and data. The idea is pretty simple: Conceptually divide the object classes between those that the user sees and touches (the view), the underlying structure (including data structures and the routines to manipulate them) that the view represents (the model), and the code that manages interactions between the view and the model (the controller).

Clear as mud, right? In our Hello, World! application, it breaks down this way. The View is the window, text field, button, and menus that the user sees and can manipulate. The Model is the underlying idea that a textual message is displayed in response to some action by the user — the particular appearance of the text field that displays the message or of the button that the user clicks (or even if it *is* a button-click that triggers the message) is irrelevent (in fact, our Hello, World! application's model is pretty barren, lacking any data structures or data manipulating routines). The Controller is the program logic that monitors the trigger condition and then changes the text message when the condition is met.

By separating things out this way, we can change the controller's capabilities (for example, what it tells the field to display) without touching the button or the field. We can change where the button and field appear in the window, as well as their sizes, shapes, and so on, without touching the controller logic. We can devise additional ways of creating the text-changing trigger conditions (that is, changing the model) without touching the view or the controller logic. And we can reduce brain-cramp in the process. Everybody wins.

have created and can modify. This color also makes the class name hard to see when you select it, as we have in Figure 1-17. Nice one, Apple.

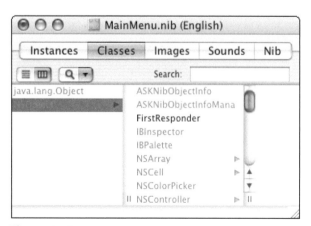

Figure 1-17
Select a base class...

2. **Select Subclass NSObject from the Classes menu (see Figure 1-18).** A new entry appears in the column to the right of NSObject in the MainMenu.nib window: MyObject. Its name is selected, ready for you to change it to something more appropriate to its function (see Figure 1-19).

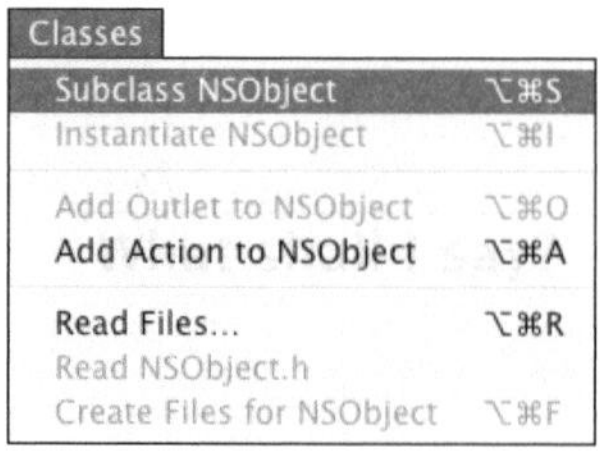

Figure 1-18
... subclass it...

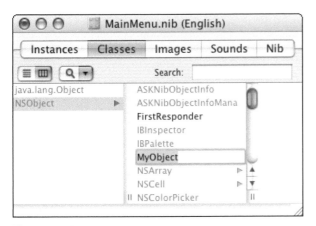

Figure 1-19
...and give it a name

Figure 1-20
Like so many of us, our controller needs an outlet

3. **Type a new name for the class.** We called ours HelloController; by convention, class names begin with an uppercase letter.

4. **Control-click (or right-click) the new class and select Add Outlet to HelloController (or whatever it was that you named your class) from the contextual menu.** A Class Info window opens showing you the attributes of your new class, with a new outlet selected so you can change its name (see Figure 1-20).

▼ Note

An *outlet* in Cocoa/Interface Builder parlance is really nothing more than an instance variable that gets added to a class. Interface Builder uses outlets to establish connections between an application's interface objects so they can exchange messages. The outlet we're creating here eventually will be connected to the text field in our app's main window so the controller object can tell the text field to change the text that it's showing.

5. **Give the outlet a name.** We called ours helloSayer. We could have called it Fred. We didn't. Also note that, by convention, outlet names begin with a lowercase letter.

6. **Click the small pop-up widget beside the outlet's type and select NSTextField from the pop-up scrolling list (see Figure 1-21).** Why? Because the app's text field is an NSTextField, and we want our controller to be able to communicate with it.

Figure 1-21
Picking an outlet type

7. **Click the 0 Actions tab in the HelloController Class Inspector window.** You see a list of actions that your controller class can take... actually, you *don't* see a list of actions, because your controller class doesn't have any yet. But you can see where the list would be if there were any items in it.

8. **Click the Add button at the bottom of the Hello-Controller Class Inspector window.** A new action appears with its name selected so you can change it. Also note that the 0 Actions tab in the Inspector window changes to say 1 Action. That's right, Interface Builder knows how to count.

9. **Give your action a suitable name.** We named ours sayTheThang: (see Figure 1-22). Note that action names, by convention, begin with a lowercase letter. They also *must* end with a colon... but if you don't supply one, Interface Builder will. It knows the rules.

Figure 1-22
An action hero is born

▼ **Note**

An *action* is nothing more than the name of a method (or of a member function for you C++ fans

out there). When a user does something to an interface object, such as clicking it, the object can respond by sending an *action message* to another object; this message becomes, through the magic of the Cocoa runtime environment, a method call with a single parameter (specifically, the ID of the sender). The action we have created here is the action message that our HelloController will receive from the app's button when the button is clicked... once, that is, we establish a connection between the button and the HelloController with Interface Builder. We'll do that shortly. In step 15, in fact.

10. **Select Create Files for HelloController from the Classes menu (the name of the class in the command will match the name you gave yours; see Figure 1-23).** A sheet descends from your Main-Menu.nib window (see Figure 1-24).

Figure 1-23
Free code...

11. **Make sure that the checkboxes for both the class's header file (ending with .h) and the implementation file (ending with .m) in the bottom-left pane of the sheet are checked, and that the files are being inserted into the right target (that is, your project), as shown in the bottom-right pane of the sheet, and then click Choose.** Interface Builder magically creates the two source files that define your class and adds them into the Other Sources folder in your Xcode project window (see Figure 1-25).

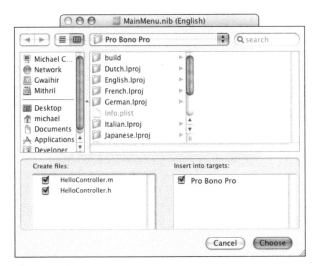

Figure 1-24
... is just a click or two away

Figure 1-25
This source is a new source, of course, of course

12. **Choose Classes ➔ Instantiate HelloController (you may need to select the class first in the Classes tab of the MainMenu.nib window).** This creates an actual instance of the class in your nib. You'll need this.

13. **Click the Instances tab of the MainMenu.nib window.** The window displays your controller object amid its collection of interface objects (see Figure 1-26). A small white exclamation mark in a yellow disk appears beside the object, which is Interface Builder's polite way of saying that the object has some yet-to-be-connected outlets.

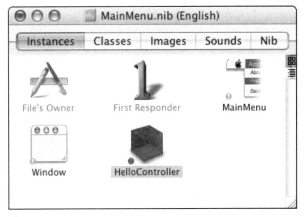

Figure 1-26
The controller, ready to be wired up

 Tip

Hover your mouse over the exclamation mark to see a tool tip that tells you exactly what Interface Builder thinks is the "problem" with your interface object.

14. **While holding down the Control key, click and drag from the controller object in the MainMenu.nib window to the text field in the Window window, and then release the mouse.** A line stretches from the controller to the field (see Figure 1-27), indicating that you've established a connection between the two objects, and the Inspector window shows the controller object's outlet list.

Figure 1-27
The controller is connected to the text field

Figure 1-28
Destination confirmed; enjoy your trip

15. **In the Inspector window, click to select the outlet you created in steps 4 through 6 (if it's not already selected), and then click the window's Connect button.** A gray button appears to the outlet's left and the outlet's destination appears to its right (see Figure 1-28). In other words, the instance variable that corresponds to your controller object's outlet now contains a reference to the text field (or, rather, it will when the application is launched and the Cocoa runtime environment rifles through the .nib file looking for things to hook up).

16. **While holding down the Control key, click and drag from the button in the Window window to the controller object in the MainMenu.nib window, and then release the mouse.** A line now stretches from the button to the controller object (see Figure 1-29), and the Inspector window shows the button's Target/Action list, which contains the controller object's only available Target/Action, sayTheThang.

17. **Click the action listed in the Inspector window and then click the window's Connect button to complete the connection.**

18. **Save your work using either ⌘+S or Save from the File menu.**

And that's it for the Interface Builder portion of our day's entertainment. You've wired up all of your app's interface objects, generated source files to play with, and now, finally, at long last, you can get ready to scratch your coding itch. We hope it was worth the wait.

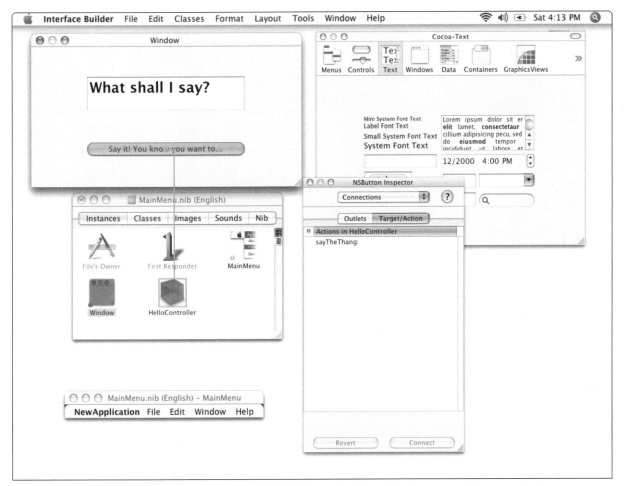

Figure 1-29
The button is connected to the controller

A LITTLE TYPECASTING

Back when we generated source files from our Main-Menu.nib file, Interface Builder produced two files, which you saw in Figure 1-25. If you named your controller class HelloController like we did, you now have a header file, HelloController.h, and an implementation file, HelloController.m. Because our project is a Cocoa application,

Interface Builder produced these files in Objective-C, an object-oriented version of the C programming language, which is Cocoa's preferred language (although you can use the Cocoa framework from Java, C++, and even a weird and wacky language blend called Objective-C++). Let's take a look at these two files, see what needs changing, and make the changes.

Note

Objective-C is a very simple superset of standard C; it's easy to pick up the basics in just a few hours, especially if you are familiar with other object-oriented programming languages. Xcode's extensive built-in documentation includes the guide, *The Objective-C Programming Language*, which can get you up to speed with the language rather quickly. To find out how to use Xcode's documentation resources, you can flip to Chapter 7.

First, we check out the header file:

1. **Switch back over to the Xcode application if you haven't already.**

2. **Double-click your controller class's header file (for example, HelloController.h) in the project window.** It should appear in the big right-hand pane of your project window; it can also be found in the Other Sources folder in the project window's left-hand pane, as shown in Figure 1-25. An Xcode editing window opens (see Figure 1-30).

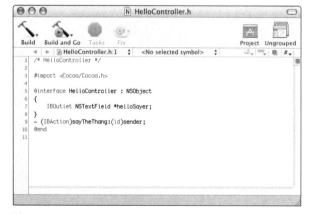

Figure 1-30
Go to the header of the class

The header file is pretty short and sweet, containing

- a comment that identifies the source;

- an #import compiler directive to bring in all the Cocoa stuff (which is much like a #include directive that avoids some recursion issues);

- an @interface statement that lets you, the compiler, and the rest of the known universe know that the HelloController is a subclass of NSObject;

- a sole instance variable, helloSayer, which is the NSTextField outlet you created in Interface Builder (the IBOutlet type qualifier lets Interface Builder and Xcode coordinate with each other as you develop your app) — note that Objective-C instance variables are included between curly braces; and

- a method declaration, sayTheThang, which corresponds to the action you added to your controller class in Interface Builder

There's nothing you need to change here. All is as it should be. You can close the editing window.

Now let's look at the class's implementation source file. Here's where you are going to write some code (Quick! Alert the media!).

1. **Double-click the class's implementation file (for example, HelloController.m) in the project window.** Like the header file, it should appear in the big right-hand pane of your project window and in the Other Sources folder in the project window's left-hand pane. An editing window opens (see Figure 1-31).

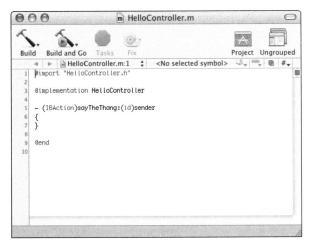

Figure 1-31
A class method, ready to edit

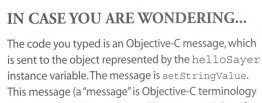

IN CASE YOU ARE WONDERING...

The code you typed is an Objective-C message, which is sent to the object represented by the `helloSayer` instance variable. The message is `setStringValue`. This message (a "message" is Objective-C terminology for what other object-oriented languages might refer to as a "method call" or "member function call") takes a single parameter: the literal string, "Hello, world!!!" (its literalness is indicated by the @ in front of it). In Objective-C, messages are enclosed in brackets to differentiate them from plain, ordinary, C function calls, which Objective-C supports as well (it is, after all, a superset of C).

2. **Following the open brace, type the following line of code exactly.** (Well, almost exactly — if you called your outlet something other than `helloSayer`, you should type the name you used instead.) The result should look like Figure 1-32:

```
[helloSayer setStringValue:@"Hello,
world!!!"];
```

Figure 1-32
A class method, finished and ready to compile

3. **Save your changes (choose Save from the File menu, or press ⌘+S).**

And that's it. That's *all* the code you have to write to make your application say "Hello, world!!!" when you click the button. Now wasn't *that* worth waiting for?

DO YOU FEEL LUCKY? WELL DO YOU?

Finally, you need to build the program and run it.

If you come from old-school Unix programming, you may be wondering about things like build files, targets, compiler options, and stuff like that there. Don't worry: All that stuff is still around, and if you have a burning desire to get at it, you'll find out how to do so later in this book (say, for example, Chapters 11 and 12). But you don't have to if you don't want to because Xcode tries to handle all of it for you, and it does a pretty good job, too. The only thing you have to do is push a button.

Oh, yes, you *do* need to know which button, don't you? Okay, um, let's see. Right. It's that Build and Go button at the top of your editing window (we may have mentioned it before... well, we're mentioning it again). Click it.

As Xcode indexes, compiles, builds, and links your application, you should see something similar to Figure 1-33 — note the progress indicator and status messages that appear at the bottom of the window. The build process may take a few seconds the first time you build your project, because Xcode has to bring together all the pieces that make up your application (which includes things like the Cocoa framework, which is no small thing), but subsequent builds (say, if you need — or want — to make any minor changes) won't take quite as long.

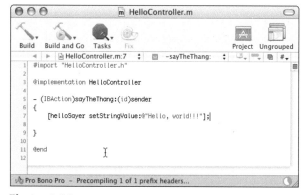

Figure 1-33
Once I built a Mac app, made it run...

Assuming you have typed everything correctly in the one line of code that you had to type, the application launches, its menu bar appears, and the window you designed with Interface Builder shows up. Click the window's button (see Figure 1-34) and see the "Hello, world!!!" message.

Figure 1-34
You don't have to shout

Woo, as they say, hoo! You've written a Macintosh OS X application. Have a cookie. Oh, and don't forget to quit the application when you're finished admiring what a fine job you've done (use the free Cocoa-supplied Quit command on the application's menu).

THE LESSONS OF HELLO, WORLD!

And what have we learned today, kids? That a copy of Xcode comes free inside each colorfully wrapped container of Mac OS X Tiger. That Xcode provides project templates that make it very easy for you to get started creating a program. That Xcode's Interface Builder application lets you do a lot of your user interface design work using simple drag-and-drop techniques instead of requiring you to create carefully handcrafted code. That the Xcode code editor lets you compile the code that you *do* have to write without switching to another mode or application. And, finally, that cranking out a sophisticated application with a fully functional, Aqua-fresh graphical user interface is pretty easy to do.

At least, *we* thought it was.

Shopping for Projects at the Builders' Emporium

In This Chapter

Make Me One with Everything • Coo-coo for Cocoa Apps
We Are Billion-Year-Old Carbon
Java Is East of Krakatoa • Frameworks and Plug-ins and Tools, Oh, My!
Checking the Receipt

Programming personal computers used to be pretty simple until they made it so darned complicated.

Back in the day, one of us (we're not saying who) wrote a full-fledged shrink-wrapped commercial application that consisted of fewer than 3,000 lines of code. Of course, when that application ran, it took over the whole computer, and it had a user interface that was the digital equivalent of a stone knife from Olduvai Gorge, consisting of arcane keyboard commands and endless single-font monospaced text scrolling off the screen: no mouse, no menus, no windows, no color, no sound, no shirts, no shoes, no service.

Today's applications require a little more polish and panache — and lots more code — if they're not to be laughed off the shelves of the local neighborhood SuperSoftwareServiceCenter. But a modern app lives in a complex computational ecosystem, and when you write one you have to include a lot of stuff that (unless you are some kind of code-monkey freak) you probably don't have the time or expertise to write yourself: window managers, network managers, memory managers, graphics primitives, font renderers, scroll bars, menus, yada, yada, and yada (where each yada stands for a whole lotta spiffy and powerful code and related digital goodies).

Luckily, you *don't* have to write that stuff: Apple provides oodles (1 oodle = 30 wholelottas) of these bits and pieces that you can use. When you begin a new project, you just tell Xcode what you want to build, and it loads your project up with all the stuff that it thinks you'll need to do it.

MAKE ME ONE WITH EVERYTHING

Just about anything that you want to build with Xcode requires more than one single file: there are header files, implementation files, resource files, library files, files full of code, and files full of... um... not code. Xcode collects all these (or, rather, collects references to all these) in a *project* file. You got a peek at this back in Chapter 1 when you built your highly original Hello, World program. Here's another peek: an instant replay, complete with slo-mo and reverse angles, to show you a clearer picture of what happens when you start a new Xcode project.

1. **Choose New Project from the File menu.** This brings up a window (see Figure 2-1) featuring our old friend from a previous chapter, the New Project Assistant, or, as we like to call our headless friend, the maitre d'ude. This time we've closed up all the disclosure triangles so you can see the plethora of choices the dude has available. A few of the choices, such as Empty Project, live at the top level of the dude's offerings because they are things unto themselves, having no variant forms... c'mon, how many kinds of empty projects do you want?

2. **Click the Application disclosure triangle (if it's not already open).** Wallah, as those with terrible French accents might say: Now you can see the various kinds of application templates Xcode has to offer (see Figure 2-2). If you thought a program was a program was a program, well, you were wrong.

Figure 2-1
A plethora of things you can build

Figure 2-2
An assortment of application templates from which to choose

WHAT THE HECK IS AN APPLICATION ENVIRONMENT AND WHY SHOULD I CARE?

In the long-long-ago, Mac programs were written in one high-level language (Pascal, if you can believe it) and/or 68000 assembly language (there were real programmers in those days, giants who were unafraid to toggle the bits in the CPU registers with their own fingers). These programs were compiled, assembled, and linked to a bunch of prewritten code known as the Macintosh toolbox, code that was frozen into the ROM of the early Macs. That was *the* Mac application environment. It wasn't an easy environment to work in (we know, we *did*), but that was okay: The Mac was so cool that programmers would do what it took to get the job done. But as the toolbox evolved and became ever more convolutedly complex and less able to meet the demands of modern computing, as Pascal became supplanted by C as the new programmers' language of choice, and as the Mac lost market share to that other, ugly platform, getting third-party developers to work on Mac applications became more and more difficult.

Mac OS X redefined the Mac experience for both the user and the developer. It scraped off the verdigris that had accumulated on the toolbox and made it easier to call from C and C++ code, it added support for modern computing concepts like preemptive multitasking and protected memory, and it added other features to make it more attractive to developers who had never worked on a Mac. Yet Apple did not want to alienate those hardy souls who had stuck with the platform through good times and bad.

For those programmers who felt like making a totally new start, Apple (courtesy of NeXT, which Apple had acquired) offered a new set of code libraries and tools based on the legendary object-oriented NeXTStep (also known as OpenStep) development environment. This was Cocoa. It was fresh and exciting. It enabled programmers to build very powerful programs with surprisingly little effort — and it was completely alien to those longtime Mac programmers who'd mastered the evil complexities of the toolbox and who weren't about to throw out all of their accumulated wisdom. For those folk, Apple created Carbon — a reworking of the traditional toolbox code libraries that eliminated their most egregious problems yet remained familiar enough so that old-school Mac programmers wouldn't feel completely lost. And, because the Internet boom of the 1990s had propelled the Java programming language into prominence, Apple came up with a way for Java programmers to join the OS X party, too.

Each of these — Carbon, Cocoa, and Java — are Mac OS X application environments. From a Mac user's point of view, they are almost indistinguishable. But each is designed to appeal to the specific types of software developers out in the wild and to lure them to the Macintosh. And the strategy seems to be working.

3. **Click one of the application project types.** Each time you click a project type, you see a description of it appear in the dude's lower panel (no, it's not his cummerbund; you can carry a joke too far, you know). For example, Figure 2-2 shows a Cocoa Application selected, and the description reads, "This project builds a Cocoa-based application written in Objective-C." Helpful, huh? Sure, unless you don't know what Cocoa or Objective-C are. (Don't worry. If you don't, you soon will.)

4. **Select an application template type and click Next.** For now, it doesn't matter which type you select, because you are not actually going to build anything with it. We're going through this whole process just for informational purposes; think of it as a dry run or an amusing waste of time. (By the way, we selected the Cocoa Application, and if you do the same, your screen will look very much like ours.) When you click Next, the dude asks you to choose a place to store your new project (see Figure 2-3).

Figure 2-3
Where, oh where, will my new project go?

5. **Type a name for your project in the Project Name field.** As you type the project's name, a message appears telling you where the dude wants to put your new project (and you know the dude is a class act because he uses words like "therein"). By default, this is the top level of your Home directory (which goes by the classy Unix name of ~/); the name that you type becomes the name of the folder that will contain your project. You can click Choose... to see the familiar standard Save dialog and use it to choose a different place to save the project, or, if you think GUIs are

for babies, you can type the path directly into the Project Directory field.

6. **Click Finish.** Aaaaaannnnd... you're done. You see a brand-new project window (see Figure 2-4) full of all the goodies that Xcode thinks you need to build your next big money-making, world-shaking software package.

▼ Tip

You can save your project at the top level of your Home as Xcode suggests, but if you are working on a bunch of different projects, or if you are channeling Felix Unger, you'll soon find that your Home begins looking a trifle messy with all those project folders scattered about. We like to keep a separate Projects folder in our Home, and put all of our individual project folders inside it. If you have a lot of projects, the Projects folder can still be a mess, but it's a much *tidier* mess, and visitors to your Home won't notice it right away (they'll be too busy snooping in your medicine cabinet).

As you can see, a new application project contains a lot of stuff. Some of that stuff is stuff you'll mess around with, some of it is stuff your code will need to refer to, and some of it is stuff that every application running on Mac OS X needs to have. Most application templates provide

- some source code files that constitute the bare bones of your program (in the right panel of the window shown in Figure 2-4 those are main.m and Pro Bono Pro_Prefix.pch);

- some library files that contain application programming interfaces (APIs) to which your code can refer (these are the .framework files in Figure 2-4);

- one or more .nib files (such as MainMenu.nib in Figure 2-4) that you'll use with Interface Builder to design your application's user interface (which is coming up in Chapter 9 — make your reservations now because seating is limited); and

Chapter 2: Builders' Emporium

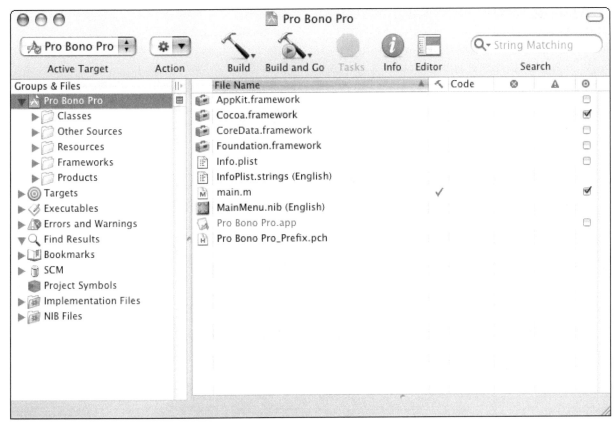

Figure 2-4
A brand spanking new project ready for you to spank

▼ **Note**

If you can't wait to get to Chapter 9, here's a quick preview: A .*nib* file contains a description of various user-interface thingies used by your app. Instead of writing code to create these thingies the way we used to do it in bad old days, you use Interface Builder to drag and drop your interface into shape, and Interface Builder writes the code that ties these things into your application. You simply add to and modify the code that Interface Builder provides.

- some files for the file system *bundle* that tell Mac OS X just what kind of application this is and other good

stuff that the Finder can make use of (in Figure 2-4, they're Info.plist and InfoPlist.strings).

The project window lets you get at these different items in different ways. You'll discover much more about the Xcode project window in the next chapter.

▼ **Note**

By the way, if you think that a project window looks a lot like a geeky version of, say, the iTunes window, well, let's just say you wouldn't be the first person to think that.

29

The files for your project are laid out on disk rather differently than they appear in the project window. Figure 2-5 shows the sample project we created previously as it appears in the Finder. The file with the name that ends with .xcode is, surprise, your project file, the one that keeps track of all the other files in your project, of the project's current state, and of various other essential bookkeeping matters that you don't want to worry about because Xcode worries about it for you. That, in short, is the file you double-click to open your project.

Figure 2-5
A project as the Finder sees it

Now, unless you plan on doing something with the Pro Bono Pro sample project you just created, you can go ahead and find the project folder and trash it. It's easy enough to make a new one, right?

COO-COO FOR COCOA APPS

If you thought that cocoa was a sweet, innocuous beverage, you've never seen a 10-year-old on a sugar and chocolate high. It's powerful stuff, indeed.

Like the drink, Apple's Cocoa is sweet stuff and incredibly powerful. Based on the NeXTStep application development environment that Apple acquired when it acquired NeXT (and with it, one Mr. $. Jobs), Cocoa makes it almost absurdly easy to write a Mac OS X program. Don't believe us? Well, the Cocoa project you created back at the beginning of this chapter can actually be compiled and run as is, without you adding a lick of code (but please don't tell us if you really *do* lick your code because we don't want to know). If you haven't trashed the project as we suggested (what? you *listened* to us? Suckers!), you can try it for yourself. Just click the Build and Go icon (shown below) in the project window and, in a few seconds, you'll see a window and menu bar for that program. Sure, it does nothing, but it does it very well.

▼ Note

There is one possible downside to building a Cocoa application: Most Cocoa applications are written in an object-oriented version of the C programming language called Objective-C. If you are a C or C++ programmer, though, don't panic. Objective-C is *very* easy to learn — most C programmers can pick it up in just a few days. And, we're told, when they do they find it quite habit-forming... much like a good cup of cocoa with a marshmallow on top.

Cocoa applications come in two basic varieties: plain and document (We bet you thought we were going to say plain and peanut, didn't you?).

- **A plain Cocoa app** is intended to let you display, and modify, existing information. For example, iPhoto is a Cocoa app that displays and lets you modify photos, but you don't *create* the photos there. When you choose Cocoa Application from the New Project dude, you get a rudimentary, fully functional application that has a main window (into which you, as programmer, can add all sorts of controls, graphics, and views of whatever data you want your users to view) and a menu bar with all the standard items on it. Not that such an app is limited to a single window, of course — you can, and probably will, add others; nor is the app's menu bar limited to the menus that the Cocoa application template provides — you can add to and modify those as well. The template is just a starting point, after all.

○ **A document-based Cocoa app** is intended to let you create, open, print, and save documents. Think of a drawing program or a word processor or a source-code editor, and you'll have the basic idea: Document-based programs let you create multiple document windows, enter and edit information in them, and

save them. Each window usually is (or can be) associated with a given data file on disk. When you build a document-based Cocoa app, you get a full-featured program that lets you create and save document windows, and a menu bar with all the standard features that a document-creating-and-editing program needs. This template supplies the files that a plain Cocoa app template provides, plus interface and implementation class source files for you to use implementing your app's documents, and an additional Interface Builder .nib file for the app's document window user interface (see Figure 2-6 for an example document-based Cocoa project).

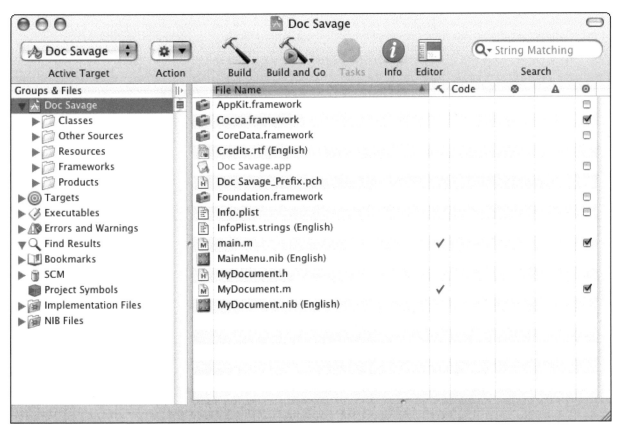

Figure 2-6
Stuff you get for free with the Cocoa document-based application template

COCOA WITH A SHOT OF JAVA

You don't *have* to learn Objective-C to write Cocoa apps; Java will do, and do quite nicely. The object models of both Java and Objective-C turn out to be similar enough to have allowed Apple to build a *runtime bridge* that lets Java code refer to Cocoa objects and methods.

Because of this runtime bridge, the New Project dude can easily offer you both a Cocoa-Java application template and a Cocoa-Java Document-based application template (see Figure 2-2). Using these, you can write your Cocoa apps in Java, employing standard Java calling conventions for all the good stuff in the AppKit and Foundation frameworks. And Xcode 2 will even show you all the Cocoa API documentation in Java format for you to consult as you write your code (check out Chapter 7).

There are some minor differences between Objective-C Cocoa and Java-flavored Cocoa, though. Probably the most important difference has to do with garbage: how you get rid of used objects. Objective-C uses a reference-counting model for retaining and disposing of objects — you often explicitly `retain` and `release` objects as they get passed into your methods. Java, on the other hand, has an actual runtime garbage collector that keeps track of objects and deallocates them when no one else wants them around any more. The Java runtime bridge handles the retain and release messages when a Java object refers to Objective-C objects.

As you might expect, the Java garbage collector and runtime bridge do exact a performance penalty when you compare otherwise identical Cocoa-Java apps to Objective-C Cocoa apps, but the penalty is pretty small. So, if you like your hot beverages with a caffeine kick, this drink may be for you.

Both the Cocoa application template and the Cocoa Document-based application template link to two main Cocoa programming frameworks: the *Foundation* framework and the *Application Kit* framework, also known as the AppKit. You can see these two frameworks listed in the project window shown way back in Figure 2-4. All Cocoa applications use the classes defined in these frameworks; they may use other frameworks as well, of course, but these two are essential.

- The **Foundation Framework** (to grossly oversimplify things) provides those object classes and protocols that Cocoa applications require but which have nothing to do with the user interface. These include object behaviors, memory management, networking, and file handling, as well as supplying bright shiny object wrappers around basic programming primitives like numbers and strings and arrays. (And in case you were wondering, the Foundation Framework has nothing to do with Isaac Asimov.)

- The **AppKit Framework** provides those things that applications require that have everything to do with the user interface: controls, windows, dialogs, menus, buttons, text, and so on. This framework comprises well over a hundred classes. Not too surprisingly, Interface Builder and the AppKit Framework are the very best of friends.

WE ARE BILLION-YEAR-OLD CARBON

Carbon is the primary elemental compound on which life as we know it is based. In Mac OS X, though, the Carbon environment is an evolutionary stage in Mac OS software development, originally intended as a temporary bridging technology to allow existing Mac OS 9 (and earlier) applications — life as Mac users knew it — to run natively in the OS X environment with minimal rewriting effort by their authors and publishers. Apple even provided a

System Extension for the old Mac OS called CarbonLib that allowed the same application to run in both OS X and earlier Mac OS releases (well, OS 8.6 and later, anyway).

Initially, most OS X applications were Carbon-based, including Apple's own offerings, such as iTunes, iMovie, iDVD, QuickTime Player, AppleWorks, and even the Finder. And, while newer apps written from scratch for OS X are frequently Cocoa-based (for example, iPhoto and GarageBand), those applications like iTunes that are in Apple's interest to keep viable in a cross-platform world are still Carbon-based and likely to remain so.

Besides cross-platform compatibility, additional reasons exist for you to consider Carbon for your application development. While you can, with a modicum of effort, leverage your C and C++ skills into Objective-C skills, you will find it more difficult to reuse existing C and C++ code libraries. Additionally, if you approach software development as a hobby or merely see it as a secondary responsibility on your job description rather than being your true calling, you might not wish to cultivate the object-oriented programming skills required for Cocoa development, and just continue to exploit your existing C, Pascal, or even FORTRAN expertise.

CARBON: WHY SOME FOLKS LIKE THAT BURNT TASTE

The true believers who came to Apple from NeXT were convinced that developers would rapidly see the advantages — there are many — of redesigning and rewriting their applications in Objective-C and taking advantage of the frameworks that are part of Cocoa (see "Coo-coo for Cocoa Apps," earlier in this chapter). What these folks failed to acknowledge, at least publicly, is that both developer community inertia and the cross-platform nature (shared source code) of most major applications made such a wholesale transition a tough sell. When Apple released Mac OS X, the company desired (heck, it desperately needed) rapid adoption of Mac OS X by the user community — the people who buy Macs. But before Apple's customers would adopt Mac OS X, it needed decent performance and lots of mainstream apps — and that really meant getting the big guys running on Mac OS X: Microsoft Office, Adobe's suite of applications (Photoshop, Illustrator, GoLive, and InDesign), Quark XPress, and their ilk.

These applications were, and still are, all cross-platform apps, and the companies that develop them believe firmly that a shared code base for both their Mac and Windows apps (and Windows really, much to our chagrin, owns the larger market) is critical in maintaining feature compatibility and for allowing simultaneous development for Windows and Mac. The lack of equivalent Cocoa frameworks and tools on the Windows side made a transition to Cocoa for such major applications a non-starter. After all, why put what would almost certainly be considerable effort and expense into maintaining and coordinating separate code bases when something already in existence was working very well, thank you kindly?

Initially, the true believers in the Apple-NeXT merger (but if you think it was an acquisition — well, have you noticed who Apple's CEO is?) held sway, and Carbon was a second-class citizen on OS X, at least relative to what Cocoa apps could do. Many of OS X's coolest things, like sheets, the Services submenu, the new Color Picker, and the new Font Picker dialog, were unavailable to Carbon apps. Gradually, though, things got better (that is, someone noticed that diversity was a good thing) and Carbon apps began to achieve parity with Cocoa, gaining the ability to access all the slick stuff that Aqua and OS X provide. After all, the marketplace spoke loudly, and the customer is always right (even when you know she's wrong).

A Carbon application's Build window is a little different from that of a Cocoa application (see Figure 2-7, showing Xcode's TickerView sample program). For example, you'll see different frameworks (Application Services, Carbon, and CoreServices rather than AppKit, Cocoa, and Foundation).

There are two Carbon application project types: Carbon Application and Carbon Bundle. The Carbon application project type uses .*nib* files for its resources and includes the three frameworks used in TickerView as well as a main.nib. A Carbon bundle is more barebones, including only the Carbon.framework and omitting the default resource and .nib files.

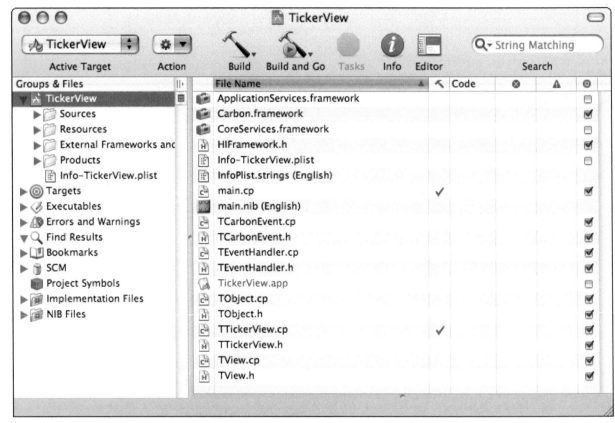

Figure 2-7
A sample Carbon application's Build window

CFM LIKES PEF AND DYLD LIKES MACH-O, GOT IT?

If you decide to dive into Carbon application development, you're going to swim past quite a few abbreviations and acronyms. Four critical examples are *PEF* (Preferred Executable Format), *Mach-o* (Mach Object format), *CFM* (Code Fragment Manager), and *dyld* (Dynamic Link Editor).

CFM and dyld are two code library managers/code loaders. CFM is a *static loader*: It determines the addresses and offsets used by variables and routines at the time you build your executable. dyld, a *dynamic loader*, resolves addresses at run-time. CFM expects PEF executables, and dyld demands Mach-o executables.

Carbon applications can be either PEF or Mach-o. But, if you want your Carbon executable to run in both OS 9 and OS X, you need a PEF (CFM) application. On the other hand, if you want to optimize your executable's OS X performance, you should create a Mach-o executable (dyld is the basic loader for OS X and, in fact, CFM for OS X is implemented on top of dyld). You can, of course, build both PEF (for OS 9) and Mach-o (for OS X) executables and package them together in the same *.app* bundle, but this usually adds significant disk overhead for your customers and increases your testing and debugging time. Note that one of the first major applications to use this two-executable approach was Apple's own AppleWorks.

JAVA IS EAST OF KRAKATOA

If you don't know already, you *should* know that the 1969 movie title, *Krakatoa, East of Java,* is wrong: Krakatoa is *west* of Java (didn't they have maps in '69?). In any case, you don't need to go all the way to the South Pacific, because Java's *all over* Mac OS X (and, no, we're not talking about the mug of latte we spilled on our keyboard, either). Mac OS X's Java runs in both native and interpreted form; you've seen something of the native variety above, when we talked about Cocoa-based Java applications.

But in addition to Cocoa-based Java apps, Xcode makes it possible for you to build a whole passel of other Java stuff. Take a look at what the New Project dude has on the evening's bill of faire (see Figure 2-8).

Figure 2-8
What kind of coffee would you like?

IT WOULDN'T BE A PICNIC WITHOUT 'EM

Building a program is not just a matter of compile and run — though Xcode may sometimes make you feel like it is. In fact, building a program (or almost any other sort of executable thingamcguffin) usually involves compiling several files, linking with several libraries, setting up bundles and other filesystem stuff, integrating some data resources, and so on. Xcode normally does all this by way of a *makefile,* which provides all those building instructions.

Makefiles, though, are tied to the operating system: A Mac OS X makefile probably won't run all that well on another platform (especially a non-Unix platform) without some modifications. While that's okay for most of the goods you build with Xcode, it's not so okay for Java executables that you might want to build in a bunch of different environments (one of the big selling points of Java being, after all, its cross-platform-deliciousness).

Ant (from the Apache Foundation, the same open-sourcerors who brought you the Apache Web Server) is a cross-platform build application that uses XML files to guide the particular build process. Because it's written in Java, Ant can run anywhere that Java does, and, because it's Java, Java developers love it. And, because Apple wants Java developers to love OS X, they've invited an Ant to their Xcode picnic.

- **Ant-based Application Jar:** With this you can build an application that the Java runtime (whether on Mac OS X or any other Java-enabled platform) can run; the application is built using Ant and packaged as a JAR file (see "Carry Moonbeams Home in a JAR").

- **Ant-based Empty Project:** Nothing to see here, because, hey, it's empty: The dude says *you* must supply your source and build.xml file — perfect for the hard-core Java do-it-yourselfer.

- **Ant-based Java Library:** Sometimes, several different Java executables share common classes and constants; with this template you can build a library that these executables can share and then seal that library up in a JAR.

- **Ant-based Signed Applet:** Signed applets include a digital signature so that users can, as it were, consider the source (that is, you). Signed applets have more privileges on a user's computer than unsigned applets, and, hence, are more dangerous.

HE'S AT THAT AWTWARD AGE

AWT is Java's *Abstract Window Toolkit,* the standard Java classes that provide platform-independent GUI goodies. Although AWT user-interface widgets and windows try their best to fit into the Aqua-fresh look and feel of Mac OS X when they run on a Mac, they *are* intended for cross-platform deployment, meaning that they often end up feeling somewhat alien and icky in use and they can't provide all the UI capabilities that a *real* Mac OS X application can. But they are portable.

Gone are the dark times when writing something in Java on the Mac would get you sniggers and sad head-shakes at your local Java Developers Conference. These days, even the Java mavens at Sun — the Home Of Java itself — tend to tote around Powerbooks, using their sleek aluminum wonders to build such goodies as:

- **Ant-based Web Start Application:** These are applications that run on the user's machine independently of the browser though they usually do require a browser for downloading them initially. They employ Sun's Web Start technology for installing applications and updates.

- **Java AWT Applet:** This template is for building a JAR-packaged applet (a Java executable that can run in a Java-enabled Web browser or in Apple's appletviewer); the applets built with this template employ AWT user interface elements (see "He's at that AWTward Age").

- **Java AWT Application:** Like the previous template, this one sets you up to build a JAR containing a Java executable (again employing AWT interface elements); but, rather than being intended for browser deployment, the executable is an application which is meant to run on its own (well, on its own with the assistance of the Java Runtime Engine).

WOULD YOU LIKE TO SWING ON A STAR

Sun, the developers of all (or, at least, most) things Java, realized relatively quickly that the GUI components of AWT had certain architectural and performance limitations. It began a project to create a more comprehensive, expandable, new, and improved set of classes for Java 2 called the *Java Foundation Classes* (JFC). This project was called *Swing*, and, because JFC is so unhip to say (what is it again? Jamaican Fried Chicken?), Java coders quickly adopted the code name for daily use. Swing is, according to Sun (though opinions differ among developers), a superset of AWT that adds many new components and services.

CARRY MOONBEAMS HOME IN A JAR

A JAR file is a Java ARchive file that lets you package all the separate files that may make up a Java executable into a single package. JARs employ the venerable ZIP file format to bundle the class files and resources that the Java executable may need into a single hunk o'data, and, because it's ZIP, that hunk can be compressed into a smaller hunk. JARs also support digital signatures for security as well as versioning information, so other Java executables can tell whether a particular JAR's contents are fresh and ready to serve.

- **Java JNI Application:** JNI is the *Java Native Interface*, which lets you combine pure Java code with platform-specific native code for performance or user-interface reasons (naturally, JNI applications are not cross-platform); use this template if you're in the mood for a JAR file-based JNI experience.

- **Java Swing Applet:** AWT is *so* Java version 1; with version 2's Swing components (see "Would You Like to Swing on a Star"), you can build a JAR-based applet with a much more advanced user interface.

- **Java Swing Application:** Similar to the AWT application template, you use this one to build a more modern Swing-based application and package it up as an application bundle.

- **Java Tool:** Finally, try this template if you want to build a command-line tool or Java library as a JAR file.

FRAMEWORKS AND PLUG-INS AND TOOLS, OH, MY!

Applications are easily the most common product you'll create using Xcode. After all, applications are what users see as icons in the Finder and employ to do their work (or fool around with for their entertainment and enlightenment). Some less obvious projects, though, are

- **plug-ins:** code modules that can be added to an existing application to enhance functionality

- **frameworks:** libraries of reusable code that you can use in multiple projects

- **command-line tools:** text-based programs invoked from the Unix command line

Whether you realize it or not, you use a lot of plug-ins in OS X. Some examples include iTunes visualizers, iMovie transitions and effects, Web browser plug-ins like Flash, Sherlock channels, the various panes in System Preferences, screen savers, and anything related to iPhoto's Export command (which you can find on iPhoto's File menu).

Frameworks, unlike plug-ins, are things that nobody but a programmer needs to know about. Your users aren't going to care a whit whether you have a framework in your bookkeeping application that is replicated in your checkbook application. Frameworks are a convenience for you, the programmer, letting you share libraries of code with your coding compatriots or among your own applications.

Command-line tools, as the name suggests, are programs invoked from a Unix command line by a user typing an arcane sequence of options and settings — an activity that Mac users really aren't that big on, which is why many

THIS PLUG WON'T FIT IN THE SOCKET

(Almost) every application's plug-in interface is different. A Photoshop plug-in won't work in iPhoto and an iTunes Visualizer does nothing for Safari. That's not to say that multiple applications might not be able to use the same plug-in — for example, Lemke Software's GraphicConverter can use many (but not all) Photoshop plug-ins. Some software developers publish their plug-in *APIs* (Application Programming Interfaces), like Adobe did for Photoshop, so that third-party developers can create plug-in products to enhance an application's functionality. What's more, you can use someone else's published plug-in API to figure out how to make plug-ins designed for that other application work with *your* application. Everybody wins! Especially you.

Apple provides template projects for some of their documented plug-in APIs such as Address Book and System Preferences. For the rest, though, you're going to have to start with a bare-bones plug-in template and import the API headers and files provided by application developers in their *SDKs* (Software Development Kits).

command-line tools are never actually seen by a user. Unix has thousands upon thousands of open-source executables that can be invoked from the command line, and most Mac users would never think to lay their hands on all that wealth. However, a clever developer (that would be you) can reuse open-source Unix command-line tool code by recompiling it for OS X as a command-line tool and then including it within his project: Just create a standard Mac interface with checkboxes, radio buttons, text boxes, and so forth, where the user can set parameters, and then simply call the embedded command-line tool to do the work, translating the Mac-friendly GUI input into the semi-intelligible parameter list that the command-line tool expects. You can find numerous examples of this approach at http://sourceforge.net including video authoring tools, encryption packages, games, and programmer utilities. AppleScript Studio is an extremely quick and popular method for creating graphical interfaces to the Unix command-line tools, as you'll see in Chapter 15.

CHECKING THE RECEIPT

Our trip to the project builder's emporium introduced us to the bow tie wearing New Project Assistant, who showed us many things we could put in our shopping cart, including project templates for making Cocoa applications, Carbon applications, Java applets and applications, code libraries, plug-ins, and various other geeky goods. In the process, we learned a bit about the different application environments that Mac OS X and Xcode support and something about their histories. In fact, we probably could spend a lot more time than we did browsing this emporium — and if it had a food court, we would!

Look in Any (Project) Window

In This Chapter

The Project window, as you may have gathered from the previous two chapters, is the center of your Xcode software development universe: It's where you summon a text editor to create or modify source files, it's where you invoke Interface Builder to construct or modify your user-interface elements, and it's where you start your builds a-building. Everything you create with Xcode, from the simplest little command-line utility to the great big honking music-enabled, video-enhanced, database-driven graphical layout suite (you know, the sort of software that Microsoft would design based on input from Homer Simpson), has its own Project window, and in that window you have access to all the things that constitute your project.

As you saw in Chapter 2, Xcode gives you a head start on assembling a project when you select a new project template, providing such goodies as necessary frameworks, a main routine, and basic user-interface elements. In addition, each template comes with a bunch of settings that control how all those pieces interrelate, and what items need to be built, and in what order. From that advanced starting point, you get to add everything else; that is, all the things that make your product unique. But if you don't know how to use the Project window in which the New Project Assistant dumps all these goodies, you won't get very far.

In order for us to explain the Project window, it would help if you had one to look at, and the best way to get one is to... wait for it... open a project (bet you saw *that* one coming!). You can use the project we created in Chapter 1 (you *did* do the tutorial in that chapter, didn't you?), or if you're bored with that project, you can pick one from among the various example projects that come with Xcode — you should be able to find *something* in the Examples folder in your Developer directory that will amuse and enlighten you.

PICTURE THE WINDOW

When you open a project document (easy to spot; they tend to have the suffix *.xcode*), the Xcode application launches, displaying a Project window like the one shown in Figure 3-1 (which happens to be the Picture Sharing Browser project in the Developer/Examples/Foundation folder) using the default Xcode 2 workspace (see "A Workspace to Play in" for an overview of workspaces).

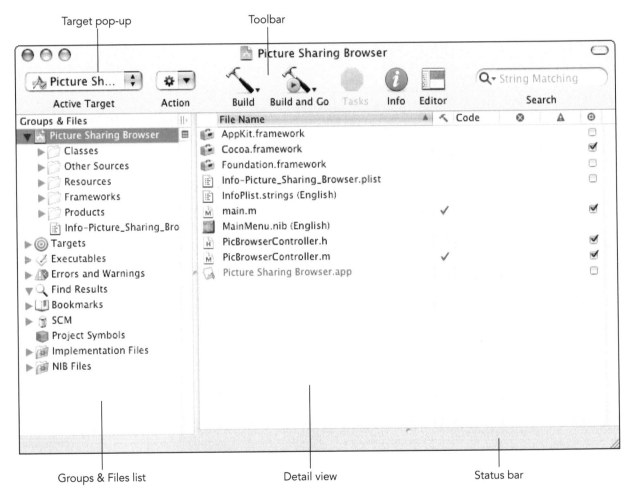

Figure 3-1
The Project window's five parts

A WORKSPACE TO PLAY IN

Not all of us like to work in exactly the same way. For example, one of us uses a trackball with his left hand (even though he throws and bats right-handed) while another of us actually likes the single-button Mac mouse and, in fact, also didn't mind the original iMac hockey-puck mouse (strange, but all too true). Similarly, some developers may like the basic layout and features of the Xcode Project window while others may want something simpler... or more complex.

The Xcode application offers three basic *workspaces* — Project window styles and layouts suited to different temperaments, working styles, and situations. The most commonly used workspace, and the only one available in earlier versions of Xcode, is the *Default workspace*; this is the Project window layout we describe in this chapter. But there are two others:

- The *Condensed workspace* (see Figure 3-2) uses a smaller window that can display several different subsets of the items that make up your project (for example, one view for files, one for targets, one for Smart Groups). Tabs at the top of the window let you switch among these views. Editing, debugging, and building appear in separate windows in this workspace.

- The *All-in-One workspace* (see Figure 3-3) jams everything into a single window that contains multiple pages: one for editing, one for building, and one for debugging. The page button in the upper-left corner of the window lets you select the different pages.

You can choose your preferred workspace using Xcode's General preferences, available from the Xcode menu. But don't do it yet; otherwise, the rest of this chapter will make even less sense than it does.

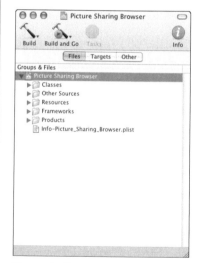

Figure 3-2
The Condensed workspace

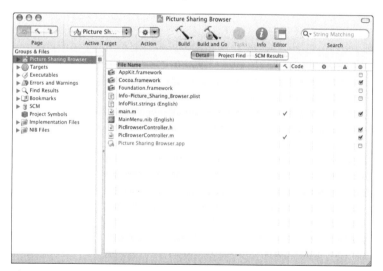

Figure 3-3
The All-in-One workspace

IF I HAD A HAMMER... WAIT A MINUTE, I DO!

Like nearly all Mac applications that offer a toolbar at the top of the window, there's a Customize Toolbar item on the View menu that produces a sheet (a *very* long sheet in this case) from which you can choose, change, and rearrange your Project window tools (see Figure 3-4).

Do a lot of debugging? Add a Debug button. Never build more than one target per project? Deep-six the Active Target pop-up and get back a few dozen pixels. Or, if you are one of those lucky souls with a 30-inch flat-screen monitor on your tweaked and fully loaded G5, you can load your Xcode toolbar up with just about every tool Xcode offers (we think: Give us a G5 and a 30-inch monitor, and we'll get back to you on that).

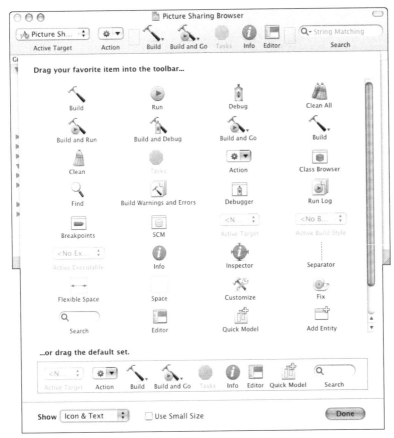

Figure 3-4
Toolbar choices galore!

Note

Don't confuse the Xcode application with Xcode itself. If you haven't figured it out by now, the label *Xcode* refers to the whole collection of tools and goodies that Apple shoves into the Developer folder; one of those goodies, the *Xcode application*, is the program that knows how to talk to all the other developer tools, and the one that manages your project.

The Project window comprises five main parts:

- the **target pop-up,** which lets you select the active target (see "Aiming at a Target" later in this chapter for more about targets);

- the **toolbar,** which contains bright, friendly, easy-to-use menus and buttons that you'll commonly use during the software development process (and, like many other Mac applications that have toolbars, you can customize the Project window's tools; see "If I Had a Hammer... Wait a Minute, I Do!");

- the **Groups & Files list,** which shows you all the pieces of your project arranged in a lot of different ways;

- the **status bar,** where messages appear when Xcode is doing something other than just waiting for you to decide what to do next; and

- the **detail view,** which shows you the details of the project items you've selected in the Groups & Files list.

If it looks a lot like a Finder window, the iTunes window, or the iPhoto window, don't be surprised — Apple likes this window style and it wants you to like it, too. Besides, this window style works really well for displaying collections of information, like albums of photos, playlists of songs, folders of files, or components of a software development project.

GROUPS, SMART AND OTHERWISE

It should come as no surprise if you read the last sentence of the previous section that the Groups & Files list functions very much like the iTunes Source list or the iPhoto Album list. Select an entry in the list and its contents appear in the detail view. Some entries sport a disclosure triangle indicating that they are a *group*. The project group appears first in the list and it organizes all your project's parts: source files, resources, headers, documentation, and so forth. Immediately below the project group, you'll find the targets group with its distinctive red-and-white bull's-eye icon. Each target describes a project variation you might want built — it might be a demo version (some features disabled), a debug version, the shipping version, or some other variation.

 Note

Xcode adds the basic groups and files required for the project template you choose, so the initial appearance of the Groups & Files list will vary depending upon the template. In most cases, you might not have to add any groups at all, just the source files required for your product, but where's the fun in that?

Your project group and the target group are called *static groups* because their contents don't change unless you explicitly change them — like a polyester shirt on a dry, windy day, they cling. Static groups are slightly more advanced than the static albums of iPhoto and playlists in iTunes — you can define subgroups and maintain a hierarchical organization of your data. For example, in your project group, you could define subgroups for header files, source files, and documentation files.

Similar to iTunes' Smart Playlists and iPhoto's Smart Albums, Xcode has dynamic Smart Groups. One such pre-defined Smart Group is the Errors and Warnings group, whose contents change to reflect the results of your most recent build attempt. If you create a Cocoa application project, you'll also see a NIB Files Smart Group.

More importantly, you can create your own Smart Groups as well. For example, you could create a Smart Group that displays only your header (.h) files like this:

1. **Choose File → New Smart Group → Simple Filter Smart Group, as shown in Figure 3-5.** A new folder icon, with the lavender hue indicative of a Smart Group, appears in the Groups & Files list and an Info window comes to the fore (see Figure 3-6).

Figure 3-5
Create a new Smart Group

Figure 3-6
Define your Smart Group in the Inspector

2. **Use the Inspector to define your Smart Group's properties.** With the Inspector you can

   - customize the Smart Group's icon by clicking and dragging a picture into the Image well or clicking Choose and navigating to an image you wish to use;

   - tell Xcode where to search for the items (select the Recursively checkbox if you wish the search to extend into nested folders of the selected starting point);

- specify the pattern or Unix regular expression to employ (we're going for a Simple Pattern of *.h in our example here); and

- tell Xcode whether to include this Smart Group in all your projects or just the current project with the Save For pop-up menu.

3. **Close the Inspector, select your Smart Group, and peruse the results of your efforts (see Figure 3-7).**

AIMING AT A TARGET

Line your sights up on the target you want to hit, take a deep breath, let half the breath out slowly, and squeeze the trigger — oh, sorry, not that kind of target. How about this: Just click the Active Target pop-up menu in the Project window toolbar (see Figure 3-1) and choose the target you want to build. Oh. You wanted something more....

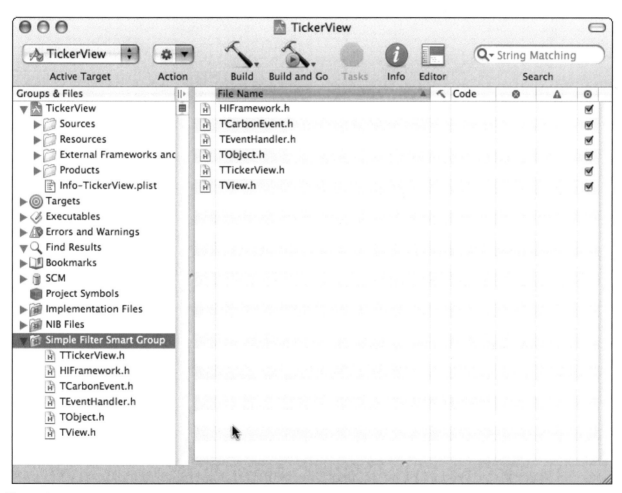

Figure 3-7
Your Smart Group's contents appear in the detail view

A *target*, as we may have said, or, at least, implied, is the thing (program, plug-in, command-line tool, whatever) you're going to build. A project can actually encompass more than one target. Let's say (and, really, how can you stop us?) you want to build several closely related applications that rely on a common framework, such as three or four self-contained solitaire games that use the same card display and manipulation techniques. You can combine these into a single project that builds both the card-handling framework and the individual games that use it by having different targets for each game.

Though we discuss building separate targets in more detail in Chapter 11 (for you Carbon lovers) and Chapter 12 (for you Cocoa sippers), here are a few take-away concepts for you to, um, take away from this discussion of the Project window:

- You select the target you want to build from the Active Target pop-up menu in the Project window's toolbar (or, if you like mousing to the menu bar, from Project → Set Active Target).

- The targets group in the Group & Files list shows you all your project's targets. You can tell which one is the active target because it has an attractive check-mark-in-a-green-circle badge decorating its icon (see Figure 3-8).

- Opening the disclosure triangle for a target shows you the various stages of the build and the order in which they occur (see, again, Figure 3-8); you can click and drag the build stages around to change the build order (after all, we're Mac users, so dragging stuff around is our birthright and Xcode understands that).

- Opening the disclosure triangle for a build phase shows you the files associated with that phase (see, yet once more, Figure 3-8).

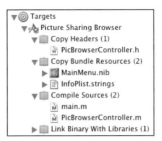

Figure 3-8
Right on target

HOW DO I BUILD THEE?

Once you've created your project; created and added all your source, resource, and ancillary files; defined your target(s), specified how those targets are built; and chosen the target you want to build, Xcode gives you many ways to customize the build process: *build styles*.

Build styles let you create multiple variations of your product without requiring additional targets. The most common reason to use more than one build style is when you want to build both a debug version and a shippable version. The complicated way to achieve this goal would be to create two targets, and the reason it's complicated is because you have to make sure that you keep both versions in sync: adding files to both targets, deleting files from both targets, and so forth. With Xcode's build styles, on the other hand, you merely describe how your source files should be processed for the different versions — all you need is one set of files, no syncing necessary. In fact, the need for building both debug and shipping versions is *so* common that Xcode automatically creates these two build styles when you create a target; Xcode calls these two styles *Development* and *Deployment*.

Note

When should you add a new target to your project and when should you add a build style? Generally, you want a new target if you are building a new product, and you want a new build style if you wish simply to modify how a target is built. For example, if your product requires additional files or different build phases, you probably want a new target; if your product simply requires different compiler settings, you probably want a new build style.

You can create, edit, and choose your project's build styles from Xcode's Project Info window.

1. **Choose Project → Edit Project Settings.** Your project's Info window appears.

2. **Click the Styles tab.** The current build style's settings appear (see Figure 3-9).

3. **Choose a build style from the Build Style pop-up menu, or create a new one by choosing New Build Style from the pop-up.** You can also delete or rename build styles by choosing Edit Build Style from the pop-up.

The Project Info window's Styles tab lets you add new settings to a style (the + button), remove settings (the - button), and edit settings (yep, the Edit button). A lot of the settings that correspond to compiler command-line options or to part of a traditional makefile live inside the Styles tab of the Project Info window, so it's one of many places in Xcode where you can be as geeky as you wanna be and still be using a GUI.

To build your target (which is, after all, what this section is about), you can click either the Build and Go or the Build toolbar icon (look back at Figure 3-1), or you can choose either of these commands from the Build menu.

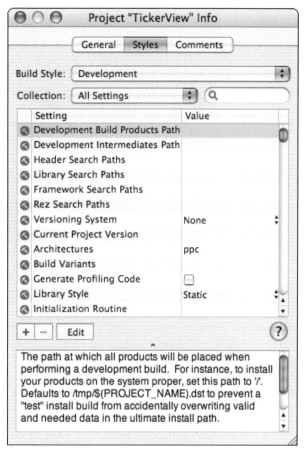

Figure 3-9
Now we're stylin'...

▼ **Note**

We'll cover deciding what files go into your project in more detail in Chapters 11 and 12. Just be aware, at this point, that there might be lots of files needed in addition to the obvious source-code files and supporting frameworks, such as images, icons, help text, preference data, sounds, and all kinds of other resources.

THE BUILD BUTTONS ARE A DIFFERENT KIND OF HAMMER

The Build and the Build and Go toolbar icons are more than just simple buttons. They're also menus, as indicated by the tiny triangles at the icons' bottom-right corners. You need to remember, though, that they don't work like most OS X menus — you have to press and hold them to display the menu; just clicking the icon is the same as choosing the first item in the undisplayed menu.

The Build button's default action (surprise!) builds your target and saves the result where your preferences specify. But there are two other options in the Build button's menu: Clean All and Clean. Both of these commands remove built and partially built end products, setting you up with a clean slate for your next build attempt. They differ thusly:

- Clean removes the built elements for the currently selected target only; and

- Clean All wipes out the intermediate results for all of a project's targets.

Like the Build button, the Build and Go button has additional options hidden away in its pop-up menu:

- Build and Run, which builds the target and then immediately attempts to run it;

- Build and Debug, which builds the target and then runs it with Xcode's Debug window open (something you may use a lot as your application gets closer to being done);

- Run Executable, which just runs the thing (and, naturally, this command is inactive if the target has not been built); and

- Debug Executable, which runs the target with the Debug window open.

 Tip
Because Build and Debug is an option you're probably going to use a lot during product development, choosing it from the pop-up menu or from the Build menu can become tiresome. We recommend that keyboard fans learn ⌘+Y and that mouse fans customize their toolbars, adding the Build and Debug button.

While the Styles tab in your project's Info window lets you control how Xcode builds that particular project, Xcode's Building Preferences (see Figure 3-10) let you specify how the build process works in all your Xcode projects. You can get to Xcode's Preferences by choosing Xcode ➔ Preferences. The Building Preferences is one of the many preferences available from the choices at the top of the Preferences window.

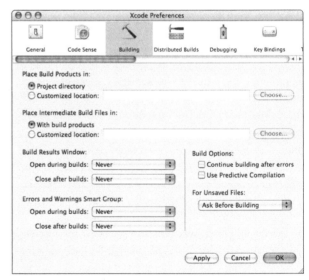

Figure 3-10
Xcode offers a number of Building-related preferences

You've already seen a version of the Build Results group of this preference pane back in Chapter 1 (the Setup Assistant showed it to you when you first installed Xcode; see Figure 1-5 if you feel like leafing back). But the Building preference pane offers many additional settings beyond those. For example, Xcode ordinarily stops the build process whenever it encounters a compilation error. Some programmers may question whether this is correct behavior, because one could fix the error, restart the build, and get stopped almost immediately by another compilation error in the very same file — after a few rounds of this stop-fix-go-stop business, irritation, frustration, and a nagging urge to chew one's fingers off become quite pronounced. For this reason, we prefer selecting the Continue building after errors option, which lets Xcode rack up as many errors as it can find, after which we can go back and fix whatever errors were encountered (or at least try to do so) in one intense bug-fixing session (which, of course, provides its own opportunities for irritation and frustration).

Another setting lets you choose how you want Xcode to proceed when there are unsaved files open. By default, Xcode asks if you want to save these files before building, but you can choose to have Xcode automatically perform a save on all open files, close all unsaved files without saving, or cancel the build so that you can deal with each file individually.

The Build Results Window preference group tells Xcode whether and when the Build Results window (see Figure 3-11) should be open. Xcode normally keeps this window closed unless you specifically open by choosing Build ➜ Build Results (Shift+⌘+B), but you can specify other settings for it. Dennis likes to have it automatically open at the start of any build and automatically close if (and he hopes when) the build succeeds — this lets him watch the build's progress a little more easily than the Project window's status bar allows (on a fast machine, the messages vanish almost before they appear), but it still gets the Build Results window out of the way when it isn't needed. Michael thinks the default is just dandy (he likes the challenge of the status

bar's flashing text). You should play with the settings to find a configuration you like.

Figure 3-11
The Build Results window tells you what happened on your latest build

Similarly, the Errors & Warnings Smart Group settings let you specify when and how the Project window will automatically select this group. Feel free to play with these settings, too; you can't break anything (unless you have a very heavy mouse finger).

As you can see, Xcode's building process is quite configurable and makes the complex task of building a modern Mac application very easy — once, that is, you've created the project, developed your algorithms, and written all your source. We can't help you with *that* part of the process, here, though: This is the Xcode 2 Book, not the Programming Book (check the cover if you don't believe us).

WE CALL THE TASKS BUTTON "BIG RED"

Why does the Tasks button look like a big red stop sign? And why is it disabled? Well, it looks like a stop sign because its main job is to stop whatever's going on. And it's usually disabled because usually there's not anything much *going* on (unless you count typing code or looking up stuff in Xcode's documentation library as "something going on").

The Tasks button becomes enabled automagically whenever you tell Xcode to go off and perform a task (like, say, building your target). When the Tasks button is enabled, all you have to do is click it to cut short whatever current task Xcode is running. That's it. Pretty simple, right? And it's a good thing, too, because you really don't want to think too hard about how to stop something when you have to stop it right now!

That's not to say that the button doesn't have its subtleties. Like the Build and the Build and Go buttons, the Tasks button also acts like a pop-up menu: Click and hold the Tasks button to see a menu (see Figure 3-12) that lets you choose which of the running tasks you want to stop, just in case more than one task is running at once (remember, Xcode is threaded and can walk and chew gum and compile and index all at the same time — well, maybe not the part about the gum).

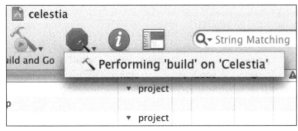

Figure 3-12
Let's call the whole thing off

And that's just about all there is to say about Big Red. He's a simple fellow, but very good to have around in an emergency.

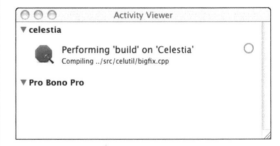

STOPPING POWER FOR THE MULTITASKER

The Tasks button is great for stopping a task — or even several tasks — that Xcode may be running on your project. But it doesn't quite fill the bill if you are working on more than one project at a time, because the Tasks button belongs to the project in the Project window, and you can have more than one of those open and doing something. For extreme workaholics like you, the Activity Viewer window is the answer (see Figure 3-13). Available from the Window menu, the Activity Viewer shows you all the currently running tasks in all the currently open projects. Click the Stop sign beside any of the running tasks and you can put a halt to it, toot sweet (and, yes, we mistakenly hit the Tasks button when we were studying French, to the deep regret of Mrs. Gagnet).

Figure 3-13
Hold everything!

411 ON SPEED DIAL: GETTING INFO

Projects, as we've seen, can contain various files of various types, and various groups of files of various types, all fulfilling various roles in the building process. And associated with each of these various files and various groups of files are various settings you may wish to view or to modify in various ways (whoops! We think we just ran over our "various" quota... time to pick a new word to beat to death).

Rather than hiding these different information viewing and setting windows in different menus and submenus (like, say, one very popular word processor of our acquaintance does), Xcode lets you get access to them with one simple button: the Info button that appears by default in the default Project window workspace. Just click the item about which you want info in the Project window — it can be anything (a group, a Smart Group, an individual file, or anything else that appears in the Groups & Files list or the detail view) — and click the Info button (or you can press ⌘+I if clicking a button is just too much trouble). Voila! An Info window appears that lets you see and change the settings and characteristics for that item. What's more, the window displays just those bits of information and settings that pertain to the specific item you chose to inspect; for example, Figure 3-14 shows the information window for a source file, while Figure 3-15 shows the information window for a Smart Group.

The Info window often (in fact, usually) provides tabs along the top that let you get at all the stuff you need to get at for the item you are viewing. A source file, for example, lets you see and change its general settings, or add additional build settings, or provide comments, depending on the tab you click in its Info window. A target's Info window, on the other hand, provides tabs for general settings, build settings, rule settings, file properties, and comments. Of course, there are some items that have no viewable or modifiable information associated with them at all, and the Info window will tell you that, too.

Figure 3-14
Source file info, courtesy of the Info button

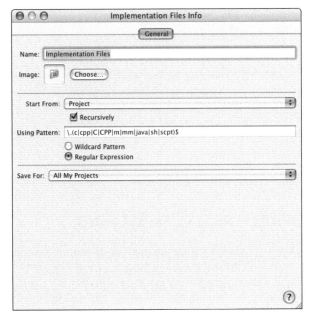

Figure 3-15
Smart Group info, also courtesy of the Info button

INSPECTOR GADGET

The Info window for any particular item belongs to that item and that item only. Click a different item and click the Info button again and a new Info window appears for that item. You can quickly fill your screen with Info windows this way (and it's a great way to avoid getting any real work done). However, you can save screen space and streamline the information-viewing process by using an Inspector instead of an Info window.

What's the difference? Not much in terms of the information displayed. However, the Inspector window is a palette that always floats in front of the other windows on the screen. It has a smaller title bar, and, most importantly, there is only one of them. With an Inspector window open, you can click any item in your Project window and the Inspector immediately shows you the information for it. Click another item, and the Inspector window shows you the info for *that* item instead.

To open an Inspector, you can press Option while opening Xcode's File menu: The Get Info command changes to Show Inspector. Or, you can press Option+⌘+I. Or you can customize the Project window's toolbar (see "If I Had a Hammer... Wait a Minute, I Do!" earlier in this chapter) and add an Inspector button.

SEARCH AND YE SHALL FIND

One of the most irritating things in life, at least in ours, is knowing that you have something but forgetting where you put it (where the *%$# are those car keys? [oh, and how is "*%$#" pronounced?]). Dealing with a complex software product involves keeping track of lots of files and, even with your stuff logically organized, tracking down a particular file or other item can still take a while. Why frustrate yourself when Xcode makes it easy to find anything in your project? Just like iTunes, iPhoto, and the Finder, there's a handy-dandy Search field in Xcode's project window, in many Info and Inspector windows, and documentation window toolbars (we'll see the documentation window later in this broadcast, long about Chapter 7).

To find a particular item in your project, just start typing in the Project window's Search field. While you're typing, Xcode hides any lines in the detail view that don't match what you have typed to that point. Apple refers to this as *filtered searching*. You're probably already familiar with this searching capability from the Finder or iTunes, and it is truly convenient for locating items. Figure 3-16 shows how one can find just those header filenames containing the letters "cal" among the multitude of files in the Foundation framework.

If your needs exceed the quick-filtered search that the Search field offers, you can always resort to Xcode's Find menu (see Figure 3-17). From here you can do all sorts of searches.

- Find In Project provides a batch search dialog with a variety of search features (see Figure 3-18) that lets you do all sorts of find-and-replace operations in your project, including limiting searches to specific types of items and even (via the Options button) filtering files using regular expressions.

- Find Selected Text In Project and Find Selected Definition In Project use whatever you have selected in a project or editor window as the basis for your search.

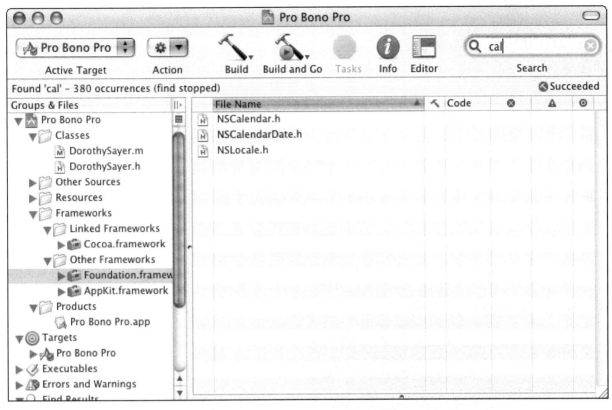

Figure 3-16
Narrowing the search

- Single File Find searches only the currently selected file and gives you a dialog to control the find operation.

- Find Next (or Find Previous if you press and hold Shift, as shown in Figure 3-17) finds the next or previous occurrence of the current search term in the currently selected file.

- Find Selected Text lets you use the current selection as the basis of your search in the current file.

- Replace replaces the currently selected text with a previously specified replacement.

Find In Project...	⇧⌘F
Find Selected Text In Project	
Find Selected Definition In Project	
Single File Find...	⌘F
Find Previous	⇧⌘G
Find Selected Text	
Replace	
Replace and Find Next	
Use Selection for Find	⌘E
Jump to Selection	⌘J
Jump to Definition	
Add to Bookmarks	⌘D
Go to Line...	⌘L

Figure 3-17
The Find menu

- Replace and Find Next replaces the currently selected text with a previously specified replacement, and then searches for the next occurrence of the search text.

- Use Selection for Find makes the currently selected text the basis for the next find and opens the project find window.

- Jump to Selection scrolls to the current selection in a currently open window (useful when you're looking at a big file).

- Jump to Definition interprets the currently selected text as the name of one your project's symbols and does a symbol lookup on it, letting you jump from your code to the header file that defines it.

- Add to Bookmarks adds the location of the current selection to your Bookmarks group, so you can quickly get back there.

- Go to Line lets you go to a specific line in the current file by line number (so very old school, but still a favorite).

All-in-all, Xcode helps you locate just about anything in your project (or in Apple's supplied documentation, as we explain in Chapter 7).

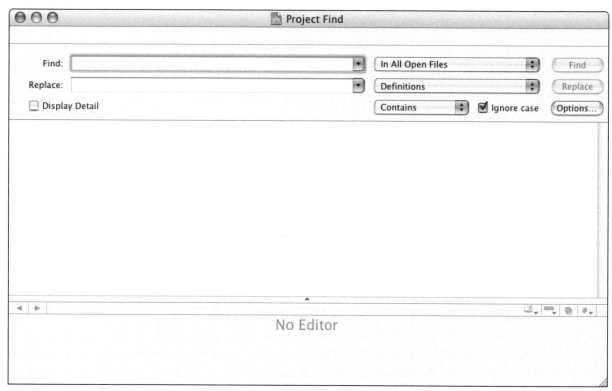

Figure 3-18
Finding can be a real batch

WHAT WE SAW

We've seen what a typical Project window looks like, perused the ways that Xcode can organize a project's files into various useful groups, cast our gazes upon targets, admired Xcode's various and sundry build options and preferences, caught sight of the big red stop sign that lets us stop something that might have gotten out of control, examined info windows and inspected Inspectors, and regarded with appreciation the extensive search capabilities built into Xcode. Now it's time to close our eyes — until we get to the next chapter.

PART II

Code Mountain

Compiler? I Hardly Know Her!

In This Chapter

We sometimes like to think of our code as really strange poetry written for a very fussy, and possibly quite mad, audience of one: the compiler. Toss the compiler a heartfelt creative effort like this little C sestet —

```
void LocalToGlobalRgn(RgnHandle rgn)
{
    Point offset = { 0, 0 };
    LocalToGlobal( &offset );
    OffsetRgn(rgn, offset.h, offset.v);
} // LocalToGlobalRgn
```

— and the compiler either nods appreciatively and produces a binary bunch of executable goodness, or it throws up its metaphorical hands and tells us that we've committed a distressing programmatical faux pas and should think about another line of employment.

The compiler is every programmer's closest friend and harshest critic: the helpful enabler who makes our code sing and the stern taskmaster who chains us to the keyboard deep into the night demanding that we fix *just one more bug*.

Few programmers regard their compilers with indifference.

Xcode would be a pretty useless development environment if it didn't come with at least one of those punctilious yet powerful programs that converts the code you craft into the programs that run. Lucky for you, it does, and a pretty fine one... or two or three.

It's all in how you count these things. Confused? Read on and we'll try to make it all clear.

A LITTLE BACKGROUND READING

We'll start with a bowl of background and a scoop or two of history on the side; feel free to skip this and the next section and head on down to "GCC, or, I GNU a C Compiler Once..." if you want to get right to the *what* and don't care (or already know) about the *why* of compilers in general.

A compiler is, at heart, a pretty simple kind of program: It takes a sequence of bytes (your code) and converts it into a different sequence of bytes (executable binary CPU instructions). This process fundamentally seems not much different from using a Captain Midnight decoder badge to translate a coded message into something understandable (in this case, understandable not by weak and squishy humans but by a silicon chip). Of course, it's not quite *that* simple in actual practice.

Humans and computers think in very different ways. The monotonous sequence of itty-bitty steps that comprise the binary instructions that make up a compiled computer program, while the sort of thing that your typical CPU chip finds delightful, most humans find both hard to follow — and incredibly boring. True, there are savants who can happily cavort through piles of compiled binary code and see the hidden beauty and power that lies therein, but these folk are as rare as those who can play 20 simultaneous games of chess blindfolded or who can tell you without thinking on which day of the week that Saint

Swithins Day falls in the year A.D. 802,701. There would be far fewer programmers if that kind of strangely shaped mind were required for the job.

Instead, most of us think in general and abstract and symbolic ways. Give us a bunch of details and we quickly look for patterns so we can stop looking at the details. Specifics bore us. The dull repetitious specificity of detail that a CPU requires is mind numbing. Humans want, say, simply to tell the computer to add two numbers; the CPU wants to know where each number is stored, where to move these numbers prior to adding them, and where to put the result once the adding is done (along with a bunch of other details). That's why we have created *high-level* computer languages like C, FORTRAN, or Java: They let us get more abstract and general in describing what we want the CPU to do, and they let us describe what we want it to do in a way that makes sense for the problem that we want to solve. For example, the FORTRAN computer language was designed to help scientists and engineers describe mathematical programs (FORTRAN means "FORmula TRANslation"), while C was designed to craft general-purpose programs and operating system utilities. Once we have written a program in a high-level language, we then use another program — the compiler — to translate our general, abstract, more-or-less human-friendly instructions into the detailed steps that make sense to the CPU.

A compiler, therefore, does more than simply translate our code into machine instructions like a software version of the Captain Midnight decoder badge: It interprets our code, analyzes it, dissects it, and looks at each part in context to figure out the best way to convert a general instruction (such as "add 1 to b") into the machine instructions that will carry the instruction out.

What's more, we don't even *want* to think about the underlying machine and its CPU at all: When we write a program in C, for example, we don't care (or shouldn't *have* to care) whether that program will run on a

PowerPC G5 CPU or an Intel Itanium or a Z-80. But the compiler has to care, because its job is to convert our high-level language programs into specific instructions for a specific CPU.

In short, we need a different compiler for each computer language we use, and we need a different compiler for each type of CPU on which we want our program to run. Unless, of course, we happen to have a compiler that handles multiple computer languages and multiple CPUs.

And *that* is what *GCC*, the compiler that comes with Xcode, is all about.

THE DESIGNER COMPILER COLLECTION

GCC used to be the *GNU C Compiler* back in the day when Richard Stallman first began developing it (see "Who GNU?"). Made sense, really: Unix and C went together like skittles and beer (no, not the fruit-candy — they're *terrible* with beer), so if you're going to build a compiler to go along with your Unix-workalike, a C compiler seems a pretty logical choice. And, like most compilers of the era, the first GCC produced code for a specific CPU (the "obscure" 68000 processor Stallman began with), but that was hardly practical for creating the components of an open-source operating system with ambitions of running on a variety of CPU platforms. Nor was the limitation to the C language practical for the hordes of programmers out there who wanted to participate in Stallman's open-source project, but who wanted to write in languages other than C.

To overcome these limitations, GCC was reengineered and transformed; even the words that the acronym stood for were changed — the *GNU C Compiler* became the *GNU Compiler Collection*, an assortment of software components that worked together to make up a complete compiler.

Today's GCC supports a wide variety of high-level programming languages and targets a wide range of available processor architectures.

WHO GNU?

The GNU Project began in 1983 as an attempt to create a completely free computer operating system, a Unix-like OS owned by nobody in particular and readily available to geeks of free will everywhere. Richard Stallman, who began the project, created the concept of *copyleft* to go with it, a licensing strategy that guaranteed that the project's products would be free to all comers to use and to develop and which would not be subject to subsequent proprietary licensing restrictions by any developers who used and improved those products. Among GNU's many subprojects were the creation of text editors, operating system kernels, and compilers for the GNU operating system. The name *GNU* is recursive: It stands for *GNU is Not Unix*. It's the sort of joke that programmers adore.

Though GNU is not Unix (which is owned in its many versions by many different companies, some of whom, even as we write, are engaging in various legal battles to decide just what Unix really is and who really owns it), it *is* based upon the general architectural principles that comprise Unix. And, through the vagaries of historical accident and common cause, the GNU Project and Linus Torvald's Unix-workalike Linux development efforts merged in the 1990s, which gave a big boost to both efforts. Apple's Darwin core, while not falling under the GNU license per se, has a similar open licensing philosophy, and many of the products of the GNU Project's many developers have found their way into the Mac world and into Xcode.

GCC achieves its magical flexibility and portability using the same method that programmers have traditionally employed to achieve the seemingly impossible: break the complex task (in this case, the task of turning high-level language code into machine instructions) into smaller, more easily solvable subtasks. These subtasks are done by GCC's *front-end* and *back-end* components. Figure 4-1 shows schematically how the compiler collection can compile two different programs, in two different languages, to run on two different processors.

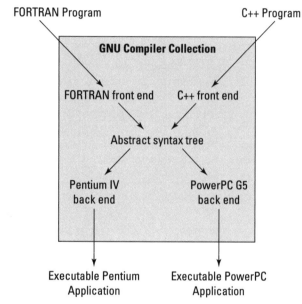

Figure 4-1
GCC's front-end and back-end compilation strategy

A GCC front end is responsible for translating a program from its high-level language form into an intermediate *abstract syntax tree* form, which represents the program's structure in a language-neutral way. A GCC back end converts this tree into the set of instructions that the target CPU understands, and, in the process, also looks for ways to optimize those instructions into the most compact and efficient form it can.

 Note

As a further example of stepwise refinement, the front end consists of multiple parts, the first of which is a lexical analyzer that verifies whether your source code conforms to the programming language specification, and the last of which is the actual translator that creates the abstract syntax tree. As software archaeologists can tell you, these front-end parts have tools called *lex* (*lex*ical analyzer) and *yacc* (Yet Another Compiler Compiler) as their progenitors.

This strategy makes providing compiler support for additional languages and CPUs much easier. A front end only has to figure out how to convert a high-level language program into an abstract syntax tree. A back end only has to figure out how to convert an abstract syntax tree into machine instructions. So, to add a new language (like, say, the dreaded and mythical Objective COBOL++), one only needs to create a front end for that language, which GCC can then employ no matter the CPU for which it is creating machine instructions. Similarly, to add GCC support for a new CPU, only a new back end needs to be created, and all of the GCC front ends can then use it. And, if the GCC back end is improved for a particular CPU, all the GCC front ends reap the benefit of those improvements. Handsome. Elegant. Intelligent. Sweet.

Most GCC distributions provide front ends for a bunch of languages, including:

- C
- C++
- Objective-C
- FORTRAN
- Ada
- Java

And there are well over a dozen back ends for GCC as well.

The GCC that comes with Xcode is formally maintained by Apple, and it includes all the C-related front ends and, not surprisingly, the PowerPC back end. Of course, other front ends are available (see "Third-Party Hearty" in this chapter); because GCC is open source, you can even use Xcode to compile them if you wish.

GCC, OR, I GNU A C COMPILER ONCE...

Compilers are always evolving, and as new versions are released, older versions tend to fall by the wayside. This, however, is not always a good thing, because sometimes the older compilers are necessary to create updated versions of programs intended to run on older systems (skip ahead a few pages and read "Compiling for Your Old Xs" for more details on how this works). In addition, developers will be less apt to use a new and improved software development system (such as Xcode 2) if the projects on which they are currently working, and which may require a specific compiler, can't be completed using the new system. Therefore, Apple always provides some older versions of its compilers when it ships a new version of its development system, and Xcode 2 is no exception.

Naturally Xcode 2 ships with a newer, improved, shinier, and silkier GCC than its predecessors, but doesn't completely exclude support for older versions. Specifically, you get support for these three GCCs:

- **GCC 2.95,** which is available via download from Apple's Developer Connection site (`http://developer.apple.com/`) for all members of the

ADC (you can become a member for the startlingly low price of free). GCC 2.95 only supports G3 and G4 processors — though G5s *can* run the code it produces, GCC 2.95 understands nothing about optimizing for the G5. However, it is the only version of GCC available that can compile for Mac OS X 10.1, so get it if you plan to do some compiling for your old Xs.

- **GCC 3.3** was the latest version of GCC that shipped with Xcode 1.5, and is still available in Xcode 2 for those developers who need it. It supports the G3, G4, and G5 processors and can compile for OS versions up to and including Panther (10.3).

- **GCC 4.0** is the newest compiler that ships with Xcode 2, and it's the one we'll talk about here.

▼ **Note**

GCC 3.1, which shipped with both Xcode 1.2 and 1.5, is no longer provided because it doesn't do anything that GCC 3.3 can't do and is not really required to support older applications and versions of the Mac OS.

The 4.0 edition of GCC is almost completely rebuilt (much like Steve Austin) to be faster and stronger and better.

- It has been optimized to be faster by employing, among other techniques, one called *single static assignments* — if you understand why this is a cool thing, good for you; if not, you don't need to know anything other than that, in terms of compiler efficiency, it is a Good Thing.

- It incorporates a completely revised C++ parser.

- It supports long doubles (essential for major number crunching on the 64-bit G5 processor).

- It provides auto-vectorization for G4 and G5 code, which, translated into something approaching

English, means that you no longer have to hand-code your programs to take advantage of Apple's Velocity Engine; GCC 4.0 analyzes your code to find those places where it can make use of the Velocity Engine and produces output code that does.

Of course, if you don't want to run with the latest and greatest, you can still use GCC 3.3, which you may want to do for existing projects you're bringing over from an earlier version of Xcode, or if you feel more comfortable with the known shortcomings of GCC 3.3 than with the unknown shortcomings of GCC 4.0. (Remember, you can always recognize the pioneers by the arrows in their backs.)

THIRD-PARTY HEARTY

According to automotive historians, you could get the Model-T in any color, as long as it was black. In Xcode, you can use GCC with any language, as long as it's some form of C. But you Fortran, Ada, and Pascal fans are not completely out of luck, because third-party compiler developers have made Xcode-compatible versions of compilers for these languages.

- **Fortran:** Aside from producing the G5 processor that is at the heart of the latest Macs (at least, as we write this), IBM also produces an Xcode-compatible Fortran compiler, Fortran-XL. This compiler supports several versions of Fortran, including Fortran 77, Fortran 90, Fortran 95, and even provides partial support for the draft standard Fortran 2003. It can generate code specifically for the G5 processor, which is not surprising given IBM's close relationship with that processor, and comes with documentation designed to slip right into Xcode's online documentation system (allow us here to refer you yet again to Chapter 7).

You can find out more about it at www-306.ibm.com/software/awdtools/fortran/xlfortran/features/macosx/index.html.

- **Pascal:** Niklaus Wirth's famous language, and one that was fundamental to the earliest Mac developers, is available in a free (as in beer — that is, it is available under the GNU license) version for OS X — Free Pascal. Based on Turbo Pascal, Free Pascal is a product of the Free Pascal project, a group of developers who are working in the spirit of the GNU and Linux projects. You can download it and find installation instructions, bug reports, and documentation at www.freepascal.org.

- **Ada:** The general public distribution of GCC provides support for Ada, the U.S. Department of Defense–sponsored language that is still the *sine qua non* for many developers working on U.S. government software projects. Unfortunately, Apple's GCC does not provide the Ada front end. Not to worry, though: An Xcode-compatible *gnat* (which is what the Ada component of GCC is called) is available from the Gnat for Macintosh project, along with debuggers and other tools. You can get it from www.adapower.net/macos/index.html.

In addition, rumblings on the Internet suggest you may be able to find Xcode-compatible versions of C# and even Niklaus Wirth's other language, Modula-2, in the near future (or even by the time this book hits the store shelves).

COMPILING FOR YOUR OLD Xs

When we were young... Heck! even after we got older, when Mac programmers talked about *cross-development*, we meant writing a product that would work on both Mac and Windows. OS X, though, adds so many features and frameworks with every new version (Puma, Cheetah, Jaguar, Panther, and now Tiger) that Apple has co-opted this venerable term to mean writing code that runs on different (earlier) versions of OS X than the one you're using to develop the product.

In the olden days, developing a backward-compatible application meant that you had to put in explicit checks for each piece of functionality you required before calling a function that wasn't available in all system releases on which you wished to deploy your product. Additionally, you had to add user interface code, such as dialogs, to explain to users of older OS versions why certain application features weren't available to them without making them feel like second-class citizens. These days, Apple wants to make it easier for you, the software developer, to develop applications for those pinch-penny ne'er-do-wells... er, financially prudent but loyal customers who have yet to upgrade to the latest Mac OS X version.

STUB LIBRARIES ARE BETTER THAN CIGAR STUBS

Generally a pejorative term, *stub* holds its head high when you're talking about stub libraries. Think of these libraries as the software equivalent of movie doubles. They contain no executable code, but look just like the originals to the linker.

You can specify which SDKs to install using the Customize option in the Xcode installer.

With Xcode, you can leverage features from different versions of Mac OS X simply by specifying the *SDK* (Software Development Kit) containing the libraries and interfaces with which you want to build. You can also specify the earliest OS X version (usually represented by the last "dot" release for that version, like 10.1.5 or 10.2.8) on which you want your product to function.

Starting with Jaguar (OS X 10.2), Apple began laying the groundwork for cross-development.

- Jaguar introduced *weak linking*, the capability for an application to launch on an OS version that doesn't *export* (make available) all the symbols to which the application code refers.

▼ **Note**

You can find a thorough discussion of weak linking and *availability macros* (macros that check whether symbols exist) in Apple's Technote 2064, at `http://developer.apple.com/technotes/tn2002/tn2064.html`.

Just in case we don't mention it again, and you're curious, technotes are stored by year of issue (tn2002), and then by an almost sequential number (tn2064), giving rise to the semiconfusing URL above. We say "almost sequential" because some technotes with earlier numbers have either been eliminated as no longer pertinent or just might never have been released.

- Panther introduced Mac OS SDKs, complete header file sets with *stub libraries* (see "Stub Libraries Are Better Than Cigar Stubs") for earlier versions of Mac OS X. This allows you to link against specific sets of headers and libraries.

- Introduced with Panther's initial Xcode release, Apple added a feature for you to specify both the earliest OS version on which your software should run and the latest OS version from which your software leverages features.

BEHIND THE SCENES WITH SDK SETTINGS

Xcode sets some internal variables (called *environment variables*) based upon your chosen SDKs.

The build environment variable, SDKROOT, tells Xcode which SDK and, as a result, which AvailabilityMacros.h file to use when determining weak linking support and sets the preprocessor macro MAC_OS_X_VERSION_MAX_ALLOWED to the version represented by that SDK. For example, 1036 would represent OS X 10.3.6 and 1040 would represent OS X 10.4.0.

The deployment OS choice sets the MACOS_DEPLOYMENT_TARGET to 10.1 (Cheetah), 10.2 (Jaguar), 10.3 (Panther), or 10.4 (Tiger). The compiler uses this setting to assign a value to the MAC_OS_X_VERSION_MIN_REQUIRED preprocessor symbol used by AvailabilityMacros.h to determine which functions are weaklinked.

The two preprocessor symbols above define a number of other preprocessor symbols and the GCC compiler references them to determine which functions are available.

- If the function is not available in the selected SDK, you get a compilation error.
- If the symbol is available, but *deprecated* (about to become extinct), the compile continues, but you get a warning.
- If the symbol is present in both the deployment and build SDKs, then all is well and the compilation continues and the build links normally.

However, you should keep the following in mind.

- If you (or a customer) attempts to launch on an OS release earlier than the deployment version and symbols are undefined, your code may not load at all.
- For the deployment version or later, your code will load, but you might get *weak references* (null function pointers) when calling functions not present in that OS release. You need to be prepared for this by either testing for a null function pointer or by checking the system version before attempting the call.

This last feature is a key one, and it is really simple to do, as the following steps demonstrate:

1. **Select your project group in the Groups & Files list.**

2. **Open an Info (or the Inspector) window for the project group.**

3. **Select an OS X version for which you want to develop from the pop-up menu, as shown in Figure 4-2.** Xcode will pretend that the chosen OS X version is the one in which you were building. For example, even though you're building in Tiger, choosing 10.3 will cause Xcode to use the Panther SDK for your development base.

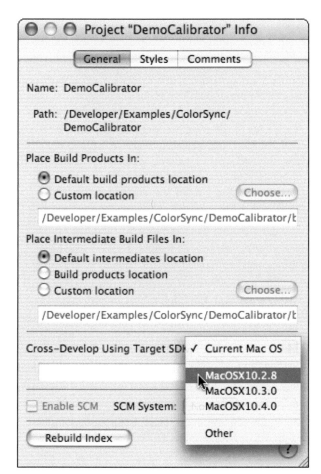

Figure 4-2
Choosing the OS X version containing the latest
APIs your software will use

4. **Click the Info window's Build tab and choose a**
   deployment version **(the earliest version on which**
   your software should run) as shown in Figure 4-3.

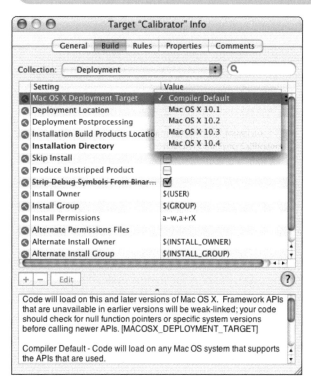

Figure 4-3
Picking the earliest OS X version on which your
software will run

Xcode uses the above two settings during the compiling
and linking build phases, respectively. The build SDK
applies to all the project's targets, but you can specify different deployment versions for individual targets. This
allows you to create separate executables for Jaguar and
Tiger, for example, without having to create separate projects and trying to keep them in sync.

A somewhat unusual state of affairs exists relative to cross-development: Carbon's APIs support it more thoroughly than do the Cocoa APIs. Apple says that this is because you don't get link errors for Cocoa apps (dynamic binding), just run-time exceptions. While this is true as far as it goes, we feel that we're more likely to overlook some incompatibilities we need to check for in a Cocoa application because of the lack of link error warnings.

There were also some significant changes made with the introduction of Jaguar. For example, C++ calling conventions changed, so if you want your code to run in pre-Jaguar versions, you need to create a separate project and build its executable with the GCC 2.95.2 compiler (SDK set to 10.1.5 and deployment to 10.1). Also, weak linking wasn't available for versions prior to Jaguar, so applications using features from later OS versions won't even load.

 Tip

Set your development build to the most current OS release you can. This will ensure that you can use such features as Fix and Continue or ZeroLink, which became available with Panther. Remember, the development build style determines what **you** have available. While building, the deployment build style specifies what your client needs and sees.

WORK YOU DON'T HAVE TO DO

Now, kids, sit back and let Grandpa tell you how good you have it with Xcode and the trials we faced when we were your age.

When we were young programmers, GUIs were only a gleam in Xerox's eye. Apple][s running DOS 3.3 and Z80s running CP/M were the newfangled contraptions to which early computer users flocked. Programs like VisiCalc were in their infancy and presented the first glimmerings of a graphic display. The pioneers who wrote those programs had to do everything involved in presenting their tables and graphs. Window frames were drawn with vertical bar, underscore, and forward- and backslash characters, and users moved around in them using the arrow keys on their keyboards instead of a mouse. We had to maintain separate branches for the drawing routines based on the type of terminal (monitor) the user had connected, because not all monitors responded to the same control and escape codes, nor did they all offer the same capabilities (such as freezing the top so-many lines).

Although machines like the Xerox Alto and Star or the Lisa from Apple were soon to appear with their built-in graphical user interface routines, they were priced far beyond a typical consumer's budget — the Lisa cost $10,000 (and that's 1983 dollars) for a machine with 512KB of RAM and a 5MB hard disk, running at 5 MHz. Your typical entry-level PDA today, selling for under $100, beats those specs by a lot. The Mac, introduced running at 8 MHz and loaded up with 128KB of RAM and a single 400K floppy, cost $2,500 and had a tiny black-and-white 9-inch screen with one-fourth the resolution of today's basic 1024×768 monitor. But, it was the first computer to ship with a well-defined and documented set of programming interfaces (and the support libraries) that let you tell the computer what you wanted to do and not have to twiddle with the low-level details of how that got done. This revolutionary offering was called the Mac toolbox and was documented in a constantly updated and expanding series of tomes known as *Inside Macintosh*. As you'll discover in Chapter 7, you now get all your programming documentation in a continually updated, easily cross-referenced electronic form. In our opinion (individually and jointly), the most useful documentation is that paralleling *Inside Macintosh* — the documentation covering all the frameworks available to you for Carbon, Cocoa, Java, AppleScript Studio, or any of the other projects you might be undertaking.

So even though this chapter is supposedly all about Xcode's compilers (wait, let's check... yes, that's what we're supposed to be talking about here), it should be obvious by now that when you are compiling your Xcode project, you're almost always going to end up compiling both your own code and a whole bunch of other stuff. That whole bunch of other stuff consists of the frameworks that Xcode provides, and that's the work that you don't have to do.

While frameworks aren't necessarily libraries of routines, they do serve the same function as static and dynamic shared libraries, providing APIs for classes, methods, functions, and other resources. Among the Xcode-supplied frameworks are groups of frameworks that Apple refers to as *umbrella frameworks*. Cocoa and Carbon are two such umbrella frameworks. Furthermore, you can also create your own frameworks, either for private or shared use. So let's take a look at the major frameworks — the ones you're most likely to be using.

 Note

While you will rarely (if ever) encounter a framework without an API, such a beast can exist, containing only resource files.

Under Cocoa's umbrella

When you tell Xcode to create a Cocoa project, you immediately see the main Cocoa frameworks: Application Kit (also known as AppKit) and Foundation (Chapter 1 provides a nice example of a Cocoa project — at least, *we* think it's nice). Other frameworks available to Cocoa projects include

- Message, for sending e-mail messages via Mail.app, and

- Web Kit, for displaying Web content in your application's windows.

Foundation is aptly named. It provides a collection of primitive classes and functionality not inherent in the Objective-C language. This is where you get conventions for object deallocation, persistence, and distribution and support for Unicode strings.

AppKit contains everything you need to implement an event-driven graphical interface. You get windows, buttons, scrollers, menus, text fields, wells, panels (which users call sheets), and so on. Needless to say (but we will, anyway), AppKit is HUGE! It contains more than 125 classes and a couple of thousand methods. Fortunately, you can create basic applications without going very deeply into how it all works or, if you're an obsessive control freak who just has to do things for yourself, you can subclass NSView and other classes, in which case you'll have to write your own drawing methods, update methods, and so on — at which point the work you don't have to do is work you've decided to do, anyway.

Carbon's umbrella casts only a little shade

The main framework provided when you tell Xcode to create a Carbon project is Core Foundation. Core Foundation's original raison d'etre was to make it easier to convert pre-Mac OS X applications into OS X applications. However, as a side benefit, Core Foundation also facilitates cross-development, not only with OS 9, but with other operating systems such as the pervasive dark force emanating from Redmond. Conceptually, Core Foundation is part of the Core Services layer that directly surrounds the heart of Mac OS X, its Mach/BSD core.

Core Foundation serves much the same function for C (and other static language) development as Foundation does for Cocoa developers. In fact, Apple states that, "Core Foundation is a library with a set of programming interfaces conceptually derived from the Foundation framework of the Cocoa object layer but implemented in the C language" (*About Core Foundation*, 2 Nov 2004).

 Note

Cocoa's Foundation framework is implemented by accessing the Core Foundation framework. This provides a level of abstraction for the Cocoa developer, while ensuring that both Carbon and Cocoa developers are working with the same primitives and that their applications will be able to share data and objects.

To accomplish the stated goal, Core Foundation implements, in C, a limited object model in which opaque types (that it refers to as *objects*) encapsulate both data and functions. These objects allow code and data to be shared among various frameworks and libraries. Additionally, Core Foundation provides common APIs for what we old-timers think of as the Mac toolbox, as well as a plug-in architecture, APIs for preferences, XML property lists, and Unicode strings and internationalization.

BACK END

For those who are curious, or who just like stories, we looked at some of the history of Xcode's compiler of choice and provided some technical background on how compilers work, following which we discussed the compilers that Apple offers with Xcode today. We went on a quick tour of other compilers available for Xcode (and were silently pleased at how supportive of Xcode the open source community has started to become) and looked at the issues involved in using Xcode 2 to work on products for older Mac OS X systems. Finally, we tripped lightly through the fields of frameworks that Apple provides along with its compilers that can save you from the arduous and redundant task of reinventing various and sundry wheels.

Living in the Editor

In This Chapter

It Came in through the Editing Window
How Do I Open Files? Let Me Count the Ways...
Split-View Editors Are Paneful • Shhh... the Editor Is Embed
You Can Get There from Here • State Your Preferences • What We Covered

If we had a nickel for every time we heard someone remark that the Mac was a "graphics machine," our pile of nickels would probably generate a gravitational field strong enough to suck your average housecat through its event horizon. Not, of course, that the Mac's graphic goodness isn't real, as a visit to almost any art and layout department at any publishing house or advertising agency could demonstrate. And Xcode, with its visual modeling tools (about which we'll learn much more in Part III), certainly makes good use of the Mac's superb graphics capabilities.

But let's face it: Programming is all about the text. C (in all its variations and guises), Java, Pascal, Fortran, HyperTalk, Lingo, ScriptX (hey, remember *that* one?), COBOL, PL/1, Lisp, APL, Forth, SNOBOL... they're all text-based languages (okay, APL uses lots of symbols and non-Latin alphabet letters, but they're still text characters), and the programs written in them all start out with fingers on the keyboard and text on the screen. Without a way to type, edit, and search text, a programmer is as hobbled as a kangaroo with a wooden leg.

That's why programmers (and kangaroo lovers) will be pleased to learn that Xcode comes with its own built-in programming editor. And it's not just a simple stripped-down text editor, either, but a full-featured and powerful text-wrangling tool that understands code and what you want to do with it.

IT CAME IN THROUGH THE EDITING WINDOW

When it's first installed, Xcode is set up to create a separate editing window for each source file that you want to edit. Figure 5-1 shows the standard Xcode editor window. You've seen it before, back in Chapter 1. You'll see it a lot more, too, before we're through.

At the top of the window is the *toolbar*. The toolbar comes prestocked with six buttons that provide some handy functions (which is, after all, what you would hope that the tools on a toolbar would do):

○ a **Build** button/pop-up menu remarkably similar to the one we saw in Chapter 3, which keeps you from having to trudge all the way back to the Project window just to build your project after making a change or two;

Toolbar   Navigation bar

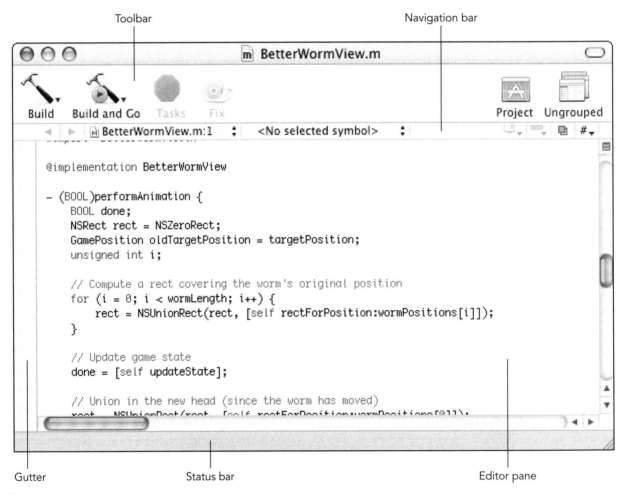

Gutter   Status bar   Editor pane

Figure 5-1
An Xcode editing window and its parts

- a **Build and Go** button/pop-up menu, also remarkably similar to the Project window's version of the same;

- "Big Red," the **Tasks** button, which we also describe in Chapter 3 (if you can't remember what it does, remember your driver training course in high school and then take another look at the button: Its function should become clear — if not, *please* stay off the public roads);

- a **Fix** button, used with Xcode's Fix and Continue feature (described in more detail in Chapter 16);

- a **Project** button, which lets you bring the Project window to the front so you don't have to search for it among the many windows you may have open (after all, why should you have to resort to, say, selecting it in the Window menu or to picking it out of an Exposé display or getting at it in any of the other ways that the Mac makes available?);

- and an **Ungrouped/Grouped** editing mode button, which lets you switch from a multiple-window editing mode (or, as the button calls it, Ungrouped mode) to a single-window editing mode (or Grouped mode) and back again.

▼Note

The Grouped mode gives you just one (count 'em, one) editing window. If you are editing a file and you open another file for editing, the second file *replaces* the file you have displayed in the editing window. The first file is still open (and, as you'll find out in the next section, you can easily get back to it), but it is not displayed — if you like, you can pretend that it is "behind" the currently displayed file. Grouped mode helps reduce screen clutter, though it does make certain tasks, like comparing two files or copying and pasting between them, rather more tedious. Still some folk like Grouped mode, and, we're happy for them (really!), but we seldom use it ourselves.

Of course, you aren't restricted to the editing windows' prefab toolbar; the Customize Toolbar command at the end of

the View menu, which, as we saw in Chapter 3, lets you modify the Project window toolbar, also lets you modify the editing window's toolbar buttons (see Figure 5-2) when an editing window is the frontmost window.

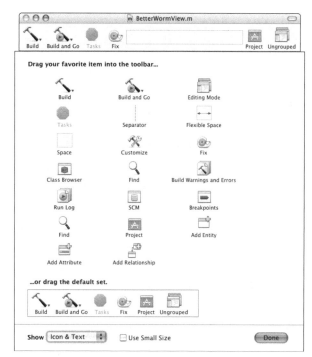

Figure 5-2
Editing the editing toolbar

At the bottom of the window is the *status bar*. Pretty sparse looking in Figure 5-1, no? That's because nothing was happening when we took this screenshot. If, on the other hand, we had been in the middle of building a project, the current state of the build process, such as the name of the file currently being compiled, would appear at the left of the status bar and a round progress indicator would appear in the right side of the status bar, as it does in Figure 5-3. Thanks to the status bar, you can continue working on a source file even as you're building a project, and you can still see what's going on with the build as you multitask your heart out.

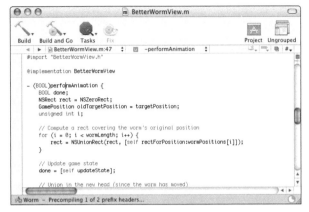

Figure 5-3
Check out the status bar now...

The *navigation bar* appears below the toolbar. This very cool feature lets you roam all over the place in your project, right from the current editing window. It's so powerful that we've devoted a separate section to describing it in this chapter, "You Can Get There from Here."

On the left side of the editing window is the *gutter*. Rather than directing the flow of runoff water and becoming periodically clogged with leaves like some gutters we've known, the editing window's gutter is designed to display breakpoints and line numbers. The reason you don't see any line numbers or breakpoints right now is that we haven't set any breakpoints in our code (setting breakpoints, a debugging technique, is covered in Chapter 16) and we haven't yet turned on line-number display in our preferences.

To see line numbers, which are very useful when the compiler tells you that you have a problem on line such-and-such, do this:

1. **Open Xcode's preferences (choose Xcode →**
   Preferences or press ⌘+,).

2. **Click the Text Editing preference icon.**

3. **Enable Show line numbers.**

As you may have noticed, you can also show or hide the gutter with this preference panel (see Figure 5-4).

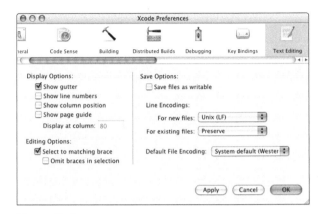

Figure 5-4
Get down with the gutter using the settings at the left of this preference panel

Last, and pretty much the exact opposite of least, is the *Editor pane* itself. Here's where your source code appears, and here's where you write and edit it. Although we're not going so far as to teach you how to type (hint: it involves pressing those buttons on your keyboard that have letters, numbers, and other symbols printed on them), we will spend a good deal of time and page space in this chapter and the next describing many of the things you can do in the Editor pane if you *do* know how to type.

HOW DO I OPEN FILES? LET ME COUNT THE WAYS...

If you read Chapter 1, you already know one way to open a file so you can edit it in an editing window: Just double-click it in the Project window. It doesn't matter which side of the Project window, either — left (the Groups & Files area) or right (the detailed view). If you can see it, and it isn't red, a double-click opens it.

JUST GIVE ME AN OPENING

Opening Quickly uses a set of predefined paths, including the paths to your project folder and certain subfolders, as well as the paths to various places in the System folder where Mac OS X keeps various frameworks. You can modify and extend the list with Xcode's Opening Quickly preference (see Figure 5-5).

1. **Choose Xcode → Preferences (or press ⌘+,).**

2. **Click the Opening Quickly icon in the Xcode Preferences window's scrolling gallery of preference panel choices (it appears at the top of the Xcode Preferences window).** A list of all the current paths that Xcode follows to find files appears.

3. **Click the + button to use a standard File dialog to select a folder whose path will be added to the list.**

Selecting the Skip panel if selection is file name option keeps Xcode from asking you to specify a path if you don't have to; deselecting it makes Xcode ask you to specify the file path every time you use the Opening Quickly command, which we think tends to violate the whole "opening quickly" concept.

Note, by the way, that the list of paths displayed in this preference panel is completely editable. You can simply type pathnames right into the list and edit them in place, if you prefer.

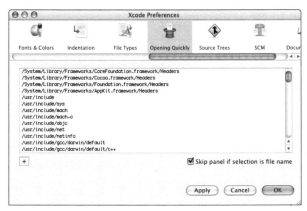

Figure 5-5
Add a path for opening files quickly

▼Note

Any file shown in red in the Project window is missing. You can't open a missing file, because there is no file to open where Xcode was told it would be. If you *know* that a file exists, and, yet, it appears in red, open its Inspector with the Get Info command and click the Choose button beneath its name. This lets you find the file and assign a path to it so Xcode knows where to find it in the future.

You can also open files directly from an editing window if the filename exists somewhere in that window:

1. **Select the filename in the window.**

2. **Choose File → Open Quickly (or press Shift+⌘+D).**

3. **Type the complete path to the file if a dialog appears asking you to do so.** Ordinarily you won't see this dialog if the selected text is recognizably a filename and if Xcode can figure out where to find it (see "Just Give Me an Opening").

You can also open the file that contains the definition of an indentifier that exists in your source code, which is useful if, say, you want to see the comments you supplied along with the definition (you *do* comment your source code, right? Right??).

1. **Select the identifier (that is, the name of a method or function).**

2. **Choose Find → Jump to Definition.** Xcode displays a list of the files that contain a definition of that indentifier; click one and the file (usually a header file) opens.

Xcode can jump to definitions quickly because Xcode indexes all the files in the project behind the scenes the first time you open a project, and it "understands" basic code constructs like function prototypes.

WHAT'S UP WITH OPEN WITH FINDER?

You may have spotted the Open With Finder command on Xcode's File menu and wondered what it does. So did we, at first, because we know that the Finder doesn't *really* open documents itself: It can open windows to show you directory contents, and it can launch applications and tell those applications to open selected documents.

It's this second thing that Xcode's Open With Finder command does; that is, Xcode examines the same information the Finder uses to decide which application should open a particular document and then tells that application to open the file. That information may consist of a filename extension, like .txt or .jpg, or it may consist of some of the metadata associated with the file in Mac OS X's HFS+ file system, such as the file's creator type.

The Open With Finder command is useful when the application normally associated with the file does something more, or different, than the Xcode editing window can do. For example, property lists (.plist) are simple XML files that you can easily edit with Xcode's editor, but the Property List Editor utility provides additional property list editing features that a normal text editor doesn't. Choosing Open With Finder on a .plist file in your project opens the file with the Property List Editor, just as if you'd double-clicked it in the Finder or used the Finder's Open command.

There are also additional file-opening tricks hidden in the navigation bar of the editing window; see "You Can Get There from Here," later in this chapter, for more on that.

Oh, and we mentioned six different ways to open files in this section, in case you were wondering.

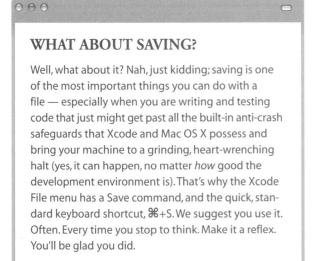

WHAT ABOUT SAVING?

Well, what about it? Nah, just kidding; saving is one of the most important things you can do with a file — especially when you are writing and testing code that just might get past all the built-in anti-crash safeguards that Xcode and Mac OS X possess and bring your machine to a grinding, heart-wrenching halt (yes, it can happen, no matter *how* good the development environment is). That's why the Xcode File menu has a Save command, and the quick, standard keyboard shortcut, ⌘+S. We suggest you use it. Often. Every time you stop to think. Make it a reflex. You'll be glad you did.

SPLIT-VIEW EDITORS ARE PANEFUL

From Dziga Vertov to Michael Wadleigh to Ang Lee, movie directors have loved splitting the screen and providing their audiences with multiple views of the same scene. Although an Xcode editing window is not quite the same as a movie screen (though wouldn't it be *awesome* if your editing window were, like, 20 feet tall?), they, too, can be split so that you can peruse and edit multiple views of the same source file — which is especially useful when your file is an incredibly hulking mass of code.

To split an editing window, you can:

- choose Split <filename> Vertically from the View menu (see Figure 5-6);

- press ⌘+" (that's a double-quote character, meaning that you also have to press and hold the Shift key if you are using a standard keyboard layout); or

Figure 5-6
Let's split!

- click the tiny split control at the top of the window's vertical scroll bar (see Figure 5-7).

Figure 5-7
The itsy-bitsy split control

When a window splits, you get two views of the same part of the file (see Figure 5-8), but, because you get twice the scroll bars, you get twice the fun: You can scroll each pane independently and quickly be two places at once. What's more, you can use the Jump to Definition command in one pane and thus be able to view, for example, both an implementation and interface file in the same window. And, because each pane also gets its own navigation bar, you can use it to view two files in the same window as well (the navigation bar is described in "You Can Get There from Here," later in this chapter).

▼**Note**

> When you use the navigation bar or some other method to go to a different file in a split window, the new file always opens in the first (either left or top) pane.

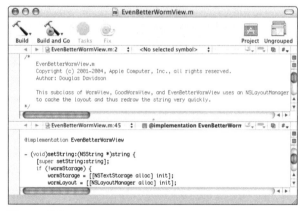

Figure 5-8
First there was one pane, now there are two

As with most Mac OS X windows that provide multiple panes, a control bar (identified by its cute little dimple) appears on the window frame between the panes, so you can drag the bar to adjust the amount of window space each pane takes up.

You can split the window horizontally instead of vertically, courtesy of the Option key. Press and hold Option as you use any of the methods described above for splitting a window, and the split becomes horizontal, rather than vertical (see Figure 5-9).

▼**Note**

> Though the View menu will lie to you and say that you *can* mix them up, you actually cannot split a window both horizontally and vertically at the same time: Splits in a window must be either *all* horizontal or *all* vertical.

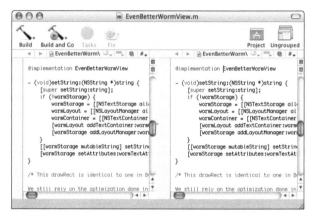

Figure 5-9
A horizontal split gives you vertical columns.
Go figure...

And finally, when you are tired of your multiview extravaganza and just want to get back to the quiet placidity of a single pane window, you can

- choose Close Split View from the View menu;

- press ⌘+' (that's a single-quote — get it? a double-quote splits, a single-quote unsplits: we call that kind of thing a *mnemonic*);

- or click the close split control (the itsy-bitsy widget right beneath the split control; it appears when the window is split).

SHHH... THE EDITOR IS EMBED

As we saw in passing back in Chapter 3, you don't have to open a separate editor window in Xcode. You can manufacture, massage, and otherwise manipulate your code in an editing pane within the project window. And not just the project window, but also the debugger window and other Xcode windows where editable files are listed (like the Errors & Warnings window) — that's what that little Editor button at the right end of the toolbar is for. Just select a file in the Detail pane (or in the Groups & Files list) and click the Editor button to see the Xcode editor *embedded*, replacing the detail view, as shown in Figure 5-10's before-and-after display. For those who like menus or ⌘+key equivalents, you can choose View → Toggle Embedded Editor (Shift+⌘+E).

▼Note

The Xcode documentation tells you that clicking the Editor button opens the Editor pane to its maximum size, but what it really means is that the Editor pane consumes all the space available in the Detail pane, not that the window resizes.

▼Tip

If you want to have the Editor and the Detail list both present at the same time, you can accomplish that as well, because the Editor pane is really just collapsed. Click and drag the little handle that appears below the Detail list or above the Editor pane in Figure 5-10, and both panes will be visible. Further clicking of the Editor button will toggle the Project window between an embedded Editor pane and a split pane that shows the Detail list above an embedded Editor pane.

The only difference between the embedded Editor and the stand-alone Editor window is that the embedded Editor doesn't have its own toolbar — everything else is exactly the same. You can split the pane, toggle lookups, display or hide line numbers in the gutter — it's all there. For those of you coming from the Dark Side, it's like Microsoft's OLE (*O*bject *L*inking and *E*mbedding) on steroids. For

those of you who have been around the Mac long enough to remember OpenDoc, the promise is realized, at least in this instance.

▼Note

Of course, Mac users are very accustomed to the true implementation of embedding with AppleWorks, née ClarisWorks. In fact, when Bill Gates was first promoting OLE at conferences and tradeshows, he used ClarisWorks as the example of how things were going to be. (We don't think his minions ever quite reached the stated goal.)

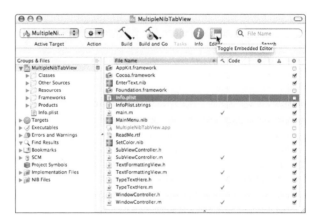

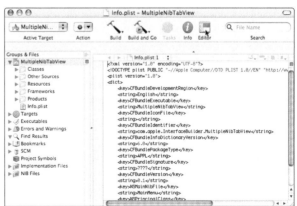

Figure 5-10
(before) Select a file and click Editor and (after) your Editor is embedded within the Project window

YOU CAN GET THERE FROM HERE

Apple has, from the very beginning, supplied a bookmarking capability in their Macintosh programmers' editors. First available with the UCSD Pascal-derivative Lisa Workshop Editor, showing up later in MPW, and making its appearance in Xcode, the bookmarking feature lets programmers mark frequently accessed locations for rapid access. One of Xcode's predefined Smart Groups is the Bookmarks group, which collects and displays all the bookmarks in a project. "But, but, but," you stammer, "what if I'm using the regular editor? Do I really have to switch back to the Project window to access a bookmark?" No, dear Reader, Xcode knows just how busy you are. Among those little buttons at the right end of the navigation bar is a pop-up list of bookmarks (the leftmost of these rightmost buttons). If your eyesight is really good or you look really closely, you'll see that the button looks like an open book. As we'll discuss here, the bookmark pop-up is just one handy tool in the appropriately named navigation bar (refer to Figure 5-1).

▼Note

Most people look at Dennis's work environment (1600 × 1200 resolution on a 17-inch CRT) and ask how he can read the tiny text and his reply is, "No problem. It's quite clear to me." However, the itsy-bitsy icons that Apple and so many others are using these days are smaller than he can easily differentiate. Maybe your eyesight is even better than his or you are using a screen with *much* larger pixels. By the way, they don't look that much more distinct to him at 1024×768 resolution on his iMac's LCD screen, so he might just have a problem with the iconographs Apple's designers created for the little buttons.

▼Tip

The little buttons on the navigation bar have tool tips associated with them. Position your mouse above one and a tip appears that tells you what the button does. So even if you can't tell what they are, Xcode can tell *you* what they are.

Creating a bookmark can be accomplished simply in a variety of ways. Each of them starts with positioning the cursor within your document. From there on, pick the method you prefer from the following:

- Control+click (or right-click with a multibutton mouse) and choose Add to Bookmarks from the shortcut menu.
- Choose Find ➔ Add to Bookmarks.
- Press ⌘+D.
- Click the Action button in the toolbar, and choose Add to Bookmarks from the menu that appears.

We generally use the first or third method, depending upon whether we're riding the mouse or the keyboard when we want to create a bookmark, but we understand that other folks don't like to memorize keyboard shortcuts and, if you don't have a multibutton mouse, you have to use two hands for the first method. Once again, Xcode leaves you lots of convenient ways to accomplish the same thing.

Similarly, you can go to a bookmark in a couple of ways. You can double-click an entry in the Bookmarks Smart Group over in the Project window's Groups & Files list or you can choose the bookmark you desire in the Bookmarks pop-up menu in an editor window's navigation bar, as shown in Figure 5-11.

You don't need to bother to set bookmarks for the functions in your code: The navigation bar includes a function pop-up, as shown in Figure 5-12, allowing you quick access to each of the current file's functions.

But, once you've found a function header, you will frequently want to access its declaration. Once again, Apple was thinking ahead for you. It has learned from past experience that function headers are among the items almost every programmer is going to want to access quickly, so

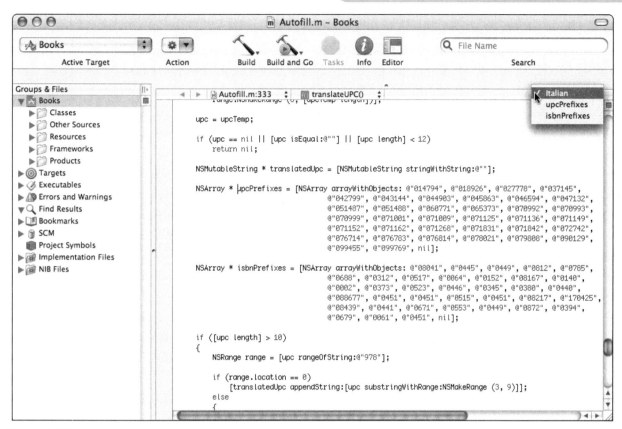

Figure 5-11
Choose your bookmark from the navigation bar

you don't have to bookmark those, either. Just use Xcode's Counterpart button (second from the right in the navigation bar). Click it in an implementation file and you get the associated header file and vice versa.

The Counterpart button is handy because it gets you to the corresponding interface or implementation file, though we have to admit that we don't use it all that often to open the interface file. We usually want to go directly to where a function is defined, so we select a function invocation and choose Find ➜ Jump to Definition (boy, do we wish that had a command-key equivalent!), or right-click and choose Jump to Definition in the shortcut menu that appears.

Of course, what we do is more a result of "old habits die hard," because it turns out that Option+clicking the Counterpart button also jumps to the function's definition.

▼Tip
To get the Counterpart to open in the same editor window, you need to select the Open counterparts in same editor option in Xcode's General Preferences panel.

There are also times you might want to open a different header file associated with the source file you're working on — maybe you want to check a method's parameter list

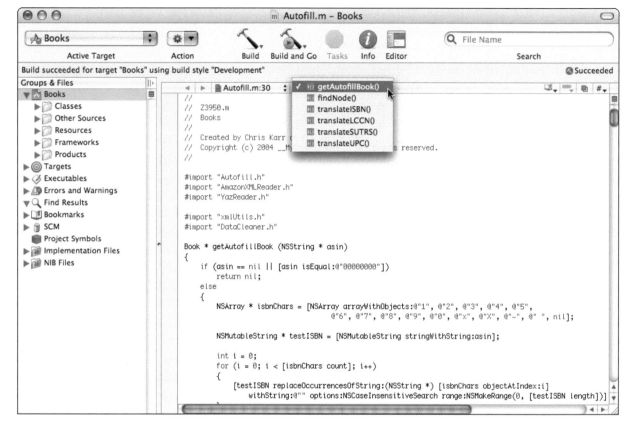

Figure 5-12
A truly function-al approach to navigation

or an object's definition. Again, Xcode makes it easy with a pop-up menu of included files available from the right-most tiny button in the navigation bar — the one with the sharp (that is, the pound, hash, number, or octothorp) symbol on it, just like the leading character in a C `#include` or Objective-C `#import` statement.

Xcode also keeps track of the files you've opened in the current window, letting you navigate through them with the back and forward arrow buttons and the file history pop-up at the left end of the navigation bar. This particular navigation aid is far more useful to those programmers who choose to employ a single editing window.

STATE YOUR PREFERENCES

No, we're not going to cover how to set all of Xcode's preferences is this short section: We've explored a number of them already, and we'll get to others in context. The "state" to which we're referring is the editing state. Using the General preference panel, you can tell Xcode how much to remember about the state of your editing session between invocations.

When you reopen a project, do you want Xcode to open all your editing windows just as they were when you quit your last Xcode session? If so, select the Save window state option in the General Preferences list of Environment options. Selecting it will enable the subordinate Remember Open Editor Windows option, which you also need to select to get full restorative power — having all the open editor windows scrolled right back to where they were when you quit from Xcode or closed the project. Figure 5-13 shows General Preferences set up to remember and restore your editing state when you reopen a project.

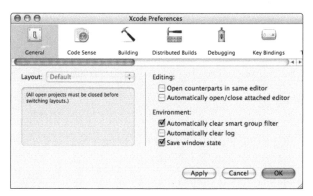

Figure 5-13
Presto! Everything reopens just as it was when you closed the project

WHAT WE COVERED

After taking a look at the layout and important parts of Xcode's editor window, we looked at some of the ways we could open a file for editing. Then we discovered that Xcode lets you split an editor into multiple panes, either horizontally or vertically. We demonstrated how the Project window can have an editor window embedded in it, and explored the ways to navigate within or between files from the editor window. We then explained how to make Xcode remember how the editor windows in your project are configured between sessions, after which we wrote this summary and then went out for lunch to celebrate the end of another chapter. You might want to do the same.

Practical Magic: Editing Features

In This Chapter

What Color Is Your Syntax? • External Editors Are *vi*-ing for Your Affection
You Know What I Mean Before I Finish Saying It: Code Completion
Automagic Formatting • #Pragma-tic Landmarks
Call It Macro-roni • In Short

Used to be, whenever someone mentioned an editor with colorful syntax to us, we might have thought of Harold Ross or Perry White or J. Jonah Jameson. Of course, that was before we started writing computer programs and discovered just how useful a text editor that "understands" something about programming could be.

We programmers are a strange breed: We may not care what color T-shirt we're wearing on any given day (or even if we remembered to change ours since last Arbor Day), but we'll argue passionately and endlessly over the merits and deficiencies of our tool sets: our compilers, our code libraries, our debuggers... and, of course, our programming editors. For, as we saw in Chapter 5, we programmers tend to live in our programming editors, spending most of the hours of the day (and night) composing and revising endless lines of code — or just staring at them in the vague hope that they will suddenly reveal to us just why they aren't doing what we darn well know we wrote them to do. So anything that can help us transform those airy, cloud-capped towers of our abstract imaginings into concrete and comprehensible coherence is welcome, and anything that can save us a keystroke or two, or that can keep us from cracking open another binder of API documentation, or that can finally help us get our latest build running so that we can kick back and get down with another session of *Halo 2* is our boon companion and friend for life.

Xcode's built-in editor, designed by programmers for programmers, has tons of advanced programmer-friendly features that very well could make it your programming editor of choice. But if not, chances are you can invite your own preferred editor (*preditor*?) to the Xcode party.

WHAT COLOR IS YOUR SYNTAX?

We're not talking about governmental levies against pornography and strip clubs, nor are we discussing profane language here (our editor — the human variety — won't let us). In a programming editor, like Xcode's, syntax coloring means that the editor displays your source code so that certain syntactic elements are rendered in a color other than the standard black. Do you want comments in a light hue, so they fade into the background when you're reading through the source code? No problem. Do you want your keywords dressed in a cool blue so that they stand out as markers, but not too much? Again, no problem. Figure 6-1 shows syntax coloring in action.

Figure 6-1

Look closely — even though it's grayscale you'll see differences in the comments and source code

▼ Note

Perhaps you can't quite make out the text color differences in the grayscale rendition of Figure 6-1. Well, we had a choice: make the book affordable, or print it in color. Guess what we chose to do? Right. And that's why Figure 6-1 doesn't convey the full impact of syntax coloring. In particular, the purple keywords look almost indistinguishable from the main source code. You may be able to tell that the comments are in green because they're lighter than the surrounding text, but, then again, maybe not. Trust us: In our original full-color screenshot, these colors were bright and vibrant and of staggering beauty.

Xcode's built-in editor lets you set color (and font, if you want) preferences for eight different classes of text in any source code that it can parse and compile — assuming that you tell it, correctly, what kind of source it's gazing upon by setting the file extension appropriately (.m for Objective-C, .c for C, .h for header files, and so on). Figure 6-2 shows you the Fonts & Colors pane in Xcode Preferences, which you invoke (you should be completely unsurprised to learn) by choosing Xcode ➜ Preferences (⌘+,).

Figure 6-2
Syntax coloring lurks at the bottom of the Fonts & Colors preference

As delivered, Xcode employs only four colors other than black:

- Comments, Documentation Comments, and Documentation Comment Keywords are green;
- Numbers and Characters are blue;
- Strings and Keywords are (dark) purple; and
- Preprocessor directives are brown.

You can change any or all of these to colors more to your liking or, if you don't like syntax coloring, you can turn coloring off altogether and view your code in vivid black and white.

▼ Note

Personally, Dennis finds the purple and brown almost indistinguishable at first glance and the green to actually stand out from the text rather than fade into the background. Thus, he customizes the colors to better suit his preferences, putting comments in silver and preprocessor directives in lavender. At least, that's what his "better half" tells him the colors are. Dennis, like some 8 percent of men (and 0.4 percent of women), suffers from partial color-blindness. And this is why Michael enjoyed tearing the wrapper labels off of Dennis's crayons when they were kids.

Your Syntax Coloring preferences setting controls how all the source files look in Xcode. Sometimes, though, you might want to turn Syntax Coloring off for a particular file, maybe just temporarily. Or you might want a file to be treated as if it were a different kind of file than its file extension indicates (maybe treat a C file as C++ so you can see quickly whether you're using any C++ keywords as identifiers before doing a conversion to C++). Xcode makes this easy via its Format ➜ Syntax Coloring submenu shown in Figure 6-3.

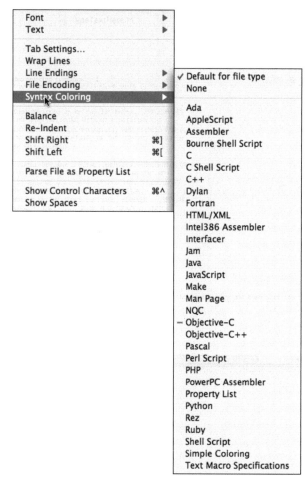

Figure 6-3
Turn Syntax Coloring on or off for a particular file, or treat that file as a different file type

EXTERNAL EDITORS ARE *VI*-ING FOR YOUR AFFECTION

Xcode's built-in editor is very good, but code editors are the programmer's red-flag equivalent to religion, politics, or sports when it comes to getting a conversation going. Herd a dozen programmers into a room, mention that a

particular text editor — *any* editor, it doesn't matter which one — is the best thing since individually wrapped cheese slices, and then quickly step out the door before the decibel level rises to tympanum rupturing levels.

Xcode's developers understand that, for some programmers (not us, of course — we're pretty easy), *the* deciding factor as to whether or not they'll develop for a particular platform often rests upon whether or not they can use their particular much-beloved and well-understood editor to do their work. Without support for external editors, Xcode would have a much harder time capturing the hearts and minds of the programming community.

In Xcode, you assign external editors based upon a file's type. For example, you can tell Xcode that opening an RTF file should launch TextEdit and that choosing to edit an HTML file should launch BBEdit. These assignments (or assignations) are made in Xcode Preferences's File Types panel.

1. **Open Xcode's Preferences (choose Xcode → Preferences or press ⌘+,) and hie yourself to the File Types pane (you'll have to scroll the list a bit to find the File Types icon).**

2. **Locate the file type you're concerned with, flipping down disclosure triangles as necessary, and click the entry in the Preferred Editor column to display a hierarchical pop-up menu, as shown in Figure 6-4.** As you see, a fresh Xcode installation offers two choices: emacs and vi, along with the ubiquitous "Other."

3. **Choose Other.** An open-style sheet appears that lets you navigate to and select your preferred editor for that file type.

After you choose an external editor, it is present in the Preferred Editor pop-up for further assignments, as shown in Figure 6-5.

THE EVOLUTION OF CODE FORMATTING

In the beginning, programmers entered their programming instructions by toggling switches on a computer's front panel. (Ummm... maybe we should ignore the prehistoric days [toggle switches], scroll past ancient history [punch cards and paper tape], forget about the dark ages [teletype terminals], and begin our story around the time that programmers started communicating with computers via terminals with screens.)

The early screens on which programmers performed their magic were black-and-white display terminals — well, actually, they were often green (or orange or yellow) on black display terminals. The point we're *trying* to make is that there were only two colors. Terminals typically displayed text in *character mode*, most commonly 24 or 25 rows of 80 characters: A terminal that could show more than 100 characters per line was the era's equivalent of the 30-inch Mac display of today. A *graphics mode* was reserved for those few programs that displayed charts or graphs. Even the expensive "color" screens sometimes found on PClones back then weren't really color as we think of it now, because they displayed just one color of text over just one background color. Of course, you could usually specify these foreground and background colors to suit your taste (or, in the case of a good friend of Dennis's, to match her outfit for that day). However, these primitive displays often *did* have boldface and underlining available to them, and some clever geeks (are there any other kind?) used those features to do limited syntax highlighting.

When the Mac finally showed up, its graphics mode was *always* on, allowing text editors to display mixtures of styles and fonts, even though the Mac's display was only black and white. Soon after the Mac débuted, an educational programming product called MacPascal was introduced, and it could automatically *format* source code: It put keywords in bold, and inserted line breaks and indentation to reflect syntactic structure. Students, hobbyists, and even professional programmers quickly saw that automatic formatting eliminated a lot of programming syntax errors, such as missing parentheses and semicolons, unmatched begin-end blocks (open and close braces, for you C language types), and misspelled keywords (it also caught undeclared variables for you, which often were merely typographic errors).

Although Apple's own development environment, known as *MPW* (for Macintosh Programmer's Workshop), didn't mix fonts and styles in a window, it did introduce parenthesis matching, where the user could double-click an opening or closing parenthesis and have everything between the bounding parentheses selected. This "balancing" function also worked for braces, brackets, and quotation marks. Once again, users found the functionality very handy in avoiding or fixing compilation errors related to syntax. While we don't know if MPW was the first development environment to offer this feature, we do know that it predated anything on the PC because it predated Microsoft's introduction of Windows. (Note that we discuss Xcode's balancing capabilities in this chapter's "Automagic Formatting.")

As color support became more pervasive, bolding, underlining, and italicizing syntactic elements gave way to coloring them. And, because there are a lot more colors available than there are distinct text styles (about 16 million colors on a modern display), even more elements could have distinct appearances.

Syntax coloring and automatic formatting tend to be far more common in an integrated development environment (IDE) like Xcode than in a stand-alone text editor (although, to be sure, some stand-alones like BareBones Software's BBEdit do support syntax coloring) because, to properly color and format code, the editor has to do much of the same work as a compiler in validating syntax: In an IDE, the editor can use the compiler's parser and lexical analyzer to facilitate the formatting effort.

Interestingly, Web designers embrace syntax coloring even more ardently than most conventional programmers. And why shouldn't they? Think of just how many tags and other markup elements there are in most HTML (or XHTML or XML) source files. Syntax coloring offers an easy way to differentiate between content and markup.

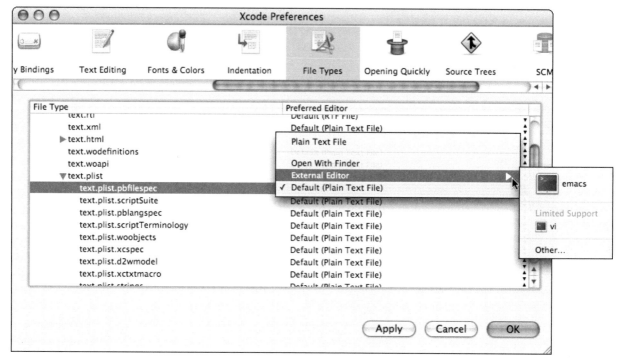

Figure 6-4
Tell Xcode which external editor you want to use for this file type

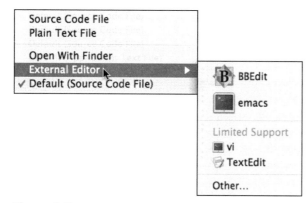

Figure 6-5
Once you select an editor from "Other," it is available in the menu

▼ **Note**

Xcode also lets you know, by its placement within the pop-up, whether the external editor provides Xcode with full or only partial support. As Figure 6-5 shows, BBEdit fully supports Xcode's editing protocols and TextEdit only partially supports them. What this boils down to in this example is that BBEdit can jump right to a specified line or selection in response to a double-click in Xcode's Detail List, but TextEdit will merely open the specified file. Similarly, BBEdit will save files in response to a build command in Xcode (assuming that you tell Xcode to save modified files), but you have to save TextEdit files manually before commencing a build.

PLUS ÇA CHANGE, PLUS C'EST LA MÊME CHOSE

Disagreeing over editors is no new phenomenon. For decades, Unix programmers (which, these days, includes all Mac developers) have been arguing vociferously over the relative virtues and foibles of Unix editors like *vi*, *emacs*, and *pico*. Let one side in the discussion (that's the word our parents used to describe a loud argument) claim that emacs is the most powerful and flexible editor *ever*, and the opposition loudly replies that emacs's marginal (at best!) superior capability is more than outweighed by its arcane complexity, and that *vi* is The One True Editor. The disagreement reflects a dilemma at the core of the Unix mind-set: Although, traditionally, Unix enthusiasts are really big on single keystroke commands, short command names (ls, mv, cp, and so on), and the *KISS* principle (Keep It Simple, Stupid!), they also love their obscure incantations — after all, *wizard* is the title to which serious Unix folk aspire. That's why we don't think this argu... er... discussion will ever end. Besides, what would be the fun in that?

▼ Tip

If you're going to use emacs as an external editor, the hidden file .emacs in your home directory must contain the following lines:

```
(autoload 'gnuserv "gnuserv-compat"
        "Allow this Emacs process to be
a server for client processes." t)
(gnuserv start)
```

(And if you don't know how to find and modify the hidden .emacs file, why are you trying to use emacs anyway?)

YOU KNOW WHAT I MEAN BEFORE I FINISH SAYING IT: CODE COMPLETION

"I love you. You... complete me," Jerry Maguire said to Xcode the first time he saw code completion in action (this scene, by the way, appears only in the unreleased supercollector's deluxe gold classic DVD edition of the film). With code completion, you never again have to say, "Just how did I spell that function's name?" or "What parameters does that method call take?"

Code completion is the expert looking over your shoulder: It watches what you're typing, compares it to its list of known thingies (a highly technical term that encompasses all the symbols in your project), and offers suggestions to complete the typing for you. Take a look at Figure 6-6 to see code completion in operation.

Having such a powerful know-it-all lurking behind you could be annoying, of course. That's why the default setting for code completion is to have it not bother you unless you explicitly ask for help. Here's how to use code completion manually.

1. **Type part of an identifier or other symbol.**

2. **Select Edit → Completion List or press Option+Escape.** A code completion list appears.

3. **Select the completion you want.** You can use the arrow keys or the mouse.

4. **Double-click the completion, or press the Tab key.** The completed item appears in your source.

Simple and sweet. And code completion cannot only finish typing out symbols for you; it can, at your discretion, also provide argument place-holders for functions and methods to save you the trouble of looking them up.

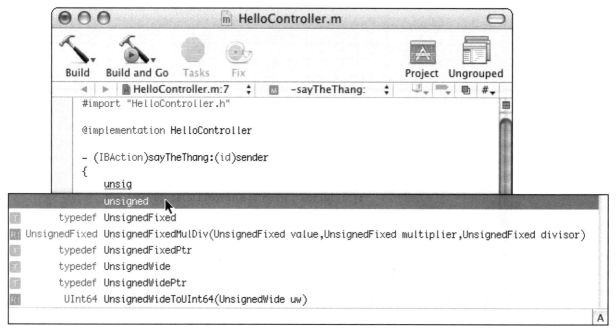

Figure 6-6
Pick a completion...

▼ Tip

At the bottom right of the completion list shown in Figure 6-6 is a button (it looks like the letter A) that lets you toggle how the list is sorted. The A indicates the list is sorted alphabetically. Click it, and the list reorders itself according to Xcode's "best guess" of which identifier you want. Oh, and the symbol shown changes to a π. Why π? We'd hazard a guess, but we're afraid it would be based on circular reasoning.

Code sense, the Xcode functionality behind code completion (see "Code Sense and Sensibility"), is such a powerful feature that Xcode has a preference panel devoted specifically to it (see Figure 6-7), and that's where you can control how code completion behaves.

- You can turn off project indexing and work without code completion and other code-sense features (we call this "doing it old-school").

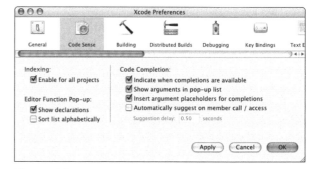

Figure 6-7
Sensible code sense settings

- With the Automatically suggest on member call / access option, you can choose to have code completion never come up uninvited, or to offer suggestions on method calls and field access.

- If you let Xcode offer suggestions, you can specify how long it waits before popping up with them. The

CODE SENSE AND SENSIBILITY

Code completion is able to perform its magic because of Xcode's extensive indexing powers. Every time you create a project, Xcode indexes the whole kit and kaboodle behind the scenes, quickly, efficiently, and unobtrusively. As a result, Xcode knows all the methods, classes, functions, and other symbols in both your project and in the frameworks that it uses. Xcode calls its internal knowledge of your project *code sense*.

Code sense is used for more than just code completion. Xcode also uses it to populate the Project Symbols Smart Group in your Project window and to let you move right from the symbol to its definition. The Class browser (described in Chapter 7) employs the code sense index, too, as does Xcode's powerful search features.

Though earlier versions of Xcode could become bogged down while Xcode indexed a project, indexing now occurs on an unobtrusive background thread; you probably won't even notice it's happening. But if you do, you can always turn it off.

default is half a second; you may want to increase that if you are a slow typist.

- You can control how much information the list shows and how much stuff it inserts into your source.

The Code Sense preference panel also controls the behavior of the editor's function pop-up, which is described in Chapter 5.

▼ Tip

If it ever seems that your project index seems somehow wrong (perhaps identifiers are missing or argument lists are out of date), select the project in your

Groups & Files list and bring up the Project Info Inspector. Then click the Rebuild Code Sense Index button at the bottom of the Inspector's General tab and all should be well.

You can also control which keys activate various code-completion features. The Text Bindings preference panel (described more extensively in Chapter 8) offers six code-completion actions to which you can attach specific key combinations (see Figure 6-8). Choose carefully, though... you don't want to pick combinations that will give you finger cramps or, worse, that will override some of the many other key bindings already assigned in Xcode.

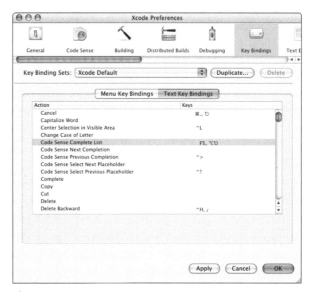

Figure 6-8
Code completion at a keystroke (or two or three or four)

AUTOMAGIC FORMATTING

We were going to call this section Indentical Twins, but our book's editor wasn't sure anyone would know what we were talking about, so we called it Automagic Formatting instead, which, in our minds, is just as opaque — but it made our editor happy, and, really, isn't that what professional writing is all about? Ahem. No matter. Whatever we call it, this section is all about the Xcode editor's ability to automatically format your code (what, in the dim, dark past was called "pretty-printing") and to help you keep track of matching brackets, braces, and other punctuation characters that come in pairs and that you can all too easily lose track of in the convoluted skeins of your code.

Unlike older, primitive computer languages where a symbol's location on a line was semantically significant (ah, punch card, how much we miss thee... not!), most modern languages are not so spatially restrictive. For example, a function formatted like this

```
static long CalcTime(WindowPtr
pWindow, Rect pData) { if
(!EmptyRect(pData)) return(0); else
return(kMaxWaitTime);}
```

and the same function formatted like this

```
static long CalcTime(
  WindowPtr pWindow,
  Rect pData)
{
   if (!EmptyRect(pData))
    return(0);
   else
    return(kMaxWaitTime);
}
```

will compile in exactly the same way. Though the latter is much easier for a human to read and comprehend, to the compiler they are pretty much indistinguishable. However, the compiler isn't going to have to read and make sense of your code nearly as often as you, so it makes sense to let the formatting help your code make sense to you — if, of course, applying that formatting isn't so much trouble that it doesn't make sense to spend time applying it. Make sense?

Xcode uses syntax-aware indenting to automatically indent your code as you compose it, using clues from the surrounding code. Syntax-aware indenting is controlled by

(what else?) a preference panel obscurely called Indentation (see Figure 6-9). By default, syntax-aware indenting is turned off, but when you turn it on, you can tweak the feature in a number of ways. With it on, the Tab key and the Return key take on magical powers.

- Pressing the Tab key (depending on the preference settings) will indent the current line to the appropriate level.

- Pressing the Return key (again, depending on the preference settings) will start a new line, indented an appropriate amount based on the preceding lines.

Figure 6-9
Let Xcode make your code pretty

 Tip

Sometimes Xcode may insist on indenting new lines to the level of previously indented lines even when syntax-aware editing is disabled. You can fix it with the Key Bindings preference: Select the Key Bindings tab and add the Return character to the Insert Newline action.

Because you may want to use a tab, say, to separate a comment on a line from the code preceding it, the Indentation preferences provide a Tab indents pop-up menu to control just when the Tab key is magic and when it isn't.

- Choose the **In leading white space** option to make the Tab key magically indent lines only when the cursor is in the white space before the text on the line begins.

- Choose the **Always** option to have the Tab key *always* indent the line (except, not really, because you can override it; see the Tip that follows).

- Choose the **Never** option if you never want the Tab key to take on supernatural powers.

 Tip

Want to override the syntax-aware indentation settings just this once? Use Option+Tab to insert a tab character no matter what the syntax-aware indenting setting may be. Use Control+I for syntax-aware indentation even when the option is turned off.

Syntax-aware indentation, because it *is* aware of the importance of certain characters in various C-ish dialects as well as in some other languages, can automatically indent lines that start with these special characters; you can turn the indenting on or off in the Indentation preferences for each of these characters (see, again, Figure 6-9). One character, the posture-challenged { character that goes by the name of *opening brace*, can have an optional additional indentation applied and can automatically supply a matching *closing brace* when it is typed (we suspect it must have been some C or Java fan who added *this* feature). And speaking of C and Java (which we were, parenthetically), single-line //-style comments can be indented and consecutive lines of them can be aligned. Now you have no excuse not to comment your code.

The Format menu provides additional control over your code's layout (see Figure 6-10). With it, you can shift selected lines left or right, or reindent the selection based upon the code's context.

Figure 6-10
The Format menu

Code indentation usually inserts (or removes) actual tab characters (our old pal, ASCII 9, alias Control+I). Xcode's Indentations preferences (again, see Figure 6-9) let you adjust how much space indents and tabs take up. Some people may like a wide indent but a narrow tab width, and Xcode can accommodate them.

You can also set Xcode's Indentation preferences to use space characters (ASCII 32) instead by deselecting the Insert 'tabs' instead of spaces option. This lets you preserve the look of the code even when it is viewed on another computer running Xcode, no matter what that copy of Xcode's Tab width and Indent width settings.

 Note

The Insert 'tabs' instead of spaces option is an Xcode preference, not a document preference. If you edit the file with a copy of Xcode configured to replace tabs with spaces, and then edit it some more on a different machine, with Insert 'tabs' instead of spaces selected, Xcode inserts tabs during that editing session — though it will leave the spaces that were inserted previously.

Xcode's Text Editing preference panel (see Figure 6-11) also provides a couple of syntax related options. Specifically, you can set how Xcode will handle certain delimiters, specifically parentheses, brackets, and braces (which the Text Editing preference refers to as "braces" because, well, it does... maybe the developer who designed this preference panel flipped a three-sided coin to pick which delimiter to feature).

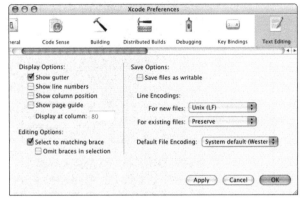

Figure 6-11
Text Editing preferences give you bracing assistance

- When the **Select to matching brace** option is selected, double-clicking a delimiter selects all the text up to, and including, its counterpart.

- When the **Omit braces in selection** option is selected, double-clicking a delimiter selects the text *between* the matching delimiters, but leaves the delimiters themselves deselected. (Personally, we'd like it if we could hold down an option or other modifier key when double-clicking a delimiter to reverse this setting temporarily, because sometimes we like it both ways.)

▼ **Tip**

The Balance command on the Format menu also selects the text between surrounding delimiters (or includes them, depending on the Text Editing preference) using the current cursor position or selection as its starting point. The traditional count-the-parentheses meditation that coders of old frequently practiced in order to find an extra (or missing) counterpart has been made much more efficient.

#PRAGMA-TIC LANDMARKS

Back in Chapter 5, you encountered the function pop-up, which made navigating to your functions a breeze. (Speaking of which, why is a breeze considered a good thing? Doesn't it depend on the direction from which it's blowing? Okay, getting a little off-topic here....) Not only can you use it to see and go to your code's functions, though: You can, in fact, add additional items to the function pop-up in your C (or C++, or Objective-C, or Objective-C++) source files (we have a lovely picture of the function pop-up in Chapter 5's Figure 5-12 in case you've forgotten what it is). It's all done by way of the magic `#pragma mark` statement.

▼ **Note**

If a C-dialect is not your native (or even second or third) tongue, a `#pragma` statement is a compiler directive, usually handled by the compiler's preprocessor before the heavy-duty compilation gets underway. The `#pragma mark` statement is ignored by compilers that don't understand it and is most often used in development environments like Xcode in order to let you set special marks in your code that will then appear in some menu or other in that environment.

To add, say, the phrase "Optional garbage functions" to the function pop-up, simply insert a line reading

```
#pragma mark Optional garbage functions
```

in your code. It appears on the function pop-up in bold, and selecting it from the pop-up selects the corresponding text in the file.

If you need to add a separator line to the function pop-up (say, to separate one group of functions from another), just insert

```
#pragma mark -
```

in your code. The hyphen becomes a menu-spanning line on the function pop-up.

CALL IT MACRO-RONI

And speaking of inserting things into your code, there are all sorts of common nontrivial bits of text that appear in source code that take nontrivial amounts of time to keep typing. The Insert Text Macro command on the Edit menu is designed for helping you avoid all that strenuous typing (see Figure 6-12).

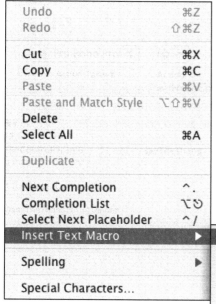
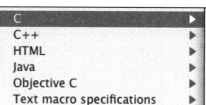

Figure 6-12
Insert prewritten text to give your typing fingers a rest

Xcode provides several submenus of carefully crafted macros that operate on, and add to, selected text. For example, selecting Edit → Insert Text Macro → C → #Pragma Mark inserts the `#pragma mark` statement that we mentioned in the previous section (look up... see it?), and selects the label so you can type your own.

Xcode currently comes with a set of C, C++, HTML, Java, Objective-C, and Text macro specifications. This last provides macros that you can use to specify additional sets of text macros. If you want to build your own set (or modify the existing sets) of macros, you can find the macro sets that Xcode provides hidden deep inside the Xcode application's package: Look into the TextMacros.xctxtmacro folder inside the package's PlugIns folder. You're a programmer; we're sure you can figure out what to do from there.

 Tip

Before you begin your macro-making experiments, make a backup copy of the Xcode application. You'll thank us for this advice.

IN SHORT

Xcode almost bends over backward to let you tailor your editing environment to your liking. You can color code by syntactical features. You substitute your favorite editor for Xcode's if Xcode's just doesn't float your boat. You can set Xcode's editor to read your code as you write it and supply suggested code-completing text. You can tailor the editor to format your code so that mere mortals can read it. You can set landmarks in your code so you can find your way back to them. And you can even employ text macros to insert and modify existing source text. Not bad for an editor that you get free in every box of Tiger.

Reference Works While You Play

Reading While You Write • I Spy an API
The Searching General's Report
The Free Mark It System • *man* Overboard
Back Cover Copy

In the beginning were a bunch of loose-leaf binders and monthly mailings. And these binders begat the "phonebook" and hard-bound editions of *Inside Macintosh*. And *Inside Macintosh* begat additional volumes, and these came in soft-cover, and in a HyperCard stack, and on CD, and were joined by the Tech Notes, and the documentation grew and was fruitful and multiplied. And the programmers beheld all the documentation in its length and its breadth and its wealth, and they gnashed their teeth and rent their garments, and they cried out, "You expect us to read all this stuff?"

And the answer came down, "No, but you should have it if you need it." And so there was Mac OS X, and there was Xcode, and with Xcode came the Documentation Viewer and the Apple Developer Connection Reference Library and the need for over half a gigabyte of hard drive space to hold it. And the programmers cried out, "Thanks. We guess...."

Macs running Mac OS X can do an awful lot, due in large part to all the code and frameworks and APIs that come with the system. Mac programmers can easily craft Mac OS X programs that handle multiple human languages and writing systems, play music and video, access multiple networks, print complex documents — all of this and much more by calling upon the system features and libraries that come with the Mac. But you gotta know what it is to use it, and running to a bookshelf groaning under the weight of all the documentation that explains these features and the libraries every time you need to look something up is no way to do that (actually, it *is* a way, but not a very smart or convenient one).

Xcode provides smart and convenient tools to help you look up what you need to look up when you gotta look something up in the hundreds of megabytes of documentation that comes with Xcode. Maybe you can't read it all — but you have it if and when you need some part of it.

READING WHILE YOU WRITE

Choosing Help ➜ Documentation opens the Developer Documentation window, presenting the main page. Figure 7-1 shows you, roughly, what you'll see. We say "roughly" because the Developer Documentation Library

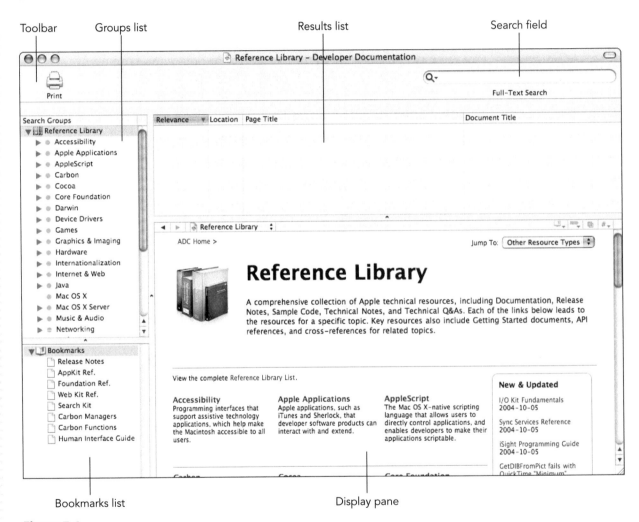

Figure 7-1
Xcode's Developer Documentation window

is an ever-growing and evolving collection that Xcode updates through the Internet when and as needed. What is here today will undoubtedly be larger and slightly changed next month, next week, tomorrow, or even in just a few minutes. So, what you see in the Groups list could change, as could the initial text in the display pane.

 Note

One thing to realize about Xcode's documentation window is that it is, in reality, an HTML browser customized with features specific to and convenient for searching and perusing technical documentation. From this, we can logically conclude that the documentation resides in HTML files. So, if you really want to do so, you can also peruse them with your Web browser of choice, but we don't think you'll find that method as satisfactory as the documentation viewer.

The small magnifying glass in the Search field is, in reality, a pop-up menu (but you figured that out when you saw the little down-pointing triangle to its right). The pop-up contains two choices: Full-Text Search and API Search (we'll talk more about this menu and API and Full-Text searches a little later in this chapter — in "I Spy an API" and "The Searching General's Report," respectively).

If you search using the Search field, the results will appear in the results list. The display pane presents whatever you've selected last from either the results list or the Groups list. The display pane should look very familiar to you, though, as it is (essentially) a read-only embedded editor pane with all the navigation bar tools presented for interface and operational consistency. You've got the Back

and Forward arrows, the recently visited page pop-up menu, the symbol pop-up menu, the bookmarks pop-up, the breakpoints pop-up (though you'll seldom, if ever, find these last three enabled or useful in the documentation window), the counterpart button, and the includes pop-up.

If you're screen-constrained, you might want to make the contents pane a little or a lot larger (that is where the documentation you seek is displayed, after all). You could hide the Groups and Bookmarks lists and the Results list, but you're probably going to need them as you go through the documentation. Or, you could plunk down over $3,500 for a 30-inch monitor and the video card to drive it (and Apple will love you if you do). Xcode also gives you some other options, but only through the contextual menu you see when Control+clicking in the contents pane (see Figure 7-2).

You'll see two or three commands in the contextual menu, depending upon whether the page in the display pane has multiple frames. They are:

- **Open Page in New Window,** which opens a new document viewer window displaying just the toolbar and display pane;

- **Open Page in Browser,** which opens the page in your default Web browser; and

- **Open Frame in New Window,** which is only present if the page has multiple frames, and which opens the frame you Control+clicked in a new document viewer window.

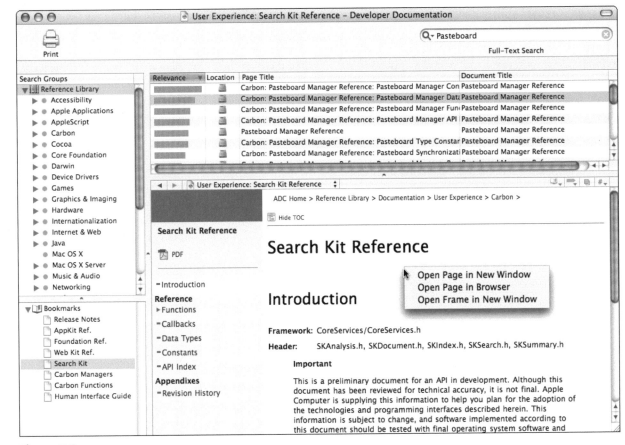

Figure 7-2
Some convenient commands are only available through the shortcut menu

I SPY AN API

Learning a computer language — any computer language — is not that hard, especially after you've done it once or twice. The size of a typical language's collection of reserved words, symbols, and syntactic constructs is really quite small. What strains a programmer's brain

as much as anything else is the need to learn all the predefined routines, constants, and data structures available in a typical development system's API libraries. It's like the difference between learning to speak English and learning the entire corpus of English-language literature. The tens of thousands of symbols defined in the various frameworks and SDKs that come with Xcode are enough to make even the most hard-core programmer a bit dizzy (that, and the continuous indulgence in caffeinated beverages and brief breaks to play the latest multiplayer shooter).

Fortunately, all of the Apple-defined interface elements and routines are documented online, and the Documentation Viewer's API Search field makes finding a routine,

class, data type, or whatever-you're-looking-for's description a matter of typing just a few characters.

First, you need to tell the Documentation Viewer that you want to search for APIs by choosing it from the Search field pop-up menu we previously mentioned (see Figure 7-3).

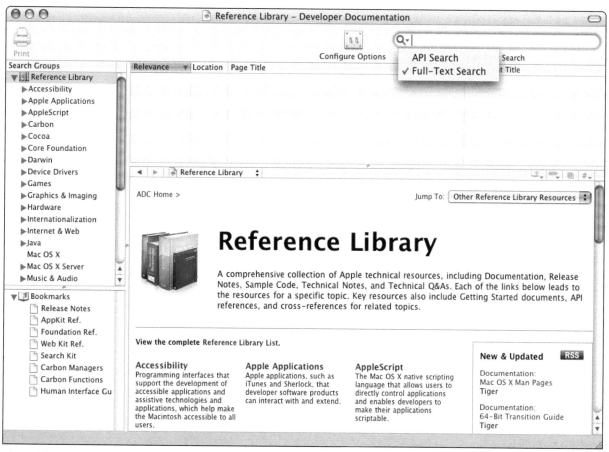

Figure 7-3
Choose a search technique

When you choose to search for APIs in the Documentation Viewer, all the available symbols for the selected Search Group miraculously appear in the search results pane (see Figure 7-4). You also see a count of the number of symbols currently found listed at the bottom of the window in its status bar; if you've chosen to search the entire Reference Library group, that number will be a few orders of magnitude larger than you can count on your fingers and toes.

However, if you have some tens of thousands of symbols listed in the results pane, it can be a pain to find the one you want, even though they are sorted alphabetically. But that's what the API Search field is for: Type the first couple of characters of a symbol's name, and the search results pane quickly changes to show just the symbols that begin with those characters. (Yes, it's just like iTunes for APIs. Rock out, dude!)

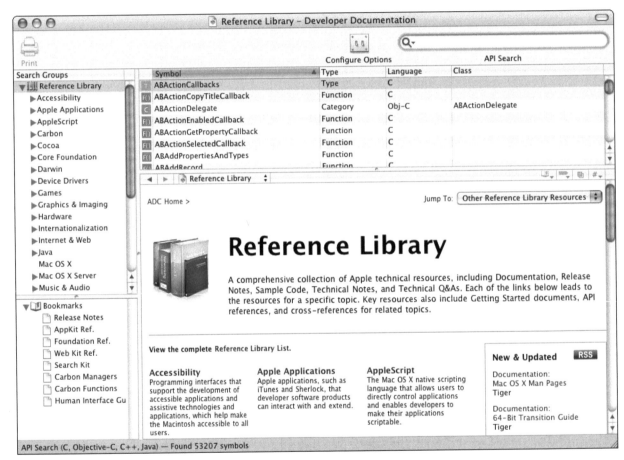

Figure 7-4
Pick a symbol, any symbol

The search results pane displays

- the name of the symbol,
- the symbol's type,
- the language in which the symbol is defined (many are defined in more than one language; for example, C++ and Java), and
- the symbol's class.

▼ Tip

You can further restrict the symbols found in an API search to a particular language by clicking the Documentation Viewer's Configure Options button. This produces a sheet with checkboxes for the languages you want included in your search: C, C++, Java, and Objective-C. After all, if you're writing your app in Java, you don't want to have to wade through all the C++ APIs, now do you?

Associated with each symbol is a special icon to let you know what type of symbol the symbol is, which is glossed by a tool-tip if you position the mouse over it (see Figure 7-5). It might seem redundant for the Documentation Viewer to provide this icon, given that its results pane also

has a column that displays the symbol's type in actual text, but, remember, this is a Mac OS X display list, which means you can click and drag columns around by their headers, and you can choose to show or hide any column by control+clicking the column header and enabling it or disabling it from a handy-dandy pop-up menu. (We weren't kidding when we said it's just like iTunes for APIs!)

The API Search field is not the only way for you to get your minimum daily requirement of API goodness. You can get it right from your source code as you're editing it: Just Option+double-click a symbol in an Editor window to have Xcode open the documentation window with the symbol's definition on display. Or you can ⌘+double-click the symbol in your source code to have Xcode open the appropriate header file with the declaration displayed front and center.

▼ Note

Xcode presents a pop-up menu of files when you ⌘+double-click a symbol if more than one header file contains the symbol (which is possible for an identifier that is defined in several different classes). In that case, select the header file you want from the pop-up.

Symbol	Type	Language	Class
ABActionCallbacks	Type	C	
ABActionCopyTitleCallback	Function	C	
ABActionDelegate	Category	Obj-C	ABActionDelegate
ABActionEnabledCallback	Function	C	
ABActionGetPropertyCallback	Function	C	
ABActionSelectedCallback	Function	C	
PropertiesAndTypes	Function	C	
ABAddRecord	Function	C	
ABAddressBook	Class	Obj-C	ABAddressBook

Figure 7-5
Every symbol has a tool-tip

THE SEARCHING GENERAL'S REPORT

We told you earlier how well we remember hauling out and pawing through the loose-leaf *Inside Macintosh* notebooks a couple decades ago. (Come to think of it, we did the same thing with IBM 370, Univac 1100, and Modcomp II binders before that.) First, we had to know which binder to search and hope the index was accurate (something that wasn't always the case), find the tab for that manager (the old term for a set of related APIs, such as *Resource Manager*), and then we would rifle through the pages (hoping) to find the information we sought, generally after a few "see also" references, frequently located in yet another manager's documentation and, when we were unlucky, in a different binder. To top it off, Apple sent out monthly updates and replacement pages that we needed to insert in the binders, removing outdated material along the way. This was one of the reasons that the index was iffy — updated index pages weren't always accurate and, when they were, they assumed that you had put everything in, every month.

Xcode makes such manual effort unnecessary (although we've had to substitute new strength-training exercises to replace using those mammoth binders as ersatz dumbbells) and its online documentation significantly reduces our physical desk and shelf space requirements. And, as we noted earlier in this chapter ("Reading While You Write"), the update process is automated, eliminating paper cuts, snap-ring pinch, and a mountain of paper going to the recycle bin (see Chapter 8 where we explain how to control the automatic updating of documentation).

Never willing to let a good UI feature be underutilized, Xcode employs the Search item interface found in a standard Help window for your full-text searches. You can type:

- a single word, such as "sheet"

- a phrase, such as "full-text search"

- a question, such as "How do I perform a full-text search?"

Okay, that last one is a variant of the phrase search, but the extra words in a question could narrow the search a bit or reorder the relevance ratings in the results list. And, as with an API search, you can also narrow your search by selecting an item in the Groups list. Doing so restricts your search to that group (and its subordinates, if any).

Tip

There's actually one more way to do a full-text search. You can select text in any editor window or pane and choose Help ➡ Find Selected Text in Documentation.

THE FREE MARK IT SYSTEM

Electronic documentation has a few limitations compared to hard copy, mostly relating to where you can read it. We mean, for example, reading on the throne (where all of us are equal), or at the breakfast table, which tends to be a lot more convenient with a book than with a computer, even an iBook or 12" PowerBook. Similarly, it's easier to read a book in bed or while lying out by the pool or on a beach — battery power is finite and electrical outlets aren't always convenient, to say little about glare or getting sand in the keyboard.

However, even with these limitations (which, frankly, have prevented our wholehearted adoption of online documentation), we've come to appreciate that the Xcode Document Viewer's benefits easily outweigh its inconveniences. For example, we don't dog-ear the pages or go through Post-it Notes or (our favorite) Post-it Flags like locusts through a wheat field, leaving a maze of markers with short, scribbled notes and no discernible organization. Next to the search and hypertext conveniences discussed previously in this chapter, Xcode's Bookmarks feature is our favorite aspect of Xcode's online documentation and will, if you're anything like us, cut into 3M's profitability. With the Documentation viewer, we just mark material we know we're going to want to see again, add a descriptive (and legible) tag, and place it easily in Xcode's orderly list of Bookmarks. No more squinting to decipher our squiggles, no more little pieces of paper or tape coming loose and making a mess, and no more trying to find that one note in a hodge-podge of 50 flags protruding at odd angles from the book — we'll suffer through not having our Xcode documentation at the beach.

Look back at Figure 7-1, and you see the Bookmarks list at the bottom left of the Developer Documentation window (just below the Groups list). The items you see in that list are the bookmarks Apple supplies to whet your appetite — they include the Release Notes for the latest edition of the ADR (Apple Developer Reference) Library, the Human Interface Guidelines, and the main links pages for the major frameworks and toolkits.

Xcode gives you three ways to bookmark the currently displayed page:

- You can choose Find → Add to Bookmarks.

- You can press ⌘+D.

- You can drag the documentation window's proxy icon to the bookmarks list.

Xcode's documentation tells you that you can also remove a bookmark from the Bookmarks list, but it doesn't tell you how (at least not at the time we're writing this). We'll tell you how and maybe our presentation here will nudge them to update the documentation. Select the bookmark in the Bookmarks list and choose Edit → Delete or press the Delete key. Pretty obvious, once you think about it, but probably not the first thing you'd try — it took us a few minutes, but we'll save you those minutes so that you can apply the time to writing the next great OS X program.

As with most lists that are under your management and control, you can reorder the Bookmarks list by clicking and dragging the item into the position you wish. As you drag an item, a line (see Figure 7-6) shows you where it will appear if you release the mouse button at that point.

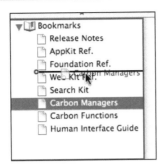

Figure 7-6
Drag and drop to reorder the items in the Bookmarks list

MAN OVERBOARD

Xcode, like the rest of Mac OS X, sits on top of Unix, and the wizards of Unix have long been accustomed to getting their information directly from the man... that is, the man command available on the Unix command line that displays the copious documentation that comes with every Unix system. Ordinarily, Mac OS X users have to open up the Terminal application to consult the various man pages available, but with Xcode you don't have to: The man pages are just a Help menu item away (see Figure 7-7).

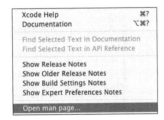

Figure 7-7
Go to the man

The Open man page Help menu item does something relatively rare for Xcode: It displays a dialog (see Figure 7-8). This dialog lets you type some text and choose whether to search for a *man page name* (which really means the name of a command-line tool) or for a *search string* (which really seems to mean a command related to a keyword... the Unix *apropos* command, essentially).

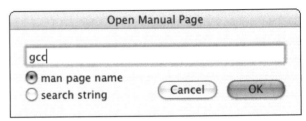

Figure 7-8
man **searches evoke a rare Xcode modal dialog**

Click OK after typing a search item in the dialog and the Documentation Viewer swings into action, displaying the relevant man page nicely formatted and hyperlinked for your viewing pleasure (see Figure 7-9).

Why would you want to consult man pages at all? Well, most of the compiler and build options provided by Xcode are based upon the command-line tools that live way down deep in the Unix layer of Mac OS X, and, in fact, Xcode even lets you specify compiler options right in the Info palette. What better place to find out about those options in all their geeky detail than by getting right down to the canonical source?

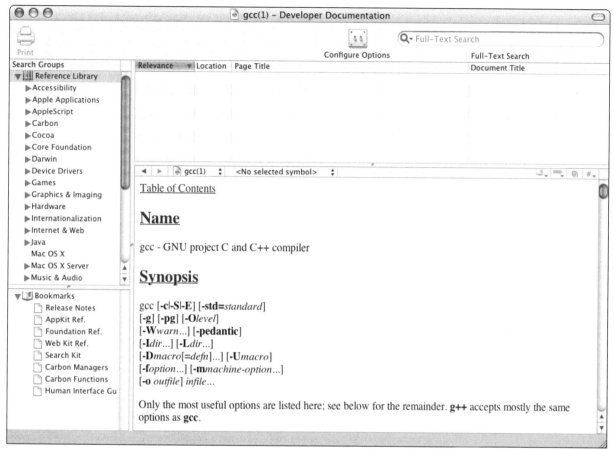

Figure 7-9
A *man* page, Document Viewer style

BACK COVER COPY

"One of Xcode's strengths is its ability to tell you what you need to know when you need to know it. Packing many manuals' worth of information behind its iTunes-like search interface, Xcode's Documentation Viewer lets you winnow down massive mountains of detail to just the facts you need, when you need them, and to mark them for future reference so you can get back to them quickly. Add in the bundled access to Unix's fabled man pages and you have a top-notch thrilling interface to the informational ride of your life!"

— Harvey Shill, *Information Weakly Monthly Review*

Still Yet Even More Preferences

More General • More Fonts • More File Types
More Paths • More Key Bindings • More Documentation
More Geeky • More to Come

The typical programmer is unique. (You like that paradox? We've got a million of 'em!) They all have their decided likes and dislikes, and they find it far easier to get their work done when things are just the way that they like them. It's not that programmers are a particularly high-maintenance group, but, like Harry's friend, Sally Albright, they simply want what they want the way that they want it, whether it's pie à la mode only with the pie heated and with the ice cream not on top but on the side, or a text editor that displays line but not column numbers and that automatically converts tabs to two spaces but uses four spaces for indents.

In recognition of this programmer fact of life, Xcode offers a *lot* of preference settings: something less than a gazillion but certainly more than your (or our) average application. We've covered a bunch of Xcode's preferences so far in those places where they're relevant, and we'll cover even more of them later in this book, too. Here, however, we're going to cover the ones that we haven't quite found a good place to discuss anywhere else and flesh out the descriptions of some that we've already covered. Call us lazy or unimaginative. We prefer to think of it as providing additional value for your book-buying dollar. Because nothing is too good for you, our reader.

MORE GENERAL

Speaking of lazy or unimaginative, what's up with the *General* preferences? They're not general so much as *miscellaneous*: Some affect the editor while others affect the Xcode environment itself (see Figure 8-1). Here's a rundown of what these preference settings do.

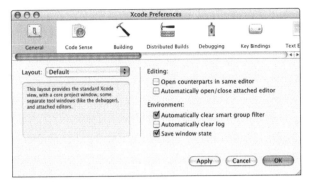

Figure 8-1

The Miscella... er... General preferences

- **Layout** — This pop-up menu lets you choose which of Xcode's workspace configurations you will use (we described workspaces in a lovely sidebar, complete with illustrations, in Chapter 3). Xcode is nice enough to provide a description of the selected workspace setting right in the preference panel (refer to Figure 8-1 if you don't believe us).

▼ **Note**

You can't set a workspace preference when a project is open; the setting pop-up becomes disabled. And the preference window will tell you why it's disabled, too, in case you can't remember this note.

- **Open counterparts in same editor** — If you're using the Counterpart button that we described in Chapter 5 to jump between a function's implementation and interface declaration, selecting this option causes the counterpart to replace the editor's current contents.

- **Automatically open/close attached editor** — Enable this setting if you want the embedded editor to immediately open whenever you select something that the embedded editor can display (we described the embedded editor in Chapter 5). For example, if you select any source file in the Project window, it appears immediately in the Project window's embedded editor.

Selecting compiler error messages or bookmarks also opens the appropriate editor when this setting is enabled.

▼ **Note**

No matter what your preferences are for embedded editors, opening a file that does not belong to any open project opens it in a separate editor window. Think about it: If the file does not belong to an open project, its editor can't belong to the project either, right? Right.

- **Automatically clear smart group filter** — Select this option to clear out the search field in the project window when you select a Smart Group in your project's Groups & Files list; this lets the Smart Group display all of its contents rather than just the ones that match whatever string you left hanging around in the search field. Xcode selects this option by default.

- **Automatically clear log** — Xcode maintains several log files, including the Run log and the Console log (available from Xcode's Debug menu). When you run an executable, Xcode adds information to those logs, such as the time of day that the executable launched or whether (and how) the executable ignominiously crashed. Select this option to have Xcode clear those logs every time you start a new session.

- **Save window state** — We described this in Chapter 5 when we discussed Xcode's editor windows, but this preference controls more than just Xcode's editor: It lets you instruct Xcode to remember the position and contents of many of Xcode's various windows when you close a project so that, when you open the project again, everything is right where you left it.

MORE FONTS

You got a look at the Fonts & Colors preferences in Chapter 5 when we described syntax coloring. Here's what some of the other options offered by this preference panel do (see Figure 8-2).

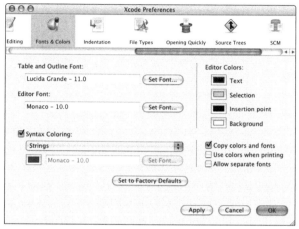

Figure 8-2
The Fonts & Colors preferences revisited

- **Table and Outline Font** — Click the Set Font button to change the font and size used for all of Xcode's various list views. The standard Mac OS X Font palette appears and lets you choose among all the fonts you have installed. The default font, Lucida Grande, is a pretty good one because it is clear, clean, and can display most of the characters in the Unicode character set, but you don't *have* to use it — which is a good thing for those of us who like a little bit of serif on our typefaces.

- **Editor Font** — This is just what you think it is: the font used in Xcode's editor windows and panes. The default font is Monaco, a sans serif monospaced font that's been with the Mac since 1984. Again, click the Set Font button to change the font and size.

> ▼ **Note**
>
> Although the current font and size for these two preferences appear in what seem to be editable fields, you can't edit their contents. You have to push the button and you have to use the Font palette. Accept it.

- **Editor Colors** — Click a color swatch to change the color used for text, selections, the insertion point (ooohhh, look... a red blinky thing!), or the editor's background. The standard Mac OS X Color palette appears and allows you to pick a color from its selection of color pickers (we like the palette's crayon picker because it tells us that the black text color is actually called "Licorice"... mmmm, licorice...).

- **Copy colors and fonts** — Check this option to have the editor's fonts and colors go along for the ride when you copy selections to the clipboard and paste them elsewhere (including into other applications like TextEdit or Pages).

- **Use colors when printing** — Useless if you don't have a color printer, but useful if you do. Checking this option lets your printout show you all the same colors you saw on the screen.

MORE FILE TYPES

We discussed the File Types preference panel in Chapter 6 when we described how to choose an external editor to use with your source files, but this panel is useful for more than just that.

For example, suppose that after you add a media file of some sort to your project's resources (say, a splash screen image or a particular funky and amusing error alert sound) you discover that the file needs some tweaking. Suppose, further, that there is a particular application that you prefer to use for such tweaking, and that application is *not* the file's default application in the Finder (for example, a .jpg file that defaults to Preview but that you like to mess with using Graphic Converter). You can select the application Xcode uses to edit media files the same way you select an external text editor (see Figure 8-3).

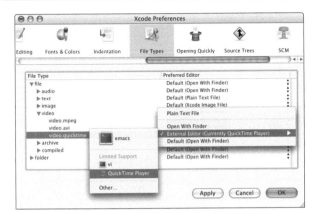

Figure 8-3
The media file needs a massage

1. **Open Xcode's Preferences (Xcode → Preferences or ⌘+,) and select the File Types icon.**

2. **Open the disclosure triangle for file, and choose the file type of interest.** Xcode provides a variety of these, including audio, video, and images. Keep opening disclosure triangles until you drill down to the exact file type that you want or until you strike oil (if you strike oil, check your G5's cooling system at once).

3. **Click the file's Preferred Editor (the column to the right), and choose the application you want to assign to it from the pop-up menu that appears.** If you're lucky and that application appears on the menu, choose it and you are done. Skip the next step. Have a caffeinated soft drink.

4. **If the application you want to use isn't listed (and it probably won't be at first), choose External Editor → Other.** A standard file sheet appears that lets you select any of the applications you have installed on your Mac. Select the one you want. Xcode, by the way, will remember this application and leave it on the External Editors submenu, so you can choose it for other file types without having to use the standard file sheet again.

YOU PUT A SOUND FILE IN MY SOURCE CODE

Keep in mind that a development project contains more than just your lovingly composed and polished source code. Applications and other executables can (and do) travel with a lot of baggage. Back in the old classic Mac days, most of this baggage was eventually shoe-horned into the app's *resource fork*, but even then most of these things would start out as discrete files — for example, sound samples, pictures, help text — which you had to keep somehow associated with your development project until such time as you did the resource shoe-horning. Today, of course, such things usually end up in the application's package (which we described in Chapter 1).

Xcode lets you keep these various non-code files as part of your project; in fact, tradition and inertia being what they are, most of these wind up being listed in the Resources group in your Groups & Files list; they are usually moved to the appropriate place in your application's package during the build phase (just open the target group in one of the more complex sample projects included with Xcode and you'll likely find a build phase or two that copies these files to the package).

Now, when you double-click the media file in your Project window, your media editor of choice will fire up and let you edit the file.

You may also want to use a different text editor for different types of source files. As we said, we cover that process back in Chapter 6, but we would like to draw your attention to Figure 8-4. As you can see, there is a whole slew of different text file types that Xcode knows about, which means that there is a whole slew of different ways to set up Xcode to handle the various text files with which you may be

Figure 8-4
Engaging in textual discrimination

working — there's no reason you can't have half a dozen (or more) specialized text editors assigned to handle half a dozen different types of text files, if you happen to have (and know and love) that many specialized text editors.

And, to wrap it all up, there are *wrappers*. Wrappers are directories or files that contain other files. (Does that sound like a package to you? Well, it should.) Wrappers differ among themselves: One type of wrapper (and the most commonly seen by most users even if they don't know that it *is* a wrapper) is an application package, but there are lots of others. For example, a .nib file (which Interface Builder creates and modifies) can be either an individual file or a directory containing other .nib files

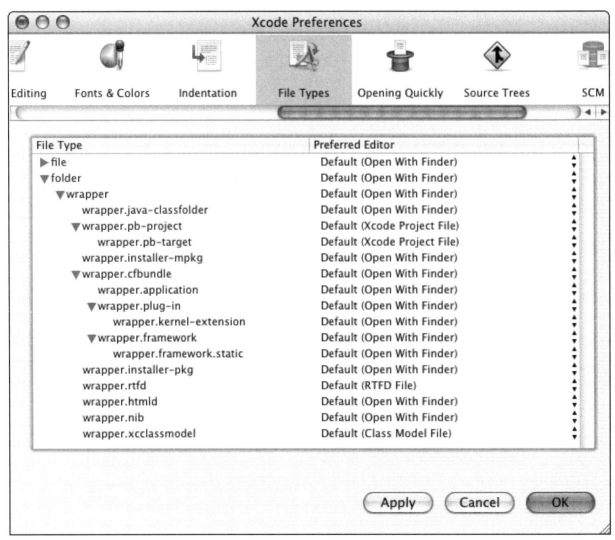

Figure 8-5
Wrap party

within it. In fact, Cocoa applications can use certain framework routines to create their own file wrappers, allowing such applications to store different types of information in a single "file" (think of a bento box — just don't overindulge on the wasabi). Xcode lets you assign different applications to open and manipulate the various wrappers included in your project (see Figure 8-5). An ambitious or driven programmer might even create a specialized application to handle certain wrapper types and then assign that application to those wrappers in other Xcode projects. This kind of customization is beyond what *we're* willing to do, of course, but we're lazy; just knowing that it's possible is enough to give us warm fuzzy feelings.

MORE PATHS

For members of a profession who, by and large, spend an inordinate amount of time indoors, programmers seem rather fond of trees (a quick search of Xcode's documentation library for *tree* turned up almost 70 hits without even breaking a sweat). Being programmers, of course, they usually tend to be referring to *conceptual* trees rather than actual earth-hugging, water-drinking, bark-covered wood things. One kind of conceptual tree is the *source tree*, which tends to be of particular interest to programmers engaged in collaborative programming projects.

Source trees let programmers who are working on the same project (but who are doing it on different machines because, hey, real programmers just *don't* share their computers) create imaginary pathways to the project files used by that project. For example, suppose Dennis and Michael are both working on their new MPEG-4 audio-editing application, *AACintosh Studio*. Now suppose they both keep the files they collaborate on in a different directory than the project directory: Dennis keeps his copies in ~/Shared with Michael/ on his machine and Michael keeps his copies in ~/Projects/Shared/Barney/ on his machine (this is because of a childhood Flintstones fixation Michael

prefers not to discuss). When, as may happen, Dennis hands off a new file to Michael in the course of their work, Xcode may try to find the file Dennis created in ~/Shared with Michael/ instead of in ~/Projects/Shared/Barney/ unless something is done to resolve the confusion. Xcode's Source Trees preferences panel is designed to do just that.

Figure 8-6 shows the Source Trees preferences panel. It lets you describe three things.

Figure 8-6
A tree grows in Xcode

- A **Setting Name.** This is the name of the tree itself. All programmers working on the same project use the same setting name; in our example, Dennis and Michael must both call their tree "Barney."

- A **Display Name.** This is the name that appears in file dialogs and other Xcode windows that refer to the file's path. This can be different for each programmer.

- A **Path.** This is the actual path to the file. Each programmer uses the path to the actual directory used for shared files on his or her machine. Michael's path is shown in Figure 8-6; Dennis's path is different.

The source tree is not specific to a particular project; it is available to all the Xcode projects on that user account on that machine. Thus, Michael can use his Barney path for several different projects on his machine if he so desires.

Once the source tree is established, it can be used every time a file is added to a project. When you add a file to a project, Xcode provides a Reference Type pop-up menu that lets you specify where the file is stored in relation to the rest of the project files; if Xcode knows about any source trees, they are shown in that pop-up menu. Figure 8-7 shows a file being added to a project using the Project menu's Add to Project command.

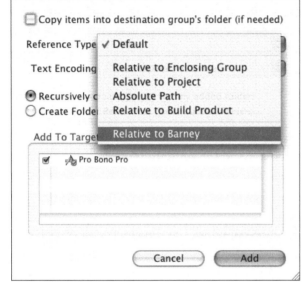

Figure 8-7
Adding a file using a tree

▼ **Note**

You can create a source tree path without creating the actual directory. However, Xcode is smart enough not to offer that source tree as an option when you add files if the path you specify for that tree doesn't actually exist. If you specify a non-existing path, and then create the directory, you may have to restart Xcode in order for it to recognize that the path now exists.

MORE KEY BINDINGS

In Chapter 6 we briefly talked about key bindings in relation to Xcode's code completion feature, and promised to tell you more about key bindings in Chapter 8. Well, here we are in Chapter 8. And here is more information about key bindings. No matter what some people (tricksy lying hobbitses!) may have told you, we like to keep our promises.

Key bindings let you assign key combinations to particular commands and operations in Xcode. And not just one or two, or even one or two dozen of them, either: Xcode lets you create key bindings for hundreds of commands — in fact, you can assign a key combination for almost any command or operation that Xcode can perform. And not just one set of bindings, either — you can create different sets of key bindings to match your project or your mood or the day of the week. It's a total geek paradise!

Figure 8-8
One preference to bind them all

For all its power, the Key Bindings preference panel is quite simple (see Figure 8-8). Xcode divides key bindings into two groups, which you choose from the tabs above the preference's main pane:

- **Menu Key Bindings,** which lets you assign your own key combinations to any of Xcode's menu commands; and

- **Text Key Bindings,** which lets you assign your own key combinations to just about anything else, including things like cursor movements, text editing, text formatting, debugging operations, source code management, and project navigation (see Figure 8-9).

Adding or changing a key binding is simple.

1. **Select the type of binding you want to add.** Menu or Text are your two choices.

2. **Select the category of binding you want to add.** In the case of Menu Key Bindings, Xcode presents them in a hierarchical list that corresponds to Xcode's menus: You can reveal or hide a menu's key bindings by clicking the disclosure triangle by each menu or submenu name. For example, you can find all the Project commands under the (what else?) Project item, and under *that* you can find the New Build Phase submenu items under the New Build Phase item. You can skip this step for Text Key Bindings because they aren't divided into categories.

3. **Double-click the key column to the right of the item to which you want to add a key binding.** If there already is a binding for that command, it is selected (see Figure 8-10).

4. **Type the key combination you want to assign.** If there is no key binding previously associated with the command, the key combination you type becomes the new binding; if there is a binding already associated with the command, your new key combination replaces it.

Menu Key Bindings	Text Key Bindings	
Action	**Keys**	
Move Down	^N, ↓	
Move Down Extending Selection	⇧↓	
Move Forward	^F	
Move Forward Extending Selection		
Move Left	←	
Move Paragraph Backward Extending Selection	⌥⇧↑	
Move Paragraph Forward Extending Selection	⌥⇧↓	
Move Right	→	
Move Subword Backward	^←	
Move Subword Backward Extending Selection	^⇧←	
Move Subword Forward	^→	
Move Subword Forward Extending Selection	^⇧→	
Move to Beginning of Document	⌘↑	
Move to Beginning of Document Extending Selection	⇧⌥\, ⇧⌘↑	

Figure 8-9
Just a few of the many text key bindings available

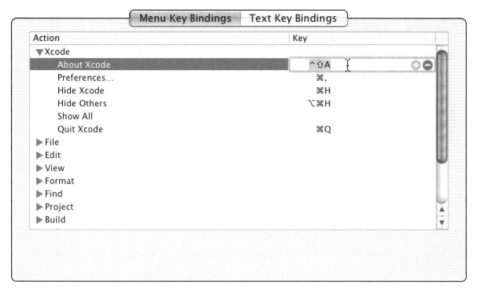

Figure 8-10
Adding or changing a key binding

"But, but, but..." you may be sputtering, "what if I want to *add* a binding to one that is already there? Or simply delete one without replacing it?" Ah, well, that gets a little trickier, but not much trickier. You may notice (and if not, look more closely at Figure 8-10) that two little buttons appear to the right of the key column when you double-click it: a + button and a - button. Click the + button to add a key binding to one that already exists, and click the - button to remove the selected key binding.

▼ Note

Xcode doesn't allow any of the Menu Key Bindings to have more than one binding; if there already is a binding for a menu command, the + button is disabled. You can, however, have several key bindings associated with any of the Text Key Bindings.

▼ Tip

With so many possible key bindings, it is pretty easy to add a binding that matches one that is already assigned to another command. In that case, Xcode removes the old binding and assigns it to the command on which you're working. Luckily, you can tell that you are about to move a key binding from one command to another, because Xcode displays a tiny message below the preference panel's main pane telling you which command is being replaced; for example, you see something like "⌘N is currently bound to New File..." if you try to bind that combination to a different command. If that happens, and you don't want to reassociate the binding, click the little - button; don't press keys like Delete or ESC to cancel, because pressing *any* key tells Xcode you want to use that key as the binding!

Xcode comes with four sets of key bindings that you can use and makes them available from the Key Binding Sets pop-up menu above the preferences main pane (see Figure 8-11).

Figure 8-11
Pre-supplied binding sets

- **Xcode Default** — The name says it all; these are the bindings that Xcode comes set up to use right out of the installer.

- **BBEdit Compatible** — This one uses the same key combinations that the popular BBEdit text editor uses; if you are a heavy BBEdit user, choosing this combination helps you avoid cognitive dissonance when you use Xcode. (Note, though, that BBEdit also lets you mess around with some of *its* bindings, so the BBEdit-compatible set probably will not match your customized BBEdit settings... Xcode is pretty smart but it's not a mind reader!)

- **Metroworks Compatible** — This set helps the legions of Code Warrior fans switch to Xcode for their development needs.

- **MPW Compatible** — This last set is for those of us who have grown gray and wizened in the service of Mac development and who still have muscle memory of all the key combinations used in the venerable Macintosh Programmers Workshop.

You can't change *any* of the key bindings in these sets, though. If you do, Xcode chides you and tells you need to make a copy first (see Figure 8-12); you *can* modify copies of the built-in sets. This, of course, is not hard to do, because the same dialog that yells at you for your transgression has a friendly Aqua Make Copy button you can click to do just that. When you do, Xcode asks you to name the new set (it suggests the name "Copy of <whatever set you are copying>"), after which you can go crazy with all your customizing key-binding wackiness.

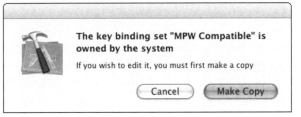

Figure 8-12
Look at, but don't touch, the presupplied bindings... or copy them and *then* touch all you like!

You can also duplicate the currently selected set of bindings (either one of Xcode's untouchable sets or one of your own) with the Duplicate... button at the top of the preference panel, and you can delete any of your own binding sets as well. How? We suggest the Delete button right next to the Duplicate... button.

MORE DOCUMENTATION

Xcode's Documentation Viewer tells you how Xcode's Documentation preferences work — as well it should. However, you probably aren't looking at the Viewer at the moment because you're busy avidly reading this book and admiring our depth of knowledge. So, to keep your eyes glued to our attractively laid-out pages, we'll describe those preferences here. They're all pretty simple.

Figure 8-13 shows the Documentation preferences. The panel has three sections.

- **Updates** — Xcode can be set to phone home to the mother ship on a regular basis to see if Apple's crack team of documentation writers have updated or added to any of the current documentation. If you don't think that Xcode can be trusted to phone home automatically, or if you regularly run without an Internet connection, deselect the Check for documentation updates option. You can always check manually for updates by clicking the Check Now button.

Figure 8-13
What's up, docs?

- **Extended Locations** — Xcode looks in various places to find the documentation that it provides in response to your questions. One location is totally hard-wired and not shown in the window: the ADC Reference Library folder that comes with Xcode. However, you can add other folders to Xcode's list of Extended Locations, which you might want to do if, for example, you purchase an additional third-party compiler and want to have its docs added to Xcode's documentation searches. Note that Xcode provides one documentation source that's not on your system: Apple's own Developer Web site (oddly, documents found on the Web appear in your default browser, not in the Documentation Viewer, even though the Documentation Viewer can display HTML documents). You can disable searches in any of the extended documentation locations by deselecting the Active option for that location, and, as the pane's tooltip tells you, you can change the order in which Xcode searches these additional locations by clicking and dragging them up and down in the list of Extended Locations.

- **Universal Access** — You use the Universal Access settings in this pane to force the Documentation Viewer to use larger type and save your eyes from bleeding as you try to read, say, 7-point type on a 108 dpi screen.

Like we said, pretty simple. Yet, satisfying.

MORE GEEKY

Then there are those preferences for which there are no Preference window panels. These are the so-called *expert* preferences, designed for those who like secret codes and Terminal sessions. You can find out what the current group of expert preferences is, along with instructions on how to change them and with details about their meanings and possible values, from Xcode's helpful Help menu (see Figure 8-14).

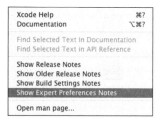

Figure 8-14
Help for the experts... you know who you are

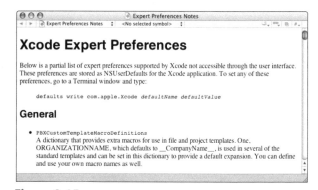

Figure 8-15
The list of expert preferences, expertly presented

The Show Expert Preferences Notes Help item shows you those notes in a non-editable window (see Figure 8-15). Right at the top of the Expert Preferences Notes you find out exactly how to change these arcane preferences: You have to open the Terminal application (in /Applications/ Utilities/) and use the `defaults` shell command to change the contents of the file `com.apple.Xcode`. The complete command takes the form

```
defaults write com.apple.Xcode defaultName
defaultValue
```

where `defaultName` is the name of one of the preferences and `defaultValue` is one of the acceptable values for that preference. Figure 8-16 shows such a Terminal session.

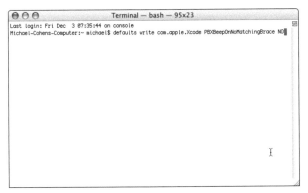

Figure 8-16
A trip to Terminal is needed to change expert preferences

▼ Note

Case is important in all the expert preference names and values. For example, `PBXBeepOnNoMatching Brace` (a typical expert preference name) is not the same as `PBXBeeponnobatchingbrace`. You must make sure to type the expert preference name exactly as documented. Remember, this is Terminal you're using, and you're on the Unix command line, which is stern and unforgiving.

What's actually going on here? Well, the Xcode preferences you've been setting all along as you've been using Xcode are stashed inside the file com.apple.Xcode.plist, which resides in your user account's Preferences folder (~/Library/ Preferences/). The `defaults` command automatically looks in this directory for a property list file (which has a .plist extension) that matches the command's first argument and then changes (or adds) the preference item denoted by the command's second argument to match the setting denoted by the command's third argument. The "adds" part is important: If you actually look at com.apple.Xcode.plist with the Property List Editor application (see Figure 8-17), you'll see that the expert preference names shown in the Expert Preferences Notes don't actually appear in the file — until the first time you use the defaults command to change them (which is exactly what we did in order to get PBXBeepOnNoMatchingBrace to show up in the screen shot).

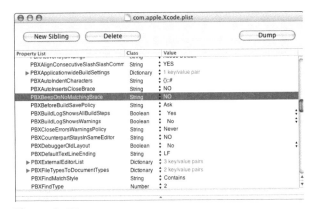

Figure 8-17
The Property List Editor can slap a GUI on your expert preferences... once you add those preferences

MORE TO COME

The number of preference settings Xcode offers is, frankly, staggering. We've documented many of them in previous chapters, but we've filled in a lot of the blanks here, describing previously undescribed settings in the General preferences, the File Types preferences, and the Key Bindings preferences. We've also described how source trees work and why you might need to set them up. We've shown you how to keep your Xcode documentation up to date and how to add to it. Finally, we've taken you into the depths of the command line to show how you can change default settings in true Unix-geek style.

And there are still more preferences left for us to cover. In later chapters, we describe various preferences related to building (Chapters 11 and 12), to debugging (Chapter 16), and to managing source code versions (Chapter 18). Right now, though, we prefer to move on to something that provides more graphic pleasure (if you're thinking what we *think* you're thinking, you really should be ashamed of yourself — this isn't that kind of book).

PART III

Drag-and-Drop
Dead Gorgeous

Interface Builder
and the Widgets of Aqua

His Nibs Has Resources • Cocoa versus Carbon Interface Objects
Interface Building Is a Real Drag • Message Therapy
Test Driving the Interface • The 143-Word Recap

It's the interface, stupid...

> — *Slogan seen on a Mac fan's T-shirt.*

The user interface has always been one of Apple's most serious obsessions. Making it logical. Making it inviting. Making it beautiful.

Crafting a user interface is no small chore. It's also something a whole lot of programmers dread doing. And why not? The underlying work that a program does, its core algorithms, are, by comparison, relatively easy to validate: Either the MP3 decodes or it doesn't, either the print engine prints or it doesn't, either the Fast Fourier transformation... er... transforms or it doesn't. But a user interface? It's as much a matter of style, of creativity, of taste, and of empathic understanding of fellow humans, as it is of algorithmic correctness. Developing interfaces is an inherently messy and fuzzy business, and it forces logic-loving programmers to confront the ugly *maybe* that lives between *true* and *false*.

Plus, it's often been just plain *hard* to wire up the code that makes the buttons click, the scroll bars scroll, the pop-ups pop up. In fact, creating a user interface purely in code feels a lot like telling an artist, by tedious verbal instruction, how to paint a particular painting ("... dip the tip of the brush in the viridian, and then gently drag it from 3.8 inches from the top of the canvas and 5.3 inches from the left, in a 2.4-inch curving path described by the following formula...").

Any tool that can make this labor-intensive work easier, that can allow you to try out different interface ideas without having to reinvent and rewire each and every widget every time, has to be A Good Thing.

Interface Builder is such a tool for Mac OS X developers. And it's a good one. It provides an extensive set of the widgets, the windows, the menus, and the other geegaws that you need to design interfaces, and it lets you supplement these with ones that you design yourself. It allows you to see your program's interface, play with it, and then redesign it quickly if it doesn't feel right. It exploits Apple's huge base of Mac OS X Aqua interface code so you don't have to do the implementing yourself, and it even helps write the code in your application that manages interface elements. Interface Builder does what its name says it does: It builds your program's interface. Not a prototype. Not a simulation. The actual thing that you actually stick into your actual app.

It's the interface, smart.

HIS NIBS HAS RESOURCES

Long before the Mac, or even the Apple II, existed, computer scientist Niklaus Wirth, who created Pascal and Modula-2 among other things, wrote an introductory programming book called *Algorithms + Data Structures = Programs* (catchy title, no?). That equation was fine for representing a program with no user interface except, maybe, for a command line and an occasional yes/no prompt. But most modern programs come with a cartload of data: the controls, the menus, the windows, the cursors, the icons, the sounds, and the images that make up the

user interface. For example, in programs designed for one operating system that hails from the Pacific Northwest, these items tend to come in separate files and can end up scattered all over the hard drive and *seem* to be separate things from the program itself... except that, without them, the program to which they belong fails to run properly, if it runs at all. In programs written for another (now obsolete yet still quite popular) operating system from Cupertino, California, these items tend to come bundled in something called a *resource fork* along with the program's executable code. However they come, the elements of the user interface are as much a part of the program as its code. *Algorithms + Data Structures + User Interface = Programs* is the modern equation.

In Mac OS X programs, the user interface elements *can* come in a resource fork, but they seldom do anymore. Instead, they come in a separate file, or in a group of files, that resides in the application's package (and, hence, like the goodies in a resource fork, don't get scattered all over the hard drive). These files are called *nib files*, or *nibs*, and are named after the company and program that first created them: NeXT Interface Builder. NeXT, of course, no longer exists (except in the form of a company called Apple Computer, Inc.), but Interface Builder is still around and is an integral part of the Xcode development environment.

To create a nib is pretty simple: As we see in Chapters 1 and 2, Xcode makes one for you when you choose certain templates from its New Project assistant. However, you often find that you need to create more than one nib. Here's how to do that:

1. **Fire up Interface Builder.** You can do that either by opening an already existing nib in your Xcode project, or you can hunt for the Interface Builder application

in the Finder and launch the program from there (hint: look in /Developer/Applications/).

2. **If you opened Interface Builder from within Xcode, choose File → New from Interface Builder's menu bar.** The Starting Point dialog (see Figure 9-1) appears (it appears automatically if you launch Interface Builder directly from the Finder or the Dock).

3. **Pick the kind of nib you want to create, optionally choose a (nonprogramming) language for it, and click New.**

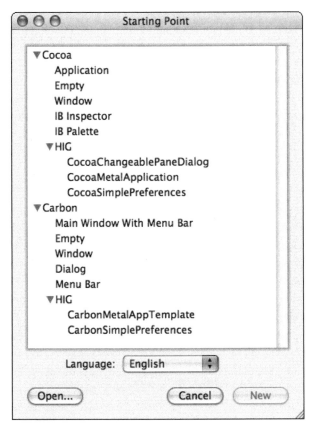

Figure 9-1
A good place to start

WHAT WE DON'T MISS MUCH

In the early Mac days, resources were created by taking a text file with a description of the resources to be created and running it through a resource compiler called Rez. What fun... especially when things like icons had to be defined as a string of hexadecimal digits. Later, Apple came up with ResEdit, which provided a GUI for creating and editing some of the basic resource types, though many still had to be described in, yep, hex.

For prototyping interface design, lots of developers (including many at Apple) used HyperCard, which came with buttons and other widgets, provided drawing tools (useful for mocking up portions of an interface), and allowed custom menus and similar features. With it, one could quickly create a rough draft of what an interface might look like and experience how it might feel to use. Unfortunately, a HyperCard prototype of an interface would then have to be painstakingly re-created with Rez or ResEdit and with a bunch of programming.

Other developers employed commercially available tools, such as Prototyper and AppMaker. AppMaker, in particular, survived into the OS X era and generated code to implement the interface. That code was usable with Metrowerks CodeWarrior to create Carbon applications in C, C++, and Pascal. But, it was last updated in December 2001 and doesn't support many current OS X interface features.

We do have to admit that we liked playing with ResEdit, and that HyperCard was a remarkable program that could do much more than simply prototype user interfaces. But we don't miss having to rely on them for our software development projects.

Quicker than you can say "quicker than you can say" (unless you speak very quickly), Interface Builder creates a new untitled nib for you, populated with the user interface elements indicated by the type of nib you chose from the Starting Point list (for example, a Cocoa Window nib comes with a window element already open).

▼ Note

The Starting Point is just that — a starting point. You can start off with, say, a Cocoa window, but that doesn't limit you to just a window. You can still add any or all of the other elements that Interface Builder has in its warehouse of gadgets and geegaws to your nib.

WHAT'S IN A NIB?

It depends on the type of nib, of course, but, generally speaking, nibs contain all the interface objects that you put into them, including their positions and sizes as you laid them out with Interface Builder. Nibs can also contain the connections you create between interface objects within the nib and even with objects stored in other nibs. In addition, nibs can contain initialization data (for example, the text in a field), so that when the nib is opened at runtime, your objects all come out piping hot and ready to serve.

Inside a nib file there is all sorts of XML stuff, and if you really want to, you can poke around and look at it. But don't change any of it... that's just about the fastest way to damage the nib as any we can imagine. Let Interface Builder do that stuff: When it comes to nibs, Interface Builder is probably smarter than you are.

Saving your new nib is just as easy:

1. **Choose File → Save (⌘+S).** A Save As sheet appears (see Figure 9-2) asking you to name the nib and, depending upon the type of nib you've created, choose a format for it. Unless you are building something for an older version of Mac OS X, you can accept the default choice. (We discuss the other choices in the next section of our thrilling exegesis in a little sidebar we like to call "Nibs Old and New.")

2. **Name the nib, click Save, and you are ready to add it to your project with Xcode's Project → Add to Project command (Option+⌘+A) at your convenience.**

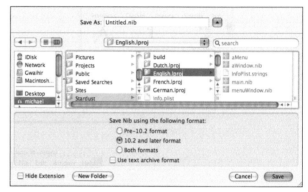

Figure 9-2
Somebody save me

▼ Note

Carbon nibs don't give you a choice of formats when you save them, while Cocoa nibs do. Also, when you save a new nib into an open Xcode project's folder, Interface Builder asks you if you want to have Xcode add the nib to the target (see Figure 9-3) in a dialog similar to the one shown by Xcode's Add to Project... command.

Figure 9-3
Include me in!

COCOA VERSUS CARBON INTERFACE OBJECTS

If you've paid attention to any of the history lessons we've scattered around this shiny tome (or if you've actually lived through — and paid attention to — that history when it was still something called "current events"), you should be aware of the two different approaches to Mac OS X development: Carbon and Cocoa. To quickly recap: Carbon is a procedural API that evolved from the classic Mac OS, while Cocoa is the object-oriented runtime environment that evolved from NeXT's NeXTStep operating system. Got that? Good. Because you're going to need to hold that distinction in mind to understand this section.

Fact of the matter is, there are Carbon nibs and there are Cocoa nibs, just like there are Cocoa apps and Carbon apps. Although it *is* often possible to use a Carbon nib with a Cocoa application (see "Integrating Carbon and Cocoa" in Xcode's documentation library), usually Carbon

apps use Carbon nibs and Cocoa apps use Cocoa nibs. Xcode's New Project dude happily provides the right sort of nib file for the type of project you choose to create, so you usually don't need to care that there is a difference. But there is. Figures 9-4 and 9-5 show, respectively, the Interface Builder nib windows for a Cocoa application nib and for a Carbon application nib.

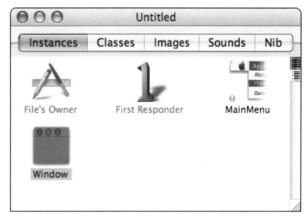

Figure 9-4
A Cocoa nib

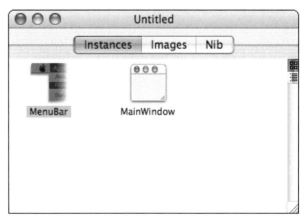

Figure 9-5
A Carbon nib

Carbon, being a procedural API, likes to handle things the old-fashioned way: by calling functions belonging to the various interface objects in order to manipulate them. Cocoa, being an object-oriented API, sends messages between objects. Furthermore, the Cocoa runtime environment embodies the concept of a *responder chain*, which passes messages (like user interface events such as mouse-clicks or key-presses) along a hierarchy of objects until an object that can handle the message chooses to handle it. Carbon nibs simply contain the interface objects along with their positioning and initialization data; Cocoa nibs contain all that as well as things like a *First Responder* object, which is the first stop along the responder chain, and whatever connections you've created between objects (more about *that* later in this chapter in "Message Therapy"). What's more, the Cocoa nib window allows you to browse the Cocoa classes and to subclass new interface

objects as you need them (after all, Cocoa *is* a dynamic object-oriented environment). With Carbon, you can use any of the interface objects that Interface Builder has to offer, but you have to do your own subclassing; note the absence of the Classes tab in the Carbon nib shown in Figure 9-5.

When a Cocoa application starts up, the Cocoa runtime automatically opens the app's main nib file (you tell Xcode which nib is the main nib in the target's Info window under the Properties tab — look for a field labeled Main Nib File). Carbon applications, on the other hand, have to open their nib files manually using the functions available in Carbon's Interface Builder Services (see IBCarbon Runtime.h in the Carbon framework and check out the example code in /Developer/Examples/InterfaceBuilder/ IBCarbonExample).

FROM RESEDIT TO INTERFACE BUILDER

If you are one of those folk looking to move an app from the old classic Mac OS to Mac OS X's new world order, you don't have to abandon all your old resource files and start from scratch. Interface Builder has a command to help you along your way: File ➜ Import ➜ Import Resource File.

Interface Builder can import certain resources from .rsrc files created by ResEdit or compiled by Rez (it can't import Rez source files). The types it can import include DLOG, DITL, CNTL, MBAR, MENU, WIND, icns, cicn, PICT, ICON, and tab#. When Interface Builder imports a .rsrc file, it converts the resources to their Interface Builder equivalents.

If, further, you are trying to maintain a Classic Mac OS version of your application, you might want to consider Resorcerer (www.mathemaesthetics.com) as a way to create your resources for both versions and then follow the directions above to get the appropriate resources into Interface Builder. Resorcerer isn't free, but it is well maintained and has been around for a long time. ResEdit, on the other hand, hasn't been updated in the current century — since well before the release of OS X.

Apple supplies a document, "Convert Resources to Nibs," that explains the process in rather exhaustive detail (hint: type "convert resources to nibs" in the Documentation Viewer's full-text search field to find this document, which is buried many levels deep in the Xcode documentation library).

NIBS OLD AND NEW

When Apple unleashed its Jaguar (also known as Mac OS X 10.2), it changed the format of nib files to allow them to store some of the newer Cocoa interface elements (such as the brushed-metal window and the circular progress gauge) introduced with that version of the system. Unfortunately, computers running Mac OS X 10.1 can't open these newer-format nib files (which use something called *keyed archiving* to store their objects as opposed to the older *sequential archiving*). This is why Interface Builder allows you to specify which format a nib file uses when you create a brand-new one: As you may have noticed in Figure 9-2 earlier, you can specify pre-10.2, 10.2 and later, or both formats.

When you choose to store a nib in both formats, Interface Builder saves the nib twice and it's up to the Cocoa runtime environment to pick the right one. Of course, elements that aren't able to be stored in the old format won't be available to the app when it runs in Mac OS X 10.1 or earlier. Also, if you choose to store the nib in pre-10.2 format only, you can still add new interface elements as you work in Interface Builder, but (and this should not surprise you) Interface Builder will not let you save the nib until you change the format to 10.2 or later.

Interface Builder has a command (File ➔ Compatibility Checking) that can help you discover what problems your app may encounter under different releases of Mac OS X (only earlier ones, of course: the future has yet to be written). Figure 9-6 shows Interface Builder's compatibility checker in action.

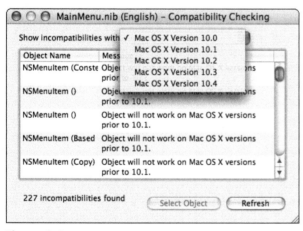

Figure 9-6
Checking compatibility

By the way, although Carbon nibs only exist in one format, apps running in older versions of the system may still have problems dealing with newer Carbon interface elements, so you really should check your Carbon nibs for compatibility as well if you intend for them to run on older systems.

Note

Even Cocoa apps may have to manually open nib files: Most Cocoa applications store only their most commonly used interface elements in the main nib and keep their lesser-used interface elements (such as, say, a preference window or an about box) in one or more supplemental nibs. You can open such nibs either by creating and using an NSWindowController object, which has the ability to open those nibs that contain windows, or by explicitly using the `-[NSBundle loadNibNamed:owner:]` method. Carbon apps, of course, can use the Interface Builder Services functions to open additional nibs, just as they do for the main nib.

INTERFACE BUILDING IS A REAL DRAG

You've had a taste of using Interface Builder back in Chapter 1 and it wasn't an accident that we chose a Cocoa app with which to demonstrate it. Cocoa and Interface Builder go back a long way together (much longer than the name "Cocoa" does, in fact), and the full beauty and power of Interface Builder can only be appreciated in that environment. Sure, IB (which is what we're going to call Interface Builder for the rest of this chapter because we're really getting quite tired of typing "Interface Builder" and we're too lazy — or too daunted by Word's peculiarities — to attempt to create a keyboard macro for it) works just dandy for creating Carbon interfaces and testing them out, and Carbon developers will still have much to gain from the next few pages — but Carbon compatibility is not really what gives IB its lustrous shine. What does is IB's ability to wire your interface, establishing connections between user interface elements and your code, so that the Cocoa runtime does as much of the event handling work as possible. As you saw in Chapter 1, with a few deft drags and drops in IB and only a tiny bit of code, you can build

a fully featured app with working menus and buttons and fields and windows.

In order to design an interface, you should have some project to which it belongs. Although you can fire up IB and noodle away to your heart's content, assembling widgets and windows and menus (and there may be some situations where that is actually what you want to do), starting from a project is a far more productive and instructive way to go. That's why you're going to run across the project we created in Chapter 1 from time to time in this chapter.

 Note

If this were a larger book, or one devoted entirely to IB, we'd be more than happy to march down the list of all IB's various features in exhaustive detail, but we only have a paltry chapter in which to cover IB, so we're only going to be able to look at the surface highlights of this surprisingly deep program (however, for a suitable advance and a nice royalty arrangement, we'd be more than happy to consider writing the Interface Builder Book; if you'd like us to do that, send your cards and letters to our publisher).

The basic windows

Figure 9-7 shows the basic IB windows displayed when you create an empty Cocoa nib (the empty Carbon nib is even emptier — we're mostly sipping Cocoa for this portion of the chapter, though we'll note Carbon differences when relevant).

There are, as you can probably see, two basic windows. The window on the left is the *Nib window*. The window on the right is the *Palettes window*, which presents palettes of various interface elements that you can use; in the figure, the Palette window is showing the Cocoa-Menus palette.

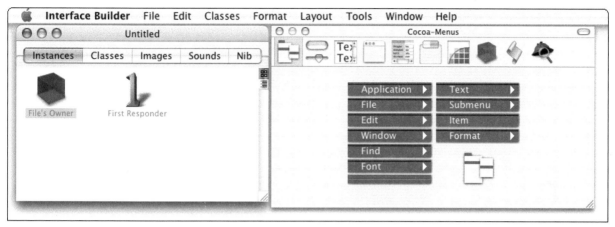

Figure 9-7
An empty Cocoa nib

The stuff you see in the Nib window is the stuff that gets saved when you save the nib. This window has several tabs:

- **Instances.** These are the interface elements your nib contains, presented either graphically or in outline form. You can switch between the two views by clicking the appropriate widget right above the scrollbar. We'll discuss the outline view a little later in this broadcast.

- **Classes (Cocoa only).** Here are all the Cocoa classes (and there are more than a few) that you can draw upon and subclass as you build your interface (see Figure 9-8). The classes displayed in black are those that are currently instantiated in the nib, either directly or as subclasses.

- **Images**, **Sounds (Cocoa only).** These two tabs contain references to additional media that you can add to your interface. Both Carbon and Cocoa nibs support images, but Cocoa lets you add sound as well. You can click and drag media onto this window

(from, say, the Finder) to add references to them to a nib belonging to an open project; if no project is open in Xcode, IB complains, because it has to find the media in the project in order to include references to them in the nib.

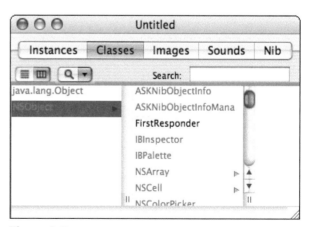

Figure 9-8
Classy Cocoa

▼ Tip

Image and sound media are not actually included in the nib. Instead, they are usually stored inside the Resources directory that is part of the application package's contents. The nib only contains references to the media, such as size, type, and format. We recommend that you add your media files to your project in Xcode first (you can click and drag media from the Finder into your Project window), and to make sure that Xcode copies the actual media files to your project directory. That way, IB automatically finds these files and shows them in the nib window, and the media will travel with the project if you move the project elsewhere.

● **Nib.** This tab lets you see and change the kind of nib you're dealing with (see Figure 9-9).

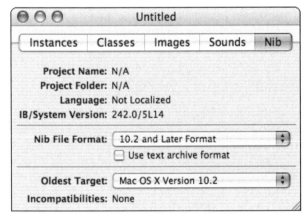

Figure 9-9
Nib settings

The Palettes window (which we want to call the Palettes palette because it is a window that floats above other non-palette windows, as traditional Mac palette windows are wont to do — but we won't, because "Palettes palette" starts to sound really silly after a while, and, besides, Apple now calls these things *utility windows*) is your storehouse of

interface elements. The elements that are available vary, depending on whether you create a Cocoa nib or a Carbon nib... if you're curious (like we were until the Man in the Yellow Hat broke us of that habit), you can take a look at the Palettes tab in IB's Preferences (choose Interface Builder ➔ Preferences or ⌘+,), which shows a list of the palettes currently available to the Palettes window (see Figure 9-10).

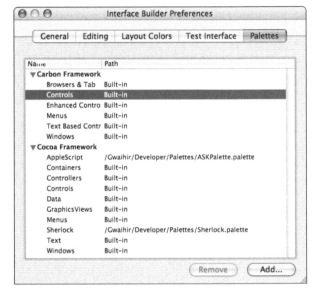

Figure 9-10
Palettes preference

Each palette in the Palettes window contains instances of related interface elements. For example, the Cocoa-Windows palette contains various style windows; the Cocoa-Menus palette contains (what else?) menus, including standard menus (like Font and Edit menus), hierarchical menus, and contextual menus; the Cocoa-Data palette contains various data view panels for things like scrolling lists; and so on. For Cocoa nibs, positioning the mouse over an item shown on a palette usually brings up a tooltip that identifies the Cocoa class to which the item belongs; for Carbon nibs, positioning the mouse usually shows the generic name of the interface element (for example, "Text View" or "Slider") that it represents.

The toolbar along the top of the Palettes window lets you choose which palette of interface elements is displayed in the window. If icons aren't your cup of tea, you can add labels to them, shrink or dispense with the icons, and adjust the order of the items in the toolbar with the

Tools ➡ Palettes ➡ Customize Toolbar command (see Figure 9-11). And, because the toolbar itself is an NSToolbar object (IB is, after all, a Cocoa app), you can also arrange the icons just like you can in any other Cocoa app that has a toolbar: just ⌘+drag a toolbar icon into the position you prefer — or, if you want to get rid of it, ⌘+drag the icon right off the toolbar and make it vanish in a puff of smoke (you can always add it back with the Customize Toolbar command).

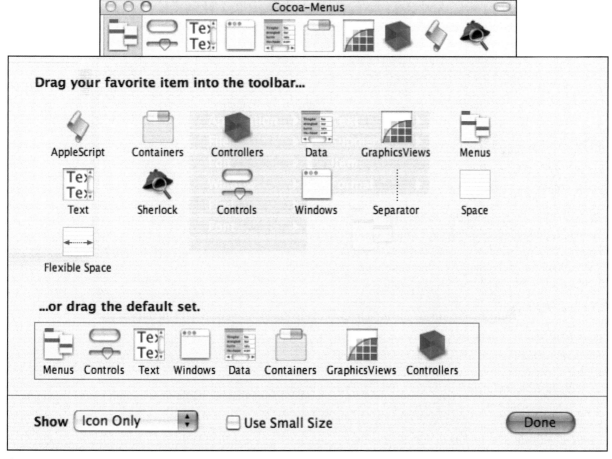

Figure 9-11
Picking palettes for the Palettes window

WHAT'S A DESIGN WINDOW?

The IB documentation frequently refers to something called the *design window*. Look as you will through IB's menus and submenus, though, and you won't find it mentioned anywhere. That's because a design window isn't part of IB *per se*. Rather, it refers to any of the windows that *you* have added to your nib and that you are designing. For example, in our sample Hello, World! application, the design window is the window into which you dragged the field and button. So when you hear us talking about a design window, what we really mean is one of the windows that you are putting together in IB. (And, by the way, if you actually *do* hear us talking about anything, we suggest you seek professional medical help because this isn't an audio book.)

Layout tools, part one

Figure 9-12 shows the window from our Chapter 1 project. As you may recall, we added the text by dragging a text field from the Palette window's Cocoa-Text palette to our window and the button by dragging a button from the Cocoa-Controls palette. That's the basic operation you use to add an interface element to a window: Click and drag something from the Palettes window to one of the other windows in IB. But it's not enough to just drop an element in a window; you really want to place it in a pleasing arrangement among the other elements. Here are some of the tools that help you do that.

- **Aqua Guidelines.** These appear and disappear as you move an element in a window to help you position the element (see Figure 9-13) in relation to other elements' centers or edges or to the window's borders following the advice given in Apple's Aqua Human

Interface Guidelines document (highly recommended reading and available for your instruction and delight in Xcode's document library). The Layout ➔ Guides ➔ Disable Aqua Guidelines command lets you disable these guides (naturally, there's a corresponding Enable Aqua Guidelines command to let you reenable them).

Figure 9-12
Remember me?

Figure 9-13
The Guidelines Aquatic

- **Layout Rectangles.** These visual aids use red solid and dashed hairlines to show you the rectangles occupied by various elements, as well as things like their text baselines or centerlines (see Figure 9-14).

Layout ➜ Show Layout Rectangles (⌘+L) brings them up; Layout ➜ Hide Layout Rectangles dismisses them.

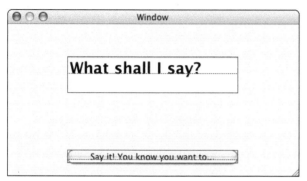

Figure 9-14
Layout rectangles

● **Guides.** You can add your own horizontal and vertical guidelines to a design window to help you arrange things to your own specifications (see Figure 9-15). Layout ➜ Guides ➜ Add Horizontal Guide (⌘+_) and Layout ➜ Guides ➜ Add Vertical Guide (⌘+|) place these blue lines on the window. You can click and drag a guide where you like simply by positioning the mouse over it; as you drag, its coordinates appear so you can see how far from the top and bottom or left and right edge of the window it is. You can hide the guides with Layout ➜ Guides ➜ Hide Guides and lock them in place with Layout ➜ Guides ➜ Lock Guides (and, naturally, there are corresponding Show and Unlock commands available once you do). You delete a guide simply by clicking and dragging it off the edge of the design window in which it appears.

PALETTES, PALETTES EVERYWHERE

The keen-eyed observer (that would be you) may notice that one isn't limited to the interface palettes built in to IB: The program can load additional palettes from disk, such as the Cocoa AppleScript and Sherlock palettes shown in Figure 9-10 (this, by the way, explains why IB's Palettes preference has an Add... button). Aside from the two non-built-in palettes shown in that figure, Apple provides some additional palettes in /Developer/Extras/Palettes/ that you can add to IB. To add one of these palettes, you can use the Add button, or you can simply click and drag it to /Developer/ Palettes/ — IB automatically looks for palettes there (it also looks in ~/Library/Palettes/, ~/Developer/Palettes/, and /Library/Developer/Palettes/ if these directories exist).

Loadable palettes are packages that contain, among other things, nib packages that, in turn, contain other nibs. We're not going to go into the process of creating an IB palette here (hint: Xcode's New Project dude has a template for IBPalettes under the Standard Apple Plug-ins heading), but just knowing that you can roll your own using Xcode (and, yes, IB itself) if the mood strikes you is pretty cool.

You can also create custom palettes, known as *dynamic palettes,* that contain items from other palettes. Unlike loadable palettes, dynamic palettes require no programming. Choose Tools ➜ Palettes ➜ New Palette to create a new dynamic palette in the Palette window, and then Option+drag an element that you've previously placed in a design window to that palette. This feature lets you create convenient working sets of interface elements. If you add multiple items to the palette with a single Option+drag, those items are treated as a single unit. Choose Tools ➜ Palettes ➜ Save to save your palette for future use.

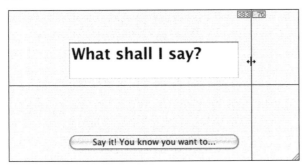

Figure 9-15
Your own personal guides

- **Alignment Panel.** The command Layout → Alignment → Alignment Panel (Shift+⌘+A) brings up this panel (see Figure 9-16) that allows you to position selected elements in a window relative to each other. We find it quite convenient when we wish to align a bunch of objects in various ways or spread them out. (It would be more convenient if its keyboard shortcut hid it when we were done, but unfortunately it doesn't.) There are also corresponding alignment commands on the Layout menu's Alignment submenu for some of its functions.

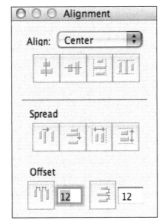

Figure 9-16
Align and spread

Adding windows

In order to drop a widget into a window, you need a window. IB's Palette window has a Cocoa-Windows (or a Carbon-Windows) palette you can use to get a window into your nib. Unlike controls and text thingies, you don't click and drag the windows from this palette into a design window — that would be silly. Instead, you add windows to your nib by clicking and dragging the window you want from the palette to, well, anywhere onscreen that you like. When you release the mouse, the window appears on your screen pretty much where you dropped it (see Figure 9-17). You can also drag the window from the palette directly into your nib window, in which case the window appears more or less centered on the screen (subsequent windows added this way appear offset from the first window).

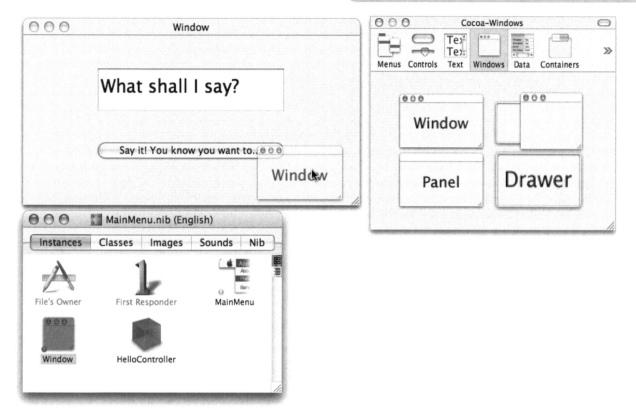

Figure 9-17
When dropped, this window appears above the other windows right where you dropped it

Adding menus

Menus are, with windows, one of the oldest and most traditional elements of a standard GUI, and over the course
of time they have evolved into various related species:
drop-down menus that drop down from an app's menu
bar, hierarchical menus (also known as submenus) that
pop out from other menu items, contextual menus
that appear in response to a right-click or control-click,

and pop-up menus that appear when a pop-up menu
widget is clicked. IB has a Menus palette for both Cocoa
and Carbon nibs to let you add these essential interface
elements to your app (though the Cocoa palette has a
wider selection from which to choose).

The menu window (see Figure 9-19) is where you click
and drag drop-down menus that you want to appear on
the application's menu bar.

DROPPING DRAWERS

In the Cocoa-Windows palette, you'll find both a drawer and a window with a drawer, neither of which is available in the Carbon-Windows palette. The window with a drawer is an example of a composite object (see Figure 9-18). When you drag and drop it, three items appear in the nib: a window (known as the parent window), a drawer (an NSDrawer object, which is a descendent of an NSResponder class), and the drawer's content view (which is a custom NSView class and which appears in the drawer's frame). IB connects the appropriate outlets for you so you can implement the drawer's behavior (we describe outlets in this chapter's "Message Therapy"). However, you may notice that IB doesn't actually present the drawer as protruding from the window to which it is attached. Instead, all IB does is present the associated content view as a free-floating design window to which you can add the widgets and other content you wish the drawer to contain. You'll have to add a widget (perhaps to the parent window) that sends the drawer the toggle message to get the drawer to function in your program.

Figure 9-18
A window with a drawer composite object

The Cocoa-Windows palette also contains a separate drawer object. If you want to add one of these to an existing window, you also need to add a custom view object to contain the drawer's contents, and then establish the appropriate connections between the drawer, the content view, and the drawer's parent window. If this seems confusing, make a new nib and add one of the drawer-window composite objects to it and take a look at how the various objects are connected. All should eventually become clear.

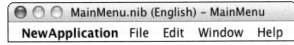

Figure 9-19
A main menu window

- To add a menu to the menu bar, click and drag the menu object labeled Submenu (see Figure 9-20) from the Cocoa-Menus (or Carbon-Menus) palette over a menu in the menu window and release the mouse. The menu appears to the right of the menu on which you dropped it. The menu comes complete with one item on it, labeled Item.

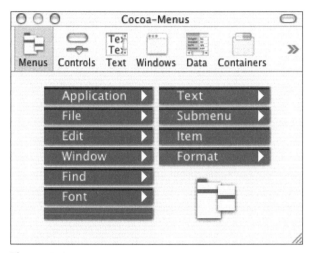

Figure 9-20
The menu palette offers menus and menu items

▼ Tip

To change the text of any menu or menu item, double-click it and type the text you want it to show.

- To add a hierarchical menu to a menu on the menu bar (or to any menu, for that matter), click and drag the Submenu item over the menu to which you wish to add it but don't release the mouse. When the menu drops down, continue dragging until the Submenu item is over an item on the menu, and *then* release the mouse. The new hierarchical menu appears below the item on which you dropped it.

▼ Tip

To reposition a menu, menu item, or hierarchical menu item, simply click and drag it where you want it to go on the menu bar or menu.

- To add an item to any menu, click and drag the Item object to the menu and release the mouse.

MENU BAR NONE

A Mac app is not a *real* Mac app if it lacks a menu bar, even if the menu bar has only an application menu with a Quit command on it. (Yes, we do know about such things as faceless background apps and shell commands, but let's face it: Although they can run on a Mac, these interfaceless things are not what comes to mind when we think about Mac apps.)

When you ask the New Project dude to whip up a new Cocoa or Carbon app template for you, or when you ask IB to start you off with a new Cocoa app, the nib you get contains a menu bar. In addition, you can use IB's Starting Point window to create Carbon nibs that contain menu bars. But, for some reason (possibly a good reason, though we haven't been able to find out what it is, good or otherwise), none of the Palette window's palettes offer a menu bar object that will let you add a menu bar to an already existing nib.

In short, IB apparently lets you have, at most, one menu bar per nib. Don't lose it. They're in shorter supply than kidneys on eBay.

▼ Tip

To remove a menu item or a menu, select it and press Delete.

- To add a separator to a menu, click and drag the separator item (it looks like a long thin line) to the item after which you wish it to appear and release the mouse.

- To associate a keyboard command with a menu item, select the menu item and choose Tools ➜ Show Inspector (Shift+⌘+I). Then choose Attributes from the Inspector window's pop-up menu (see Figure 9-21) and assign the key equivalent and appropriate modifier key(s).

Figure 9-21
Add menu item key equivalents in the Inspector's Attributes pane for the item

 Note

In addition to the Submenu, Item, and separator elements in the palette, there are various labeled menus in the Cocoa and Carbon menu palettes, such as File, Edit, and Application. These menus come prestocked with the appropriate commands; for example, the Edit menu has Undo, Cut, Copy, Paste, and other commands already on it. You can, of course, rearrange, rename, and delete these items — however, the User Interface Police may come to your house in the dead of night and take you away for some serious reeducating.

Adding a pop-up menu to an interface is quite easy... except that you don't use the Menus palette to do it. Instead, you need to bring up the Controls palette and click and drag the pop-up menu button (called an NSPopUpButton in Cocoa nibs or a PopUp Button in Carbon nibs) from it to your design window. The pop-up button comes with three menu items already in it (and all named Item). To modify the items, double-click the button in your design window and then edit the items just as you would for any other menu. You can also click and drag additional items, submenus, and separators to the button's pop-up menu from the Menus palette.

Layout tools, part two

You've seen how you can click and drag the handles associated with an interface element in a design window to adjust its size. However, if you want truly fine-grained control, there's nothing like specifying exact dimensions and location information numerically. IB lets you do that and totally indulges your obsessive-compulsive tendencies.

To get at an element's size controls, you need to bring up the Inspector window (Tools ➜ Show Inspector or Shift+⌘+I). The size controls for the selected interface element can be seen by choosing Size from the Inspector's pop-up menu. Figure 9-23 shows the size controls for our Hello, World! app's button.

The size controls adjust the coordinates of the element within its enclosing view. You can set coordinates for both the element's frame and its internal layout (Cocoa) or for its layout rect and control bounds (Carbon). You can also choose the corner of the element that the x and y coordinates in the pane represent by selecting from the pop-up menu associated with the coordinates: you can choose top/left, bottom/left, top/right, or bottom/right.

COPING WITH CONTEXTUAL MENUS

In a Cocoa nib, you can add a contextual menu to an interface element, such as a button or field, with a few steps:

1. Click and drag the item that looks like a tiny menu from the Menus palette to your nib window.

2. Control+drag from an element in your design window (the one to which you want to assign the contextual menu) to the menu icon in your nib window. A blue line connects the two, and the Inspector window appears, showing the Outlets pane for the interface element with the menu outlet selected (see Figure 9-22).

3. Click the Connect button in the Inspector window, and wallah! The contextual menu is now attached.

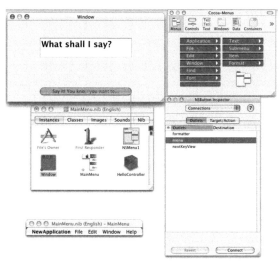

Figure 9-22
Attaching a contextual menu

You can add additional menus to a Carbon nib that you can then use as contextual menus in your Carbon code, but IB won't connect them for you as it does for Cocoa nibs. You'll have to write the code yourself.

If you connect a field to a contextual menu in Cocoa, you need to disable editing in the field with the Inspector's Attributes pane; otherwise, the field will show the standard editing contextual menu instead of your contextual menu when it is right-clicked or control-clicked.

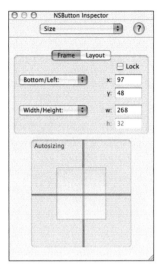

Figure 9-23
Size matters

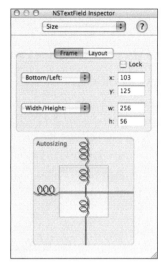

Figure 9-24
Springs and struts control autosizing and positioning

The size of the element is set in the Inspector's width and height fields; you can also set a maximum width (MaxX) and height (MaxY) in the same fields by choosing from the pop-up menu associated with the fields.

Then there are springs and struts. Your car has them. So do many of the elements in your Cocoa nib (sorry, Carbon fans). Springs and struts allow your elements to adjust — or not — to changes in the size of a window. IB calls this *autosizing*. Figure 9-24 shows how the autosizing pane looks for our sample app's text field after we've made a couple of clicks in it.

In the autosize pane, straight double lines (struts) denote fixed positioning or sizing; loopy lines (springs) denote autosizing or autopositioning. You change a strut to a spring, and back, by clicking it.

The lines in the inner rectangle control the element's size: Springs let the element grow or shrink as the view enclosing it grows and shrinks. Note you can constrain the autosizing to just the horizontal or vertical axis (and for some elements, like buttons, only for the horizontal axis). The lines in the outer rectangle control the element's position relative to the enclosing view's border. Struts keep the element nailed to whatever position is specified in its x/y coordinate settings; springs let it float to accommodate window size changes. Again, note that you can have the element float relative to any one edge of the view, to some of them, or to all of them.

The best way to explain autosizing is not to explain it but to see it in action. You can do this with IB's Test Interface command, which we cover in "Test Driving the Interface," later in this chapter. It's lots of fun and a great way to avoid getting real work done... and we're *always* up for some healthy procrastination.

INSPECT YOUR GADGET

The Inspector window may not be the one-stop shopping center for modifying your interface elements, but it definitely packs a lot of power. This utility window is context sensitive: It changes to reflect whichever element is currently selected, so you may want to have it hanging around somewhere on your screen at all times as you bop around your interface. With it you can change or view:

- The attributes of an element, such as its name, appearance (different options appear for different kinds of elements), and behavior. For example, you can change the kind of button a button is with the Attributes panel of the Inspector.

- The connections between elements. You've had some exposure to these earlier in this chapter and in Chapter 1; we'll talk much more about connections in "Message Therapy."

- The size of an element, as you have just seen in this section.

- Its bindings. Again, we'll talk about bindings in "Message Therapy."

- The attributes of the class to which the element belongs (double-click one of the classes listed in this panel to see the class inspector for it).

- The Help tool-tip associated with the element.

- The AppleScript events the element can handle.

- Associated Sherlock information for the element.

Changes that you make to an element in the Inspector window happen immediately; there is no OK or Apply button. However, Undo on the Edit menu undoes any change you make with this window, so the penalty for messing around to see what something does is not as severe as it might be (of course, we *always* recommend that you save your work before you embark on a voyage of exploration).

Other palettes

Aside from the menu, window, and control palettes we've just covered in varying detail, there are several other palettes of interface elements available in IB. Some of them are Cocoa-specific and some are Carbon. Also, as we've seen, additional palettes can be added to IB, either supplied by Apple, third-party developers, or even you, so the following is by no means an exhaustive catalog (it's more like a cable-TV listing summary).

- **Carbon-Enhanced Controls.** This palette consists mainly of view-based controls from Carbon's HITool-box, including things like a movie view for displaying QuickTime movies, image views, sliders, and other controls that aren't in the standard Carbon toolbox (the one that is shared with classic Mac OS apps).

- **Carbon-Browsers & Tabs.** Look here to find tab view panels, group boxes, and data browser elements (both list and column view).

● **Cocoa-Text.** You can find various text-entry and display widgets in this palette, including things like a search field, a combo-box, form elements, and both a currency and a date formatter.

▼ Note

The currency and date formatters allow you to turn a normal text field into one that formats and validates user entries and currency or dates. You use a formatter by clicking and dragging it onto a field that's in your design window; the Inspector's Attributes pane lets you specify the formats you allow and display.

● **Cocoa-Data.** This palette supplies various data views (for example, column and table views), along with specialized cells that can be displayed within these views. For example, if you need to create a column view that has a column with dates and another with combo-boxes (one for each date), you can assemble it from this palette. IB is smart enough to allow you only to drag data cells to the kinds of views that can accept them.

● **Cocoa-Containers.** Plain and tab view boxes can be found here, as well as a custom view. This last is a plain NSView object that you use when you create a subclass of NSView in the nib window's Classes tab; after you add a custom view to your design window, you use its Inspector to assign the subclass you created so that, at runtime, Cocoa swaps in your subclass (which, of course, you implement in your source code) for the custom view.

● **Cocoa-GraphicsViews.** If you need to draw into an OpenGL context, you can use the NSOpenGLView found here. And if you need to embed a Web browser view in a window, the WebView is just the ticket (at runtime it uses Mac OS X's underlying Web Kit framework — the same one used by Safari).

● **Cocoa-Controllers.** The collection of controllers found here make it possible to implement the Model-View-Controller paradigm used in most Cocoa apps, and which, you may recall, we described and demonstrated in Chapter 1. Unlike the elements found in the other palettes, these elements are invisible... they don't go into a design window or a menu or any other part of the user interface that users can see; instead, they arbitrate interactions between user interface elements and your application's data-processing objects. Two controllers, NSManagedObjectContext and NSTreeController, support Tiger's new Core Data libraries (we discuss Core Data in Chapter 10).

Someday, we think it would be fun to write an app that uses every single item on every single palette. But today is not that day.

MESSAGE THERAPY

A bunch of objects in a nib does not an interface make. They have to have some lines of communication established between them and the application so that, say, when a button is clicked the application knows that it has been clicked and can take appropriate action. Carbon apps handle the communication one way; Cocoa apps another.

Carboniferous communication

In the Carboniferous era, Pangea began to form, animals developed the ability to lay eggs with shells, huge fern forests appeared on land, and applications started using application signatures and control IDs to allow for communication with controls and other widgets.

In a Carbon app, whenever a menu is selected or a button is clicked, an event is sent to the application indicating what has happened so the app can decide what to do about it. Included in the event data for controls is information identifying which control is involved and what type of command is being sent. The identifying information includes a *signature* (usually the four-character signature belonging to the app itself), a control *ID* (which is unique for each of the program's controls), and a command identifier. These items can all be set in IB for the Carbon controls you add to your nib.

How you do this, as you might expect (especially if you read the caption to Figure 9-25), involves the Inspector. For Carbon controls, the Inspector provides a Control pane, which provides fields that allow you to specify the selected control's signature and ID. You can also specify the command that the control represents (by choosing it from a pull-down menu) and that, when it gets sent to your app, comes in the form of, yes, another four-character code (though IB can show you this code in decimal form if that is your heart's desire).

For menus, the event includes both the menu ID and which item on the menu has been chosen. You have to know (and let your code know) which menu items go with which commands for any given menu, but, at least, you can use the Menu Inspector's Attributes pane to assign a Menu ID to each of your menus (although you can also set those programmatically at runtime from your app when you load the menus). Figure 9-26 shows a Menu Inspector.

Figure 9-26
Inspecting the menu

In short, the amount of interface communication support IB supplies for Carbon apps is really rather primitive, but that is in the nature of Carbon itself: It's a procedural API designed so that you can (and usually must) do most things for yourself. This gives you a whole lot of control over things like controls and how they behave in your app, but it means you have to do a good deal of work.

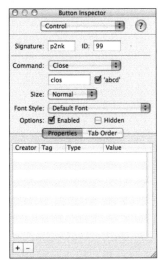

Figure 9-25
Identify the control with the Inspector

Cocoa confections

Cocoa takes most of the work of handling a user interface out of your code and lets the Cocoa runtime environment do most of the work. It's really pretty sweet (even without the marshmallows).

Rather than relying on an Event Manager (and an event loop or a WaitNextEvent function such as you might find in a Carbon program), the Cocoa objects that make up various interface elements come with the necessary methods and internal data structures to let them send messages to each other. A Cocoa button, for example, can "know" both that it has to send a specific message when it has been clicked, and where to send that message. Cocoa interface objects acquire this knowledge when you establish their various connections as you build your app's interface in IB. There are two main concepts you need to understand (and to which you were introduced as you built the sample application in Chapter 1): *target-actions* and *outlets*.

- **Target-actions:** A target-action is a message that a Cocoa object sends to a specific target. In our sample app from Chapter 1, the button in the app's main window sends a message (which we defined) to a controller object (which we created) whenever the button is clicked. Cocoa buttons already know to send messages when they're clicked; sliders already know to send messages when dragged; menu items already know to send messages when selected. You don't have to do anything. You simply choose the target (some other object... often a controller object of some sort that you create, as we did in our sample app) and define the message (the action). You provide both the action's implementation in the target (in your source code) and the name of the action message (in IB). Of course, you can only add target-actions to objects that

are subclasses of Cocoa classes, because target-actions are methods that you have to implement, but IB makes it pretty easy to subclass Cocoa objects... it even has a menu choice for that very purpose.

▼ **Note**

More than one object can send the same action message to a target; for example, we could have also added a menu item to our sample app to send the same message to the app's controller that the button does.

- **Outlets:** An outlet is nothing more than an instance variable belonging to an object that contains a reference to some other object. Some objects come with outlets already in them, ready for you to fill with some reference, but IB makes it easy for you to add outlets to any object in your nib that you have defined (as with target-actions, you can't add an outlet to a predefined Cocoa class, but you can add outlets to subclasses of them — in fact, that's how you usually add outlets). An object like a controller will use an outlet to call a method in some other object. In our sample app, the controller has an outlet that points to the app's text field and it uses that outlet to send the field the setStringValue message (which NSTextField objects understand).

▼ **Note**

A controller could use the same outlet to send a different message to that outlet in response to some other target-action message that the controller has received — for example, a different button could send a clearItOut message to our controller, and we would then code the controller's clearItOut method to send a message to the text field, by way of the same outlet, to display an empty string.

To summarize, the process works like this: An interface object sends an action message to a target object, and the target acts upon the message, either by sending an appropriate message to one (or more) of its outlets or by doing some other processing.

Target-action and outlet connections are both established by Control+dragging from one object to another. Figures 9-27 and 9-28 show, respectively, the outlet from our app's controller being connected to the text field, and the target-action from our app's button being connected to our controller.

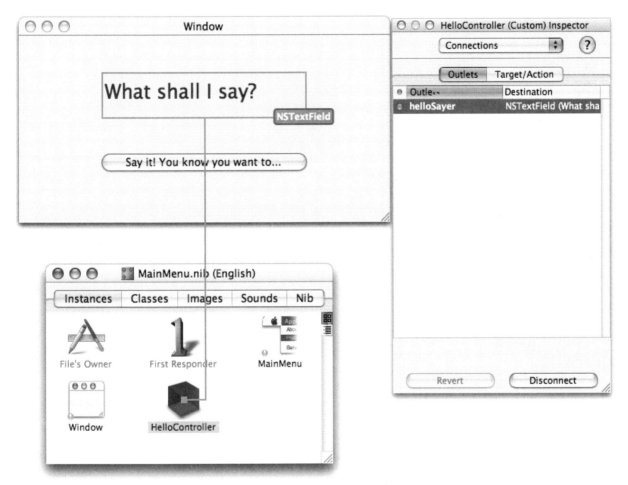

Figure 9-27
Establishing an outlet

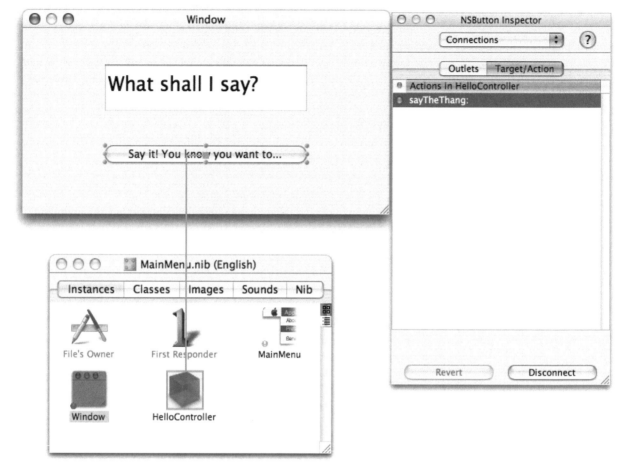

Figure 9-28
Establishing a target-action

Here's how you add an outlet to a user-defined subclass (like our controller) so that you can use it:

1. **Select the class in the nib window's Classes tab.**

2. **Choose Attributes from the Class Inspector's pop-up menu.**

3. **Click the Outlets tab.**

4. **Click the Add button.**

5. **Give the outlet a name.**

Figure 9-29 shows our sample controller being given a new outlet.

Figure 9-29
Adding an outlet to a subclass

Creating a target-action in a user-defined subclass is quite similar to adding an outlet:

1. **Select the class in the nib window's Classes tab.**

2. **Choose Attributes from the Class Inspector's pop-up menu.**

3. **Click the Actions tab.**

4. **Click the Add button.**

5. **Give the action a name.**

Figure 9-30 shows our sample controller being given a new action.

Often, though, it becomes somewhat tricky to click and drag the connections from one object to another, especially in those cases where the interface objects may be embedded inside some other objects. This is where the nib window's Instances outline view comes in handy

(see Figure 9-31). The little icons above the nib window's scrollbar let you switch between outline and icon view.

Figure 9-30
Adding an action to a subclass

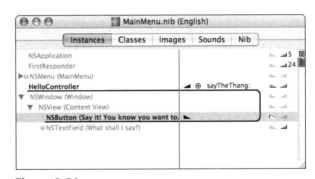

Figure 9-31
Outlining the instances in a nib

The outline view displays the nested hierarchy of all the objects in the nib on the left, and their associated target-actions and outlets on the right. Outlets are denoted by the small wedge widgets sloping down to the right;

target-actions are denoted by the small wedge widgets sloping upward to the right. Click a widget to see the connection. As you can see in Figure 9-31, the target-action in the helloController is actually connected to an outlet in the button (yes, a Cocoa button object has an outlet that it uses for the purpose of sending target-action messages to an object).

Just as you can Control+drag from an object in the design window or menu windows to other objects in order to establish connections, you can Control+drag between objects directly in the outline view to connect them. Figure 9-32 shows such a connection being made.

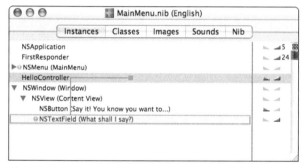

Figure 9-32
Connecting in the outline view

Once you've defined the subclasses you need and created all the connections between them and the various interface objects, you still have no code until you tell IB to write it for you. We saw the process in Chapter 1: Just choose Classes ➔ Create Files For <name of object> (or Option+⌘+F). IB creates the files in the open Xcode project that contains the nib upon which you are working.

▼ **Note**

IB can't create the files in the project if the project isn't open in Xcode. It will simply write them out to disk, offering you a Save dialog to specify filenames and locations.

BIND FOR GLORY

You may have noticed that the Cocoa Inspectors contain a panel for *bindings*. Bindings are relatively new Cocoa technology added to Mac OS X 10.3 that simplify the creation of the Model-View-Controller paradigm in your applications. Bindings use special controllers that implement key-value binding to bind a value in one object to a property in another object. These come in very handy when, say, a change to some interface element (like a slider) needs to result in updates to several other objects at the same time (say, several text fields). It is really beyond the scope of this book to explore how bindings work, but you can find out all about them in Xcode's documentation library. Just do a full text search on "Cocoa bindings."

The important thing to note about Cocoa bindings is this: Using them means you'll have even less code to write. And that means more time for other things, such as having a life.

▼ **Caution**

You probably don't want to choose Create Files For if you've already done so previously and then made changes to the implementation and/or header files, because IB will overwrite your work.

TEST DRIVING THE INTERFACE

As you are building an interface in IB, you sometimes may have an uncontrollable urge to see how it looks and acts. One way to do that is to write out all your subclasses, code your target-action methods, and build the program and run it (Cocoa), or save your nib and do a whole heck of a lot of coding and then building (Carbon). And, sooner or later, you'll have to do something like that. However, we always prefer later rather than sooner (fear of commitment? basic slothfulness? an unwillingness to go off half-cocked? Yes, all of these, depending on the day and phase of the moon).

IB can offer you a test drive of your interface by way of its File ➜ Test Interface command (⌘+R) so you don't have to prematurely code and build. Choose the command and, suddenly, all the IB windows vanish except for the windows you've created, and the IB menu bar is replaced with the one in your nib. Then, go ahead and click, drag, type... whatever it is that you want to check out. Interface testing is especially useful when you want to see how your auto-sizing settings work when your apps windows are resized.

Of course, the testing is rather limited: buttons will click, but target-actions won't be acted upon. (How could they be? They might not have been coded yet, and even if they have been, how would IB know how to run them?) Still, you can see all your menus and buttons, try out tabbed and scrolling views, and a bunch of other stuff. Even bet-ter, if you've established any Cocoa bindings, you can also test those out. It won't be your complete app, but it will be a nice simulation.

▼ **Note**

The amount of testing you can do with a Carbon inter-face is somewhat more restricted than it is for Cocoa; for example, tabs controlling tab views won't function when testing a Carbon interface. That's the nature of Carbon. It *wants* you to work for your rewards.

When you finish, just choose the Quit command from your application's menu and you'll be back in IB again.

What's that? You mistakenly omitted the Quit command in your app? Heh. IB also places a Dr. Frankenstein-approved switch near the right side of your menu bar when you test an interface. Click *that* to get back to IB.

And that's all there is to it.

THE 143-WORD RECAP

In this chapter we first discovered that a nib is where you store your application's interface elements and explained how to make one. Then we explored the differences between Carbon and Cocoa nibs, and learned in the process that while Carbon and IB work well together, IB and Cocoa were, literally, made for each other. We next spilled a huge amount of ink describing how the various layout tools, palettes, windows, and interface objects avail-able in IB both work together and with Xcode. We took a closer look at the kinds of things that IB's palettes have to offer and then explained how to create connections between the interface and your application, including details about how Carbon's signature and ID labeling of interface elements work, and how to create outlets and target-actions in your Cocoa app. Finally we described IB's Test Interface feature.

Hanging Out with the Supermodelers

A Touch of Class Modeling • Model Making 101
How to Data Model • Model Making 102
How Our Date Went

"Hobbits delighted in [genealogical charts], if they were accurate: they liked to have books filled with things that they already knew, set out fair and square with no contradictions."

— from the prologue to *The Lord of the Rings*, J.R.R. Tolkien

If you've ever been up against a new object-oriented API and tried to find your way through its thicket of classes and subclasses and sub-subclasses, you know how useful a visual aid — some sort of a chart or diagram showing how all those pieces of API relate to one another — can be. Although Xcode's helpful class browser is a nice start, it doesn't provide The Big Picture that we crave. And when it comes to dealing with the data structures that those classes and subclasses and sub-subclasses supposedly manage... well, scanning down a list of structs and instance variables scattered among a bunch of class descriptions may be someone's idea of fun and enlightenment, but it sure isn't ours.

Of course, in theory, all you really need to program your Mac (or any computer) is a text editor and a compiler, and there are those programmers out there (and you know who you are) who consider anything more visually stimulating than *vi* and *gcc* as simply extraneous gilding on a superfluous lily. But we like pretty pictures. A whole lot. It's why we're using a Mac in the first place. And that's why we like the new visual development tools for class and data modeling that Apple has added to its Xcode toolbox.

With Xcode's class modeling tool, we can finally see (not just read about and try to visualize) how the classes in a program or API relate to each other. With the data modeling tool, we can finally see, and, in fact, design the storage structures — and the relationships among them — that an application requires. With these two visual modeling tools, we can finally let our right brain get in on the programming fun that our left brain has been exclusively enjoying for so long, and see pictures of the things we already knew, set out fair and square with no contradictions.

It's enough to make the hair on our hobbit toes curl.

A TOUCH OF CLASS MODELING

Classes. As we've just said, keeping track of all of them and figuring out how they all relate to one another, even in a relatively simple little project, can be a real, bona fide, 100 percent prime premium pain in the fundament (if you know what we mean, and we think you do). Apple has heard these (metaphorical) cries of pain from countless developer derrieres and has provided fast-acting relief in the form of its new visual class modeling tools in Xcode 2.0. You can find them in Xcode's equally new Design menu (see Figure 10-1).

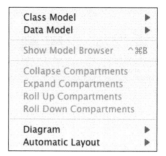

Figure 10-1
Classy design tools on the new Design menu

The Class Model tool allows you to get a quick view of your project's classes and their relationships to one another, as well as gives you a powerful design and navigation tool. In Xcode 2, class models come in two basic varieties:

- a *Quick Model*, which is designed simply to show you what's what in your code, and which we describe in this section; and

- a *User Model*, which you not only can view for fun and profit, but also can manipulate to help you design your project; we describe User Models in the next section, "Model Making 101."

PLUGGED-IN POWER TOOLS

The Class Model tool (and its good buddy, the Data Model tool, which we describe later in this chapter) relies upon a sophisticated modeling engine to provide its graphical smarts, and is included with and directly accessible from the Xcode application itself in the form of a plug-in (if you simply *must* poke around to satisfy your curious cravings, you can find it in Library/Application Support/Apple/Developer Tools/Plug-ins). Xcode, as it evolves, will rely more and more upon plug-ins to provide new and improved development tool support: Simply drop in a new plug-in and you're good to go.

Just as important, from a work-flow perspective, plug-ins provide their capabilities directly within the Xcode environment — unlike such longtime favorite Xcode tools as Interface Builder (see Chapter 9), plug-ins provide much closer integration between the tools and Xcode's editing and building capabilities: For example, changes made in your project's source can be instantly reflected in a Class Model display... as you'll see in the following text.

A Quick Model is exactly what the name implies: a quickly created model that shows you the class hierarchies for a project, target, framework, or group. To create a Quick Model, simply select one of the groups in your project... you can even select the target if you like. Then choose Design ➔ Class Model ➔ Quick Model. Faster than you can recite the names of the 15 brightest stars visible in the Northern Hemisphere between June and August, Xcode draws a class diagram for you (see Figure 10-2).

A Class Model window consists of a basic Xcode editing window's shell, but instead of containing source text it contains a class browser (similar, but definitely *not* identical, to the Class Browser available from the Project menu) coupled with the actual class diagram itself.

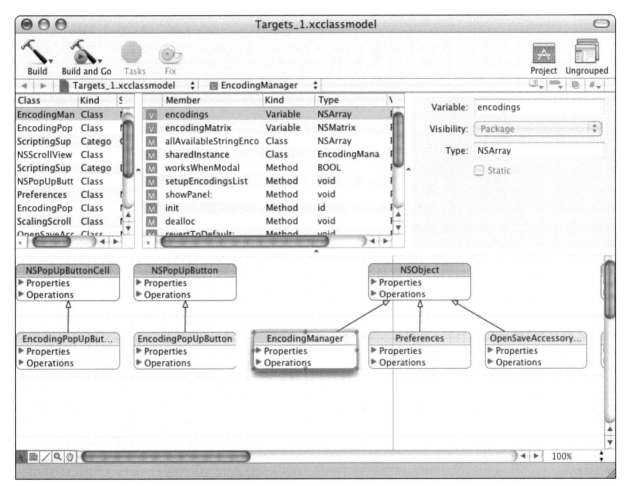

Figure 10-2
Quickly modeled classes from Apple's TextEdit source code

SO WHAT'S IT GOOD FOR?

Come on, you're kidding, right? A Quick Model is a great way to get a handle on someone else's code. Load a project into Xcode, select the target, make a Quick Model, and (zap!) you have an instant snapshot of how that project is conceptually organized, regardless of how the actual definitions and declarations are scattered among the various source files.

 Tip

To see the full splendor of the Quick Model diagram, you can hide the model browser by choosing Design ➜ Hide Model Browser (Control+⌘+B). When the browser is hidden, the command intelligently changes to Show Model Browser (the keyboard equivalent remains the same, of course).

A Quick Model shows you all the classes (and categories and protocols) of the selected group or target, as well as the first parent outside the group — a real time- and space-saver, because you probably don't want to see the entire Cocoa or Carbon class hierarchies every time you model a bit of your code. For each class (or classlike thingie... let's call them *entities* from now on, because that's what Apple calls them), you can see

- its name,

- its properties (that is, its instance variables), and

- its operations (that is, its methods).

 Note

The Quick Model is not a completely static representation of your code at the time you create it. If you move some files from the group of files being diagrammed to another group, or move another set of files into the

group, the model diagram adjusts itself right before your eyes to reflect the new state of your project.

When the model is drawn, each of the displayed entities' properties and operations are collapsed to save screen space. You can see the individual properties and operations belonging to a class by clicking the disclosure triangles in each entity box, or you can click to select an entity and choose Design ➜ Expand Compartments — this is particularly handy if you have selected more than one entity (see Figure 10-3). Similarly, you can collapse a compartment by clicking its disclosure triangle again, or by choosing Design ➜ Collapse Compartments to close the compartments of a selected entity (or selected multiple entities).

▼ **Tip**

If you have no entities selected in the class diagram, the Expand Compartments command becomes Expand All and the Collapse Compartments command becomes Collapse All. Of course, choosing Expand All creates a much more crowded and confusing diagram, and, for a complex class model, can take a bit of time — on the other hand, the Collapse All command is quite useful for cleaning up after yourself following a madcap session of model exploration and expansion.

Similar to the Expand and Collapse commands are the *Roll Up* and *Roll Down* commands. Choose Design ➜ Roll Up Compartments to collapse the entire selected entity box (or boxes) into just an entity name label; choose Design ➜ Roll Down Compartments to get access to the entity's properties and operations again (and, of course, when no entities are selected, you can roll up or roll down all the entities in the diagram using the Roll Up All and Roll Down All commands on the Design menu).

You can also rearrange the diagram to suit your viewing needs, printing requirements, or aesthetic predilections by clicking and dragging one or more entities to wherever you like: The lines connecting the entities to their ancestors or

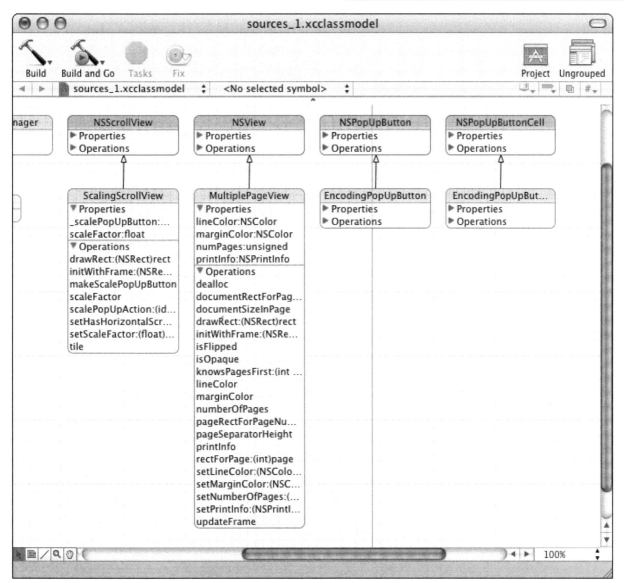

Figure 10-3
Several expanded classes

descendents adjust themselves accordingly. There are, in fact, a number of commands on the Design menu's Diagram submenu for fine-tuning the appearance of a class model — you have alignment commands, size commands, and other layout commands similar to those you might find in any drawing program. You can even add comments to your diagram. (Comments? Do real programmers ever *write* comments? You bet your sweet patootie they do!)

MAKING A MOVE ON A MODEL

Aside from just being oh-so-neat and informative to look at, a class model diagram is also a very useful code navigation tool. You can get to the definition or declaration of any class, property, or operation by simply clicking to select it in the diagram and then choosing Design ➔ Class Model; the Class Model submenu has choices that will take you where you want to go (see Figure 10-4).

Also, remember that class model diagrams contain the immediate parent classes, if any, of the group of classes being diagrammed (for example, the model of a group that defines a direct subclass of NSScrollView will also include NSScrollView). This means that class models often contain classes that come from an Apple framework, and for such classes, you can select Design ➔ Class Model ➔ Go to Documentation to see that entry's docs in the Reference Library that comes with Xcode.

If, however, a trip to the menu bar taxes your mousing hand too much (and if you're running a 30-inch flat panel, it just might... but don't complain to us about it!), you can simply position your mouse pointer over an item in the diagram to see a faint, iTunes-ish arrow icon appear to the right of the item's name, along with a tool tip telling you the name of the entity to which the item belongs (see Figure 10-5). Click that iTunes-ish arrow and you'll be magically transported to the item's definition code. Or you can Control+click (or right-click) any item in the model to get a contextual menu with all sorts of navigational choices, too.

As the old punch line doesn't go, you *can* get there from here.

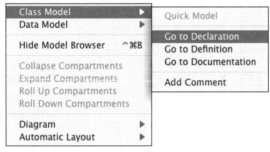

Figure 10-4
One way of getting to the source

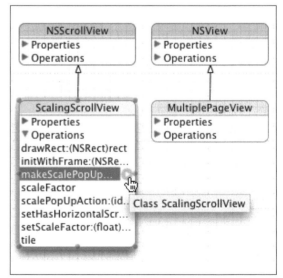

Figure 10-5
Another way of getting to the source

LANGUAGE AGNOSTIC; CURRENTLY TRILINGUAL

When the Class Model tool debuted at Apple's World Wide Developers Conference in 2004, it was described as being *language agnostic*; that is, it could diagram a project's class structures regardless of the language(s) used to write the project. And it's true... as long as the language is either Objective-C, C++, or Java — at least for now. But because the Class Model tool is a plug-in, it seems likely that the tool's linguistic proficiencies will increase over time. In fact, we're rather confident they will, because Apple actually told developers at the conference that it has plans to do so. And when has Apple ever lied? (By the way, we want modeling support for AppleScript!!)

 Note

Quick Models are automatically generated and laid out based upon your source code each time you choose the Quick Model menu item, and, most important, they are *not* saved with your project. So, if you make any changes to one (for example, dragging entities around, expanding certain compartments of specific entities, adding comments), those changes vanish like ethics in the House of Representatives when you close the model window or the project. However, User Models, which we describe in the next section, *are* saved with the project, and *that* makes the class model layout tools we've just discussed *much* more useful.

At the top of the model view is the familiar navigation bar that you've seen in so many Xcode editing windows so many times before. In a class model window, however, the function pop-up lets you select from among the entities displayed in the diagram: when you choose an item from this pop-up, the diagram pane scrolls the selected entity

into view and selects that entity both within the diagram and in the window's model browser (if you haven't hidden the model browser, of course).

 Tip

If you happen to be more of a keyboard than a mouse jockey, you can use a model's type-ahead feature to get where you want to go: Type the first few characters of an entity's name to center the diagram on it.

MODEL MAKING 101

Quick Models are designed to give you a quick view of your project's classes, protocols, and categories and how they are related; User Models are designed to let you track them on a file-by-file or group-by-group basis. Unlike Quick Models, User Models are stored in files as part of your project (the files are of type .xcclassmodel, if you are interested). This means, of course, that any changes you make to the layout of your model are saved as well. What's more, though you can only have one Quick Model at a time, you can have multiple User Models in your project, each of them focusing on a particular group or set of files.

To make a User Model, follow these steps:

1. **Choose File → New File (or type ⌘+N).** A New File Assistant sheet slides out of your project window (see Figure 10-6).

2. **Scroll down to the Design category, select Class Model, and then click Next.** The assistant offers you a chance to give your file a name and habitation (see Figure 10-7).

3. **Give your model file a name.** You can also choose a different place than the project file in which to store the file if you wish. Click Next.

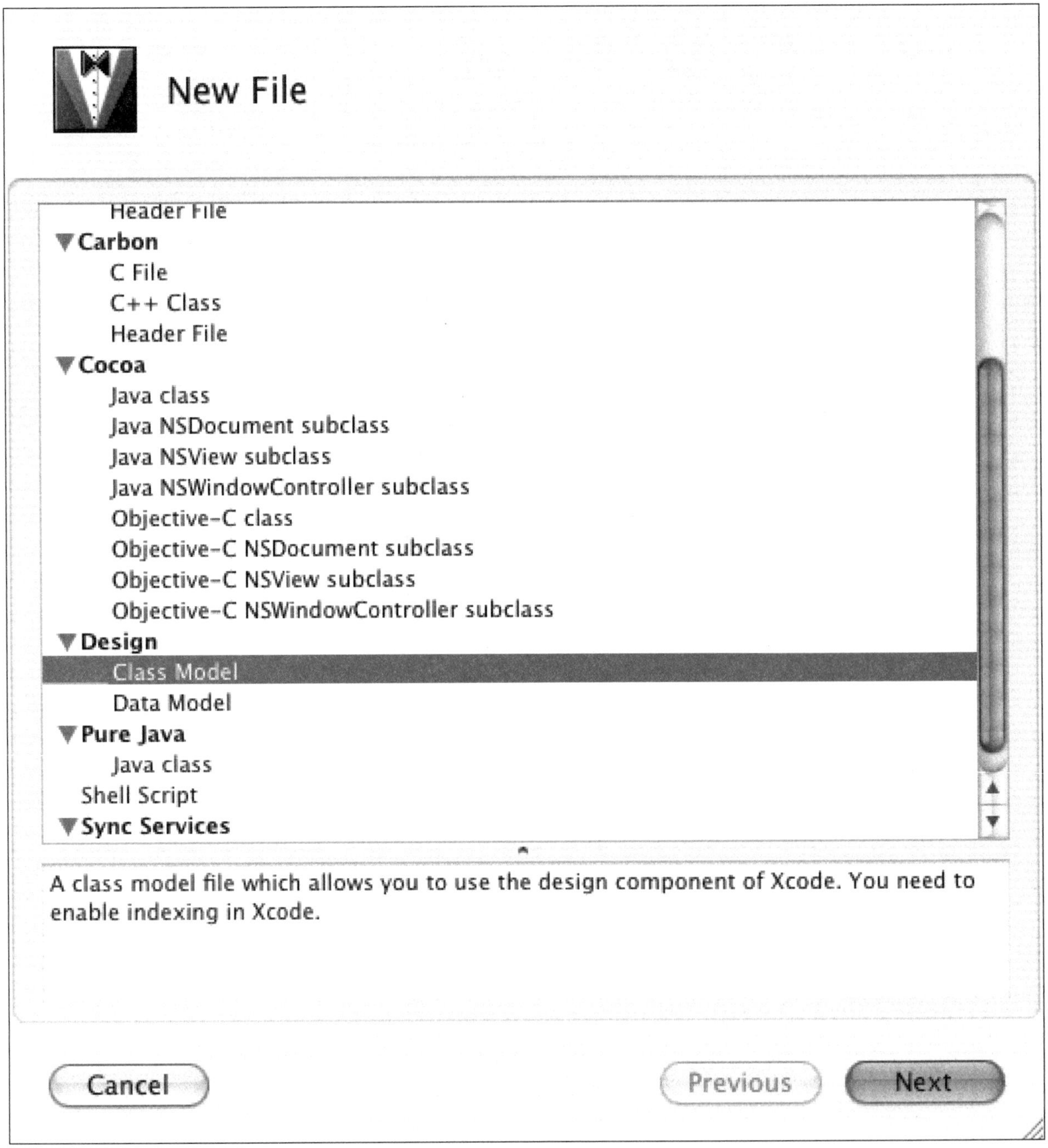

 New File

Header File
▼ **Carbon**
    C File
    C++ Class
    Header File
▼ **Cocoa**
    Java class
    Java NSDocument subclass
    Java NSView subclass
    Java NSWindowController subclass
    Objective-C class
    Objective-C NSDocument subclass
    Objective-C NSView subclass
    Objective-C NSWindowController subclass
▼ **Design**
    Class Model
    Data Model
▼ **Pure Java**
    Java class
  Shell Script
▼ **Sync Services**

A class model file which allows you to use the design component of Xcode. You need to enable indexing in Xcode.

Cancel   Previous   Next

Figure 10-6
The New File dude

WHAT IT TAKES TO BE A MODEL

In order to build a class model, whether of the User or of the Quick variety, Xcode makes use of the code index that it builds in order to provide many of its other smart services, such as Code Sense. This is why, for example, when you create a new User Model, the New File Assistant informs you that creating a Class Model file requires you to enable indexing.

There are a few other limits, too, related to language and file organization. For example, if you have your C++ headers in a .c file, the Xcode indexer (which believes what your file extensions tell it) won't consider the header to be a C++ header and therefore won't include the declarations as part of the class hierarchy properly. Generally, if your classes don't appear listed in your Project Symbols Smart Group, you shouldn't expect them to show up in your model either.

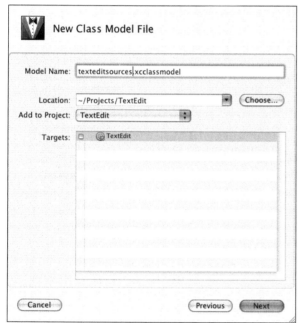

Figure 10-7
Your model wants a name and a place to live

▼ Note

If you select the checkbox beside any of the targets listed in this sheet, the model file will be included in the target as one of the resources to be copied into the executable's package. Why would you want to do this? Beats us... but you can.

4. **The assistant offers to let you assign files and groups to your model (see Figure 10-8).** Select the group(s) or file(s) that you wish to include in the model from the column on the left, and then click Add.

▼ Note

As the sheet tells you, adding a group to the Selected Items list allows the model to include or exclude classes dynamically when the files defining those classes are added to or removed from the group. Explicitly adding files to the Selected Items list, on the other hand, includes the files' associated classes in the model, whether they are part of a particular group or not.

5. **Click Finish.** You now have a User Model to use as you see fit.

Once you have created the model, you can open and manipulate it at any time by double-clicking its file in your project window.

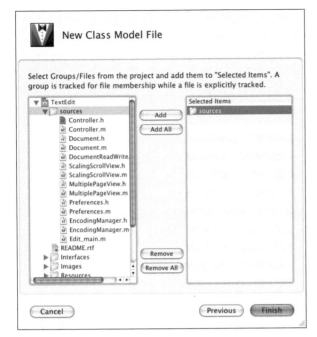

Figure 10-8
Add items to your model

A User Model lets you do just about anything you can do with a Quick Model, with the wonderful enhancement of actually being persistent: Any changes you make to the model will be saved when you close it (unless, of course, you tell Xcode not to save the changes in the dialog that appears whenever you close the model). Because the model is persistent, you can make better use of the Diagram and Layout items on the Design menu... and you can make better use of the tools that appear in the bottom left of the model window (see Figure 10-9):

- the **Selection tool,** for selecting, dragging, and toggling disclosure triangles in the model;

- the **Comment tool,** which lets you drag out comment boxes on the diagram, into which you can type your own descriptions of what various parts of the model mean;

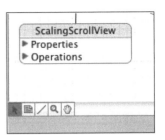

Figure 10-9
Model tools

- the **Line tool,** which, actually, you can't make any use of, because it is completely nonfunctional for class models... however, it turns out to be very useful for Data Models (see the next section);

- the **Zoom tool,** which lets you zoom in and out of the diagram quickly (click to zoom in, Option+click to zoom out, and drag to zoom directly to the area dragged); and

- the **Scroll Canvas tool,** which lets you drag the diagram around the model window instead of forcing you to fiddle with scroll bars.

When you save a User Model, the model remembers which categories were expanded or collapsed, which entities were completely rolled up, the positions of all the entities in the diagram, and the relative scroll position of the model window.

Once you begin working on an OOP project with the Class Model tool, you'll probably end up wondering how you got along without it for so long.

HOW TO DATA MODEL

There's been a big, ugly hole in the whole object-oriented programming paradigm for a long time: data.

Don't get us wrong — OOP and the concepts related to it (for example, design-by-difference, model-viewer-controller,

BENEATH THE HOOD OF A MODEL

What sort of legerdemain makes Xcode's modeling capabilities possible? It's a little-known (except for those who know it well) technology called Unified Modeling Language (UML). Beneath both Xcode's Class Model and Data Model tools is a UML-enabled engine that stores, retrieves, and manipulates the model according to the UML specification. We're not about to go into just what that specification is nor are we going to describe what it can do (especially because we have merely glanced at the spec and already our eyes have developed a thick, translucent glazing similar to the one you might find on a Krispy Kreme doughnut). You, however, can check the UML specification out for yourself at www.uml.org. When you finish reviewing it, tell us how thick the glaze on your eyes becomes.

message-passing hierarchies) are wonderfully fruitful ways to approach a wide variety of programming problems. But sooner or later, the data being manipulated by all the clever classes to be found in a typical OOP library, such as Cocoa, will need to be saved to disk, and, once saved, sooner or later will need to be retrieved as well. And those storage and retrieval processes, as the well-worn textbook cop-out goes, have usually been "left as an exercise for the reader." (Need some windows? No problem. Menus? Have a stack of 'em right here. Widgets? Gotcha covered. Persistent data store? Whaaaaa?!?) It seems that almost every programming project that requires a data storage and retrieval mechanism has had to reinvent the mechanism each and every time.

Well, toss up a handful of confetti and come join the celebration: Xcode 2 and a Cocoa-flavored API that debuted in Tiger called *Core Data* are bringing data design and storage to the object-oriented programming party.

Here are some of the key concepts you need to understand Xcode's data models:

- **Schema.** In a nutshell, this is what Xcode's Data Model tool helps you to create and manage. Figure 10-10 shows an incredibly simple schema as represented in an Xcode data model.

▼ Note

The Data Model tool lets you create a schema from scratch, derive it from source code, or import it from an XML file.

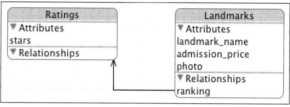

Figure 10-10
An incredibly simple schema

- **Object graph.** This boils down (at least so far as Core Data and data modeling are concerned) to the data objects and the relationships among them that your program processes as the program is running. In other words, it's the schema brought to life.

- **Entities.** Schemata (yes, that *is* the plural of schema) are made of these. Entities have a *name*, (usually) a *class*, and *properties*, which, in turn, comprise *attributes* and *relationships*.

- **Attributes.** You can think of these as data values: a number, a string, a picture, an array of various objects. An entity can have many different attributes. The entity named Landmarks in Figure 10-10 has three attributes.

- **Relationships.** These connect one entity to another and can be *one-to-one* or *one-to-many*. Often

SO WHAT IS CORE DATA, ANYWAY?

To begin with, it's a framework. More specifically, it's a framework that descends from the Cocoa framework, because it comprises classes that descend from the root class of all Cocoa classes: NSObject. Even more specifically, it's a framework that provides general solutions to data storage, retrieval, and management problems.

In particular, the various Core Data classes are designed to help you

- store and retrieve data objects from external data stores (for example, disk files);

- group, filter, and organize data as it floats around in memory;

- represent the data in your bright and shiny user interface;

- manage the whole nasty business of undo/redo (a feature which we've always loved to use in other applications, and which we absolutely dreaded implementing in our own apps, because, frankly, it's almost always really, really *hard* to do well); and

- handle data-value sanity-checking (such as supplying default values, making sure that the data are of the appropriate type and in the right range for the purpose you intended).

Significantly, Core Data has been designed with Xcode's data modeling capabilities in mind. Though it may be possible, at least in theory, to write Core Data–savvy programs in other development environments, the fact is that the data model files created by Xcode's Data Model tool are as closely tied to Core Data as Cocoa's interface smarts are tied to the nib files created by Interface Builder.

In short, if you want to use Core Data, you want to use Xcode. And if you want to make use of the models created by Xcode's Data Model tool, you probably want to use Core Data.

a relationship also has a corresponding *inverse relationship* in the related entity that points back to the first. In Figure 10-10, Landmarks has a one-to-one relationship with Ratings, but there is no inverse relationship.

- **Fetch specs.** These are associated with entities, but don't appear in the data model diagram; they do appear in the model browser, though, as you shall see. If attributes are like variables, fetch specs are like methods; you can also think of them as database-type queries into your data that you can prebuild and associate with the entity. Xcode lets you specify two types of fetch specs: *fetched properties* and *fetch requests*.

And speaking of the model browser... the Data Model tool offers a model browser similar to the model browser that the Class Model tool provides. This browser lets you manipulate the entities and their properties very deeply and precisely. Figure 10-11 shows the model browser for our incredibly simple schema.

In its default form, the browser consists of three panels:

- The leftmost panel contains a list of all the entities in the model, along with some associated information.

- The central panel contains a list of details associated with the entity or entities selected in the leftmost

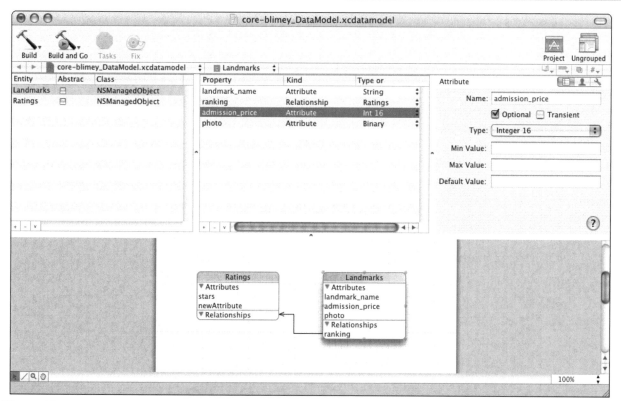

Figure 10-11
Browsing our incredibly simple schema

panel. Typically, it shows the properties (attributes and relationships) of the selected entities. It can, however, show subsets of these, or it can show fetch specs (as we describe a bit further on... patience, Grasshopper).

- The rightmost panel is the *detail editor*, which lets you edit specific, um, details belonging to the properties selected in the central panel.

Keep in mind, though, that the detail editor in the model browser is not the only place you can edit your entities' details. Both the data diagram and model browser's panels are quite alive. For example:

- You can click and type to change the name of an entity or one of its properties right in the diagram, and the model browser will reflect the change.

- You can click and type to change the name of an entity or property in its respective list in the browser. The diagram will reflect the change.

- You can use the pop-up widgets in the Type column of the property list to change a property's type without resorting to the detail editor.

In addition, you can change what the central panel shows (see Figure 10-12).

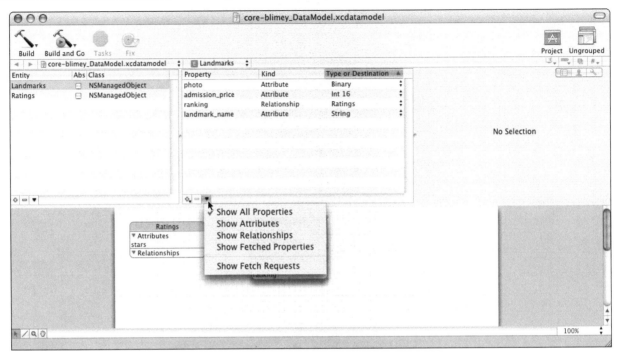

Figure 10-12
Changing the face of the model browser

Click the pop-up menu widget at the lower left of the model browser's central panel, and you can choose to have the panel show specific types of properties or fetch specs.

MODEL MAKING 102

As we mentioned in a note a few pages back, Xcode lets you build a data model in several ways. One of the more useful ways, especially for those of you working on an existing product and wanting to take advantage of all the good stuff that Core Data brings to the party, is to derive the model right from your existing source code.

First, it helps very, very much if your app is written in Objective-C and uses Cocoa; the first version of the Data Model tool assumes as much. But if your app meets these simple requirements, here's what you do:

1. **Choose File → New File (or press ⌘+N).** As we've seen on similar occasions, a New File Assistant sheet slides out of your project window (see Figure 10-15).

2. **Scroll down to the Design choices and select Data Model. Click Next.** The New File dude, as you've seen before with class models, wants you to name the data model file and choose a place to save it (see Figure 10-16).

THE FETCHING PREDICATE EDITOR

Xcode provides a *predicate editor* to edit fetch requests and fetched properties. When you choose to view a fetch spec, the middle panel becomes a list of fetch specs and the detail editor becomes a fetch spec editor (see Figure 10-13).

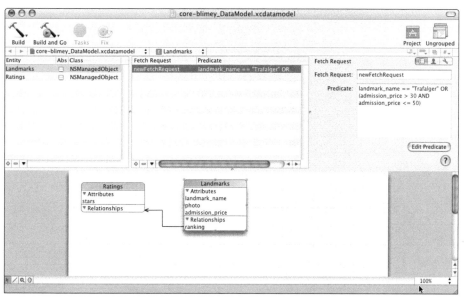

Figure 10-13
Fetching editing features

You can type your predicate algebra statements right into the Predicate box in the detail editor... or you can use the detail editor's cool predicate editor by clicking Edit Predicate (see Figure 10-14).

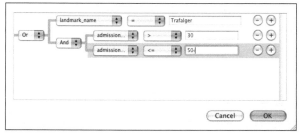

The predicate editor looks a lot like iTunes' Smart Playlist editor after it went to graduate school. You can add or remove individual clauses with the plus and minus buttons, and the pop-up menus allow you to add **and** and **or** clauses, attribute and relationship names, and expressions to the spec. You can also drag the head of a clause to move it to somewhere else in the statement.

Figure 10-14
The very cool predicate editor

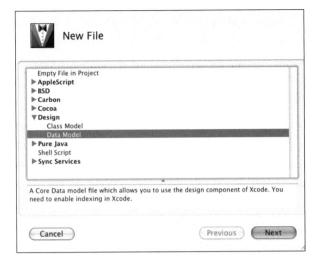

Figure 10-15

Add a new Data Model file (positronic brain not included)

▼ **Note**

> Unlike the class model creation process, the New File Assistant for Data Models includes the model in the project's target by default, which is why the checkbox beside the target in Figure 10-16 is checked. Your Data Models need to be included in your app for the Core Data routines to use them. You should leave this box checked unless you have a good reason not to (and such reasons don't include, "I felt like it").

3. **Type a name for the model and click Next.** If you like, you can also change where to save it before you click Next, but we usually don't bother, because the model file is really another source file and belongs with its comrades in our opinion.

4. **Select the source files that the assistant uses to build your model from the leftmost list.** You can select one or more groups or files — the assistant consults the project's index for class definitions in the selected files and lists them in the Available Classes list

(see Figure 10-17). The class and instance variables in these definitions are used to create the appropriate entities, attributes, and relationships.

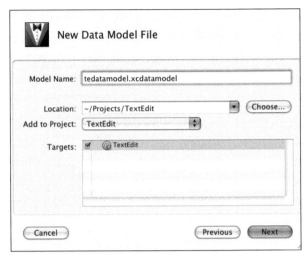

Figure 10-16

Name the model and add it to the target

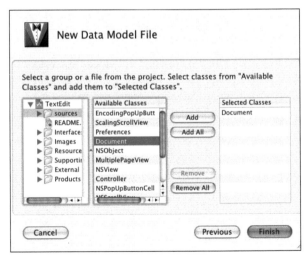

Figure 10-17

Picking your classes (it's just like college!)

5. **Select one or more classes from the Available Classes list and click the Add button.** This populates the Selected Classes list (we bet you can figure out what the Add All, Remove, and Remove All buttons do).

6. **Click Finish.** In two shakes of a wool-bearing herbivore's tail, a model file is born, and a window appears showing you your new data model in all its shining glory (see Figure 10-18).

Of course, adding a data model to an existing project does nothing for you if you don't also add the Core Data framework to your project and write the classes and other code necessary to implement your data-handling routines (with Core Data's help, natch). We're not, of course, going to go through the gyrations you'll have to perform in order to add Core Data wonderfulness to your project, because that (along with discussions of things like *managed object contexts* and *key-value coding* and Core Data's relationship with Cocoa

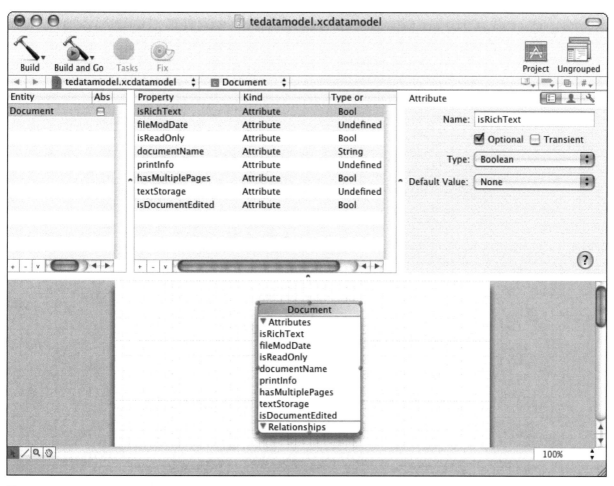

Figure 10-18
A new Data Model to manipulate

CALL MOM

We said earlier that "the model file is really another source file" and we meant just that. When you build your program, Xcode not only compiles your own source files, but the model file as well (see Figure 10-19).

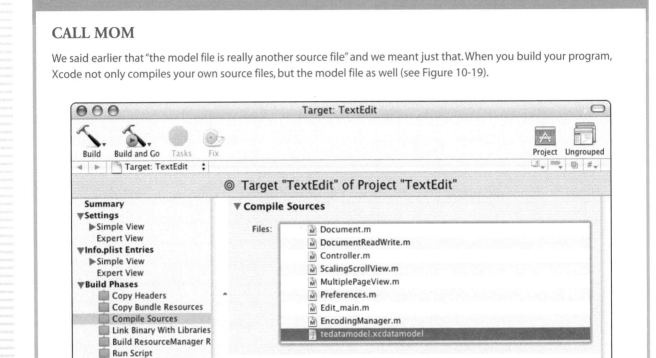

Figure 10-19
A model to be built

Although the model file is not a C or C++ or Objective-C or Java file, and although the GNU compilers don't actually touch it, the `.xcmodeldata` file is still processed and the results placed in your target. What happens is that all the information in the file that Xcode uses to present the model to you and allow you to edit it is stripped out, and the model data is optimized so that Core Data can more easily handle it. The result is a `.mom` file, which is included in your compiled project's package along with other resources. It's this resource file that Core Data will call upon when your app loads in order to create the necessary memory structures to hold your data. Think of it as a nib for managed data.

Bindings) belongs to a book about Core Data programming, which this volume isn't. However, you can get an idea of how a Core Data application is organized and works by making a new one from one of Xcode's templates (see Figure 10-20).

Figure 10-20
A new Core Data application project waiting to be created

Xcode, as it does with Cocoa applications and Cocoa-Java applications, provides two templates for Core Data apps: a Core Data application (for apps that don't create and manipulate documents) and a Core Data document-based application (for those apps that do). Figure 10-21 shows a fresh-baked Core Data project just as it came from

the oven. As you can see, the project contains a new, empty data model file, as well as two source files (in Figure 10-21 these are `corianderAppDelegate.h` and `corianderAppDelegate.m`), along with the necessary frameworks, property lists, and nibs that the project needs.

▼ Note
We've opened up certain groups in the project in order to let you see where Xcode puts various things.

In fact, you can build and run this new project, though it will not do anything interesting. After all, the data model it contains is completely empty, so there's not much for the app to do. However, it is easy enough to add entities to the model — just open the model file up and choose Design ➜ Data Model ➜ Add Entity (Control+ ⌘+E). And, once you have an entity, it's easy enough to add an attribute to it: Select it in the model and choose Design ➜ Data Model ➜ Add Attribute (Control+ ⌘+A). And, once you have a few entities, you can add relationships with Design ➜ Data Model ➜ Add Relationship (Control+ ⌘+R). Or you can Control+click or right-click an entity in the diagram and choose the Add command you want from the contextual menu.

Once you have an entity or two or three or more in your model, you can use Interface Builder to construct user interfaces that manipulate the data represented by the model — without writing a single line of code. Figure 10-22 shows a simple data entity we created for the app shown in Figure 10-21.

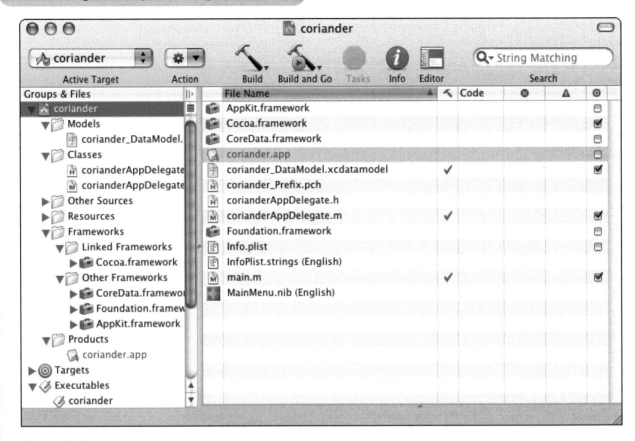

Figure 10-21
A new Core Data application project ready to be fleshed out

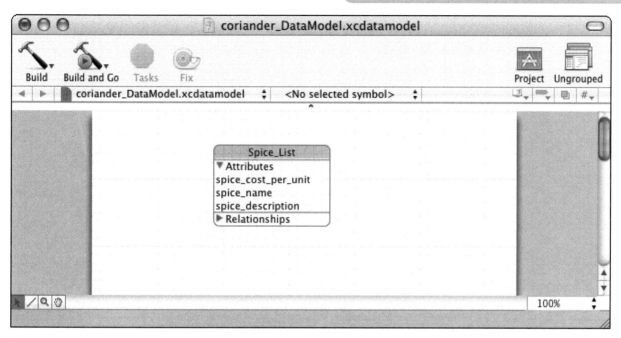

Figure 10-22
A spicy entity

Here's how you build a working UI for something like this:

1. **Open the nib file that comes with the project (double-clicking will do it), so that Interface Builder displays it.**

2. **In the data model diagram, Option+drag the entity for which you want to build an interface to the application's window in Interface Builder.** (It helps a whole lot if you arrange your screen so you can see both the diagram window in Xcode and the app's window in Interface Builder.) Interface Builder presents the dialog shown in Figure 10-23.

Figure 10-23
This happens when you Option+drag a data entity to Interface Builder

3. **Click one of the buttons in the dialog; we chose the Many Objects button.** The result is shown in Figure 10-24.

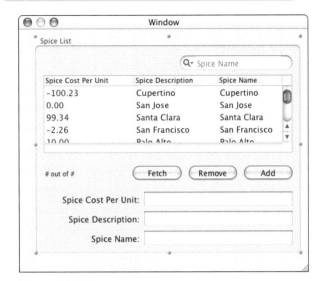

Figure 10-24
Interface Builder knows about data models

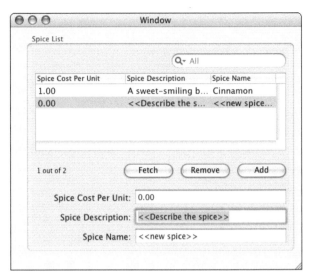

Figure 10-25
Completely functional Core Data app with no code required!

4. **Save the changes in Interface Builder, go back to Xcode, and build the project.**

Figure 10-25 shows the application that we built in action. The Add and Remove buttons work just as you would expect... in fact, most of the interface works exactly as it should: You can even sort the columns, resize them, and move them around, just as Apple's Human Interface Guidelines describe how such things should work.

▼ Note

You can remove items from the interface with Interface Builder (say, for example, the Fetch button) and the app you build will still function. Much of the functionality you get comes courtesy of Core Data and Cocoa Bindings. You may want to select the interface that Interface Builder created and check out the Bindings pane in the Inspector to see more of what's going on under the hood. It's fun and educational, too.

HOW OUR DATE WENT

We began our date with the supermodelers by looking at the types of class models that the Class Model tool creates (Quick, for ephemeral overviews, and User, for use when actually designing a project). We showed how to create a Quick Model and described the elements of a class as displayed in a model diagram: *name*, *properties*, and *operations*. Then we looked at the various ways to manipulate and navigate a class diagram, which was lots of fun. The next part of our date involved building an actual class user model and included a tour of the tools available for playing with it. After dinner and a movie, we took a long moonlight stroll and talked about data models. In the process, we introduced our date to the new Core Data framework and recounted the basic concepts involved in data modeling (how we both laughed when we learned that the plural of *schema* is *schemata*!). We spent some time window-shopping with the data model browser and oohed and aahed at the beauty of the modeler's shiny predicate editor. Our date was tickled when we built a data model from an existing project, and was really impressed when, with the clever help of our wingman, Interface Builder, we created a new project and constructed a Core Data app, complete with working interface, without writing a single line of code. That's where the date ended, but we hope we can go out again next week.

PART IV

If You Build It,
It May Run

Doing It Old School in Carbon

I Got a C++ in Programming
It All Depends • Status Symbols
Totally RAD-ical Techniques
Build Log

To New-Agers of a certain age, *carbon* evokes thoughts of being a golden stardust child setting out on a trip down to Yasgur's farm. Perhaps that's what Steve Jobs was hoping programmers of a certain age might be flashing on when he announced the creation of Carbon: the traditional classic Mac toolbox and libraries cleaned up, retooled, and modernized for Mac OS X.

It was, and had to be, a heck of a sales job. Switching to Mac OS X and the NeXT runtime software libraries that rested between the (mostly) familiar Mac interface and its underlying Unix foundation meant that programmers who had spent years developing Mac programs and learning the Mac toolbox's quirks and secrets suddenly had to move to an entirely different way of doing things — and few were willing to go there. The Carbon libraries were designed so that they might not have to: Apple claimed that about 80 percent of existing Mac code could move to Carbon unchanged, and that the rest would only require some modest tweaking. In addition to providing programmers with an API bridge to the future, Carbon was also designed to let developers build a single application that would run in both OS 9 with the CarbonLib shared library installed (actually, in OS 8.1 or later) and in OS X. Carbon, in fact, was described as "the basis of all life" in characteristic Jobsian hyperbole, though there were some dissenters who felt that Carbon actually referred to coal, the fossilized remains of something formerly living.

Whatever.

In fact, Carbon did make it easier to move old Mac (Pascal, C, and C++) code to the new Mac OS X without programmers having to learn all the new (old) NeXT-based libraries and the

Objective-C language in which they were written (and which Apple began to call Cocoa) — even though, in many cases, the transition wasn't quite as easy as Apple claimed it would be. But when, inevitably, developers also began demanding Carbon access to more of the new Mac OS X features that the original Carbon libraries didn't support, Carbon began looking less and less like the old Mac toolbox and more and more like a C++-compatible version of Cocoa. Plus, as more OS X-specific features were desired, it became necessary to build a different kind of executable, called a *mach-o* (for the Mach underpinnings, not because it was more manly), for use in OS X. Many of the best-known and largest-selling Mac OS X applications are still Carbon applications, including Adobe Photoshop, Microsoft Office, Quark XPress, Quicken, AppleWorks, and iTunes.

Today, Carbon provides just one of the many ways to program Mac OS X. There's now little that can be done in Cocoa that can't be done in Carbon (and vice versa). Carbon is particularly attractive to C and C++ programmers who have a significant investment in old Mac code and in shared, cross-platform C and C++ application libraries. If that sounds like you, read on....

▼ **Note**

If you see amazing similarities between this chapter and the following chapter, it's probably because they are amazingly similar. Chapter 12 covers almost exactly the same material, but from the perspective of a Cocoa programmer. You can skip right to Chapter 12 if Cocoa is more your cup of tea.

I GOT A C++ IN PROGRAMMING

Xcode's templates include basic build instructions that will serve for almost any application you want to build. You can specify additional targets and Xcode will know how to build those as well after analyzing the dependencies (see "It

OBJECT-ION, YOUR HONOR

We've been saying C++ a lot because C++ is object-oriented and, so far as the trade press and industry pundits are concerned, the future of C programming. But, at its heart, the Carbon interfaces and framework aren't really C++ — they're good old-fashioned C. And therein lies the rub in getting Carbon and Cocoa to full equality and interoperability — the Cocoa framework is object-oriented and numerous assumptions are made concerning what can invoke Cocoa methods.

All Depends," later in this chapter). Xcode sometimes seems as all-knowing as Santa: It knows what to do with your project's files and targets; it knows which compiler(s) to use, which files to copy and to where, which frameworks and libraries need to be linked, and in what order to perform its tasks; it may even know when you've been sleeping, and when you've been awake (so be *good* for goodness' sake!).

The process of taking all your project's pieces and constructing your end product is called the *build process* and, quite unoriginally, the mechanism the build process employs is called the *build system*. Chapter 3 introduces the target concept, and targets are the build process's roadmaps to creating products. Although Xcode's build system can produce many different target types, we're concerned here with Carbon-based applications. Now, your Carbon application target might depend upon subordinate targets, such as a proprietary framework or a Unix command-line tool. Xcode ensures that subordinate targets are current and available in the process of building your application.

That targets are roadmaps (or recipes or blueprints) is an important concept, because we poor English-speaking folks are accustomed to correlating the word "target" with a goal or a physical entity. Fortunately, a target and the product are very closely related, almost like gestation and an embryo. The target organizes the build process's four inputs:

- Each target includes a list of input **files** that need to be processed (compiled, copied, and so on) to create the final product.

- The operations required to process the above-mentioned files are organized into **build phases**. Each build phase includes a list of files and a task to be performed on those files, for example, preprocessing headers (see "Totally RAD-ical Techniques" later in this chapter), compiling sources, or copying resource files.

- Just how a build phase is performed is controlled by variables called **build settings**. Compiler options are examples of build settings as are the paths to where files are copied.

- To determine which build settings are to be employed is the province of **build rules**. The most common example of a build rule for a C++ Carbon project is that files with the .cp extension are to be compiled as C++ sources. Build rules only apply to the Sources and Resource Management build phases.

Associated with a target is a *product type*, describing the build process's output product. Xcode uses the product type to establish the default build settings, which build phases will take place, and how the product will be structured. It all goes something like this:

- You create a project and Xcode establishes a number of build phases for you, based upon the project template you selected.

- As you add your source files to the project, Xcode references its build rules to determine in which build phases the files belong.

- Xcode references its dependency graph (see "It All Depends," later in this chapter) for the target to determine in which order the build phases should be executed. This ensures that files produced by one build phase that are needed by another build phase exist when that second phase begins. For example, if you haven't compiled your source files yet, the object files won't exist for the link phase.

- The build progresses and, assuming that there were no errors, your product comes into being. (If there were errors, you fix them and restart the build.)

If you click a target's disclosure triangle in the Groups & Files list, you'll see the build phases displayed in the order in which Xcode will perform them, as shown in Figure 11-1 (using the ScrollView example provided with Xcode in the Examples folder's Carbon folder).

You can reorder the build phases by clicking and dragging them into a different order, and you can remove a build phase by selecting it and pressing the Delete key or by choosing Edit ➜ Delete. Xcode tells you how many files are involved in a particular build phase through the parenthesized number to the right of the build phase (for example, the "(7)" after Copy Headers in Figure 11-1). Click a build phase's disclosure triangle to see a list of that phase's files (or just select the build phase and see the list appear in the detail view).

▼ Caution

You can click and drag the build phases into a different order, but be sure you know what you're doing! Rearranging them in such a manner that an input necessary for a particular build phase hasn't yet been created will cause your build to fail.

If all you could do was reorder or delete build phases, that would be useful, but it would leave a gaping hole — after all, as prescient as Xcode's designers might seem, they

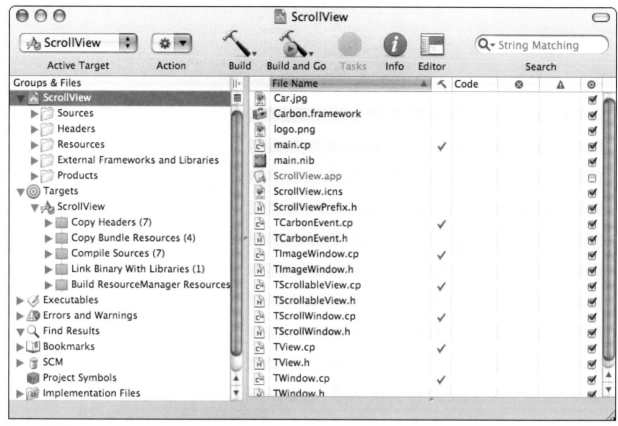

Figure 11-1
Build phases appear in order, subordinate to their target, in the Groups & Files list

aren't omniscient. You might have to run shell scripts to prepare some of your files, for example. You can add a build phase in a specific position by selecting the phase you want it to succeed, and choosing the build phase type from the Project ➜ New Build Phase submenu (or Control+click the phase you want to follow and choose from the contextual menu's Add ➜ New Build Phase submenu).

The two most likely build phase candidates for addition are a Copy Files build phase and a Shell Script build phase.

 Note

Thanks to drag and drop, you don't have to decide which phase you want the new one to follow ahead of time. You can neglect to select a phase when creating the new build phase and the new phase will be added at the end. Then, when you've decided its position in the logical sequence, just drag it into place.

Obviously, next to knowing which files Xcode is supposed to copy, a Copy Files build phase really needs to know *where* you want them copied. Adding the files is easy: Just select them and drag them to the Copy Files build phase entry in the Groups & Files list. Specifying the destination, though, requires a bit more thought. Once again, the Info/Inspector window is your specification portal. When you create the Copy Files build phase, Xcode immediately opens the window shown in Figure 11-2.

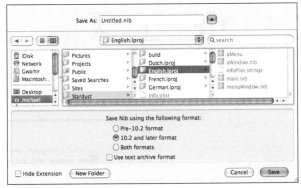

Figure 11-2
Specify where your files get copied in the Copy Files Info window

The Info window's Destination pop-up menu gives you three general destinations:

- an Absolute path in the file system that you specify in the Path text box,

- the same location as where the built target is to be placed, or

- a folder within your product's bundle (the Resources directory is the default location).

▼ **Tip**
You can specify a subdirectory within the chosen bundle directory in the Path text box.

If you don't want the files copied during development builds, select the Copy only when installing option.

The Shell Script build phase is useful when you want some task or tasks performed whenever you build. For example, notifying members of your test team that a new build is ready is easy to do by invoking a script to send mail — maybe even by executing an AppleScript (this is also how you can let your boss know that you're doing more than just playing *Starbase Defender* in your cubicle). Similarly, you could invoke a script to create a disk image that contains your build results. Figure 11-3 shows the Info window for a Shell Script build phase.

Here's how to specify a Shell Script build phase:

- Tell Xcode which Unix shell your script is written for in the Shell text box.

- Type your script in the (large) Script text box. If you only want the script executed on deployment builds, select the Run script only when installing option.

- Add the input files for your script in the Input Files list and the output files in the Output Files list (use the plus and minus buttons to add and remove items from the lists). If you don't specify any output files, the script executes every time you build; however, if there are output files specified, Xcode checks to see whether the input files were created before or after the output files to determine whether to execute the script.

Tip

You probably aren't going to want to have to type (or paste) scripts into the Script text box — Xcode's editor has surely spoiled you by this time. Besides, you probably want to debug the script before you set this phase up. So, once you have your script ready, use a source `scriptname.sh` entry in the Script text box, replacing `scriptname.sh` with your script's filename.

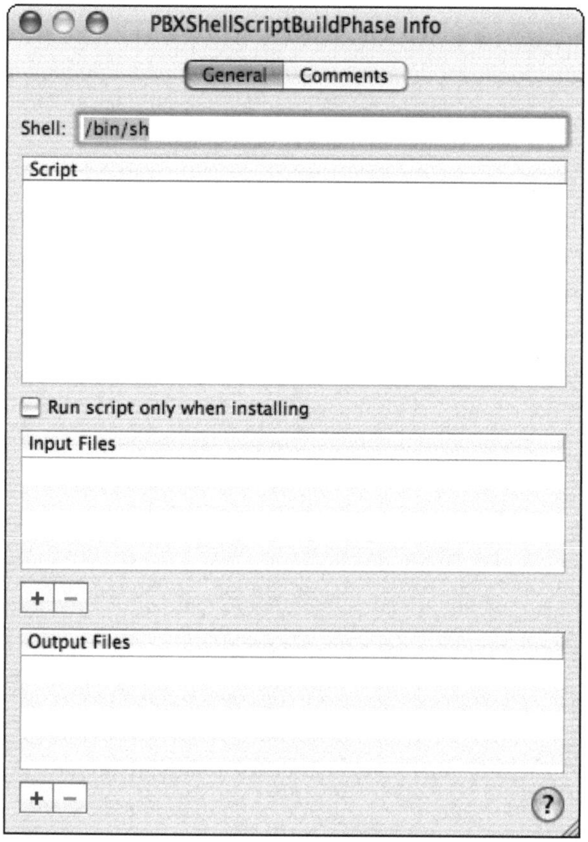

Figure 11-3
Set your Shell Script build phase parameters here

IT ALL DEPENDS

In anything larger than a trivial example project, you're undoubtedly going to have multiple source files, including many header files that get included in one or more source files. You might even have multiple intermediate targets. If you had to recompile and rebuild everything in your project every time you made a minor change to fix a bug or add a feature, you would be wasting a lot of time and computer cycles that could be better spent playing Halo or surfing the Web. Fortunately, Xcode is smart and only recompiles files that have changed or files that depend on files that changed. It performs this voodoo by creating a *dependency graph*, a structure it consults to ensure everything downstream from your change gets rebuilt to incorporate the change. Figure 11-4 illustrates a very simple example of how Xcode knows what to do when you make a small change at a low level of your project's code. In case you don't recognize the code, it is the ScrollView example project that comes with your Xcode installation.

▼ **Note**

Because Xcode doesn't actually provide a way to show you a dependency graph (maybe it's just shy), we've performed a "Find In Project" for `#include` statements in all the ScrollView project's .h and .cp files. Then we picked one, TView.h, that had a cascading impact to use for the example. Keep your eyes open for occurrences of TView.h in the figure; after all, it's what Xcode keeps an eye on when we make a change to it.

Making a change in TView.h impacts TView.cp and TScrollableView.h, the latter of which in turn impacts TScrollableView.cp and TScrollWindow.cp. Xcode knows this and will recompile all three .cp files before linking (or running, if you're doing a development build with ZeroLink as described later in this chapter in "Totally RAD-ical Techniques").

Figure 11-4
Part of ScrollView's dependency hierarchy

WE'VE COME A LONG WAY, BABY

More than 20 years ago — ancient history, in technology terms — in the BM (Before Mac) era, I (Dennis) worked at a company named Ashton•Tate that created and sold the leading database product for the IBM PC, an application named dBASE III. dBASE III was written in C, but the DOS-based compilers of the day were awkward command-line tools, the editors were horrific, and DOS wasn't a very good environment for automating a build process, so we did most of our development work on a DEC VAX minicomputer running BSD Unix because of the wealth of (also command-line) tools Unix offered. One of the most important of these was the make command because it was very easy with Unix's scripting to automate a make depend step that created and incorporated dependency lists into the makefile, allowing us to speed our edit-build-test cycle tremendously — of course, having a cross-compiler on the VAX that built Intel 8086 binaries didn't hurt. Using the DOS-based development tools of that era meant it was usually easier to just recompile and relink everything when you changed anything, lest you forgot one of the .c files that depended on a particular .h file you just changed.

In the mid-1980s, a small Boston-based company named Think Technologies released a couple of development environments for the Mac: Lightspeed Pascal and Lightspeed C. Compared to their competition, they deserved the name because the edit-compile-test cycle was so fast. This was due, primarily, to the introduction of the *project* concept — which kept track of dependencies behind the scenes and only compiled what needed to be compiled and relinked very quickly. In very short order these compilers became the most popular development tools for the Mac platform, easily surpassing even Apple's MPW (Macintosh Programmers' Workshop) environment, which was available for free — most developers were willing to part with cash for a fast and easy-to-use tool, even if it was somewhat less capable than the platform producer's free tool. (Actually, many developers of major projects adopted a hybrid approach, doing their development work with the Think products and then doing distribution builds with MPW to take advantage of slightly superior code optimization and linking.) A couple of years went by and Think dropped the Lightspeed name, rebranding the products as Think C and Think Pascal. Then Think Technologies was gobbled up by Symantec and the compilers' market shares rapidly dwindled: Metrowerks' CodeWarrior product became the de facto standard because Symantec was incredibly slow to get on the PowerPC bandwagon (and when it finally did so, it was with a version that had none of the polish to which Think customers were accustomed). Metrowerks provided the support and responsiveness that had originally been part of Think's success.

With development systems like Xcode and, previously, CodeWarrior and Think C, we don't even have to construct the dependency graph, table, or list (depending on how a particular system chooses to implement dependency tracking) — and a good thing, too, because today's applications are orders of magnitude larger and more complex than was dBASE III, one of the largest commercial applications of its time. After all, dBASE III fit on a single 5¼" floppy disk (or two, if you want to count the support files and examples that were on a second floppy). By contrast, database products like FileMaker Pro or Microsoft Access (Windows only) take up a couple hundred megabytes — well over 100 times the size of dBASE III.

STATUS SYMBOLS

Different developers have different needs and desires (and not just in terms of development systems, contrary to what *some* people may think), and so Xcode offers several,

increasingly more detailed, approaches to tracking a build's status as it progresses. The simplest and least detailed feedback mechanism is the project window's status bar, shown in Figure 11-5. The left side of the status bar displays the step currently being performed and, when the build

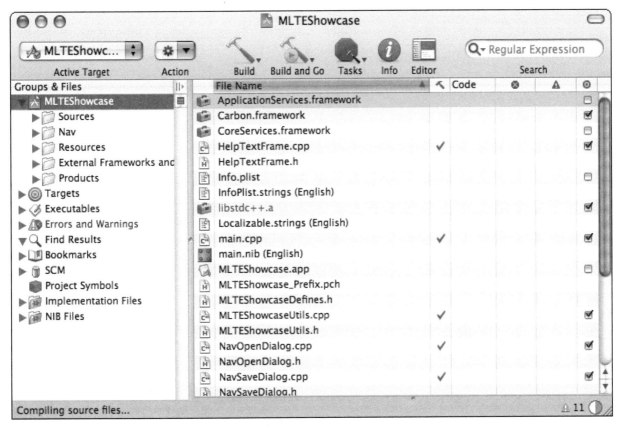

Figure 11-5
The status bar at the bottom of the Project window tells you what's going on

attempt is complete, the right side of the status bar will indicate whether the build succeeded or failed, as well as whether there were any errors (okay, this only happens with a failure) or warnings.

If you want to see more detail, you can open the Build Results window. There are three ways to bring the Build Results window front and center:

- You can set your Building Preferences to have the Build Results window open during builds as described in Chapter 3.

- You can double-click the status bar's Succeeded or Failed item.

- You can choose Build ➡ Build Results (Shift+⌘+B).

The Build Results window is shown in Figure 11-6. By default, the Build Log pane is hidden, but we're showing it here so that you can see what happens when the Show Build Log button is selected.

The Show Build Log button is one of four buttons at the left side of the separator between the Build Results pane and the Build Log pane. From left to right they are:

Figure 11-6
Xcode's Build Results window

- **Show build steps:** When this button is clicked, each step of the build process is detailed in the Build Results pane. When it is not selected, only steps that produce errors (or warnings) are shown.

- **Show warnings:** Click this button to have warnings displayed, or turn it off to only display errors.

- **Show build log:** Click this button to show the Build Log pane.

- **Auto-open Build Results window:** This is a project-specific override to the Building Preferences described in Chapter 3 and lets you specify when the Build Results window automatically opens and closes for this project only, regardless of how your Building Preferences are set.

 Tip

As we note in Chapter 3, we tend to have the Build Results window open at the start of each build so that we can see what's going on without having to track quickly flashing text in the status bar and automatically close if there are no errors or warnings. You might like these settings as well or, if a window opening and closing proves distracting to you, you can try some other combination. Mix and match to find what works best for you.

As always, double-click an error or warning and Xcode obligingly presents the offending file, scrolled to the offensive line, in either an embedded editor pane or an editor window, depending upon how your Editing Preferences are set.

TOTALLY RAD-ICAL TECHNIQUES

RAD is Rapid Application Development, and it is not so much one particular technology or one specific set of techniques as it is the Holy Grail that programmers have been seeking since the first bit was twiddled. Some backstory...

Very early in our programming careers, Michael and Dennis both worked at JPL (the Jet Propulsion Laboratory) in La Cañada, California — we were even in the same building on the same floor, albeit in different groups, for a while. It was there that we learned from various managers that almost every good programmer is a little bit lazy — but lazy in a good way. Because our egos make us want to believe that our managers were truthful when they told us we were good programmers, we'll tell you about "good lazy" from our perspective.

Good programmers like to produce code that works and does what it is supposed to do, when it is supposed to do so; however, they really hate to go back and rework code they've already written to remove bugs or shoehorn in functionality that they omitted the first time through. Therefore, good programmers will do the upfront work to make sure that they've dotted their *i*'s and crossed their *t*'s — the Design tools described in Chapter 10 assist greatly in that effort. In other words, programmers will expend a lot of effort making tools for themselves to automate repetitive, tedious, and mind-numbing tasks down the road. Think of those tools as the products of great programmers, created for their most appreciative audience — their peers.

But programmerly laziness also means that programmers want to speed up the edit-build-debug cycle so that they spend less time twiddling their thumbs. Xcode offers several features to help you cut down on the thumb-twiddling habit. Two of them are hardware related and won't be available to all of you.

- If you have a multiprocessor Mac (like a dual-processor G5), you can set your Building Preferences for the number of concurrent tasks you want Xcode to perform. Xcode will then allocate tasks to separate processors when and as they are available.

▼ Note

Apple obligingly sets the Building Preferences default here to "Best for this machine" for you, so if you have a dual-processor G5 (or G4), you're already set to take advantage of this feature. The only reason you might want to change the setting is if you plan to be doing something fairly processor-intensive concurrently with your builds and don't want Xcode hogging both processors.

- If you have multiple Macs on your network all with the same version of Xcode, you can use the Distributed Builds Preferences to have multiple-networked computers operate in parallel, each building a part of the project. (We, being merely poor starving authors who spend almost all our time writing about software, rarely have the time to develop a project that's large

enough to make us bemoan the fact that we can't afford multiple systems across which to distribute a build — but we will bemoan it anyway [*n.b.*: hardware donations from our devoted readership are *always* appreciated]).

Three other speed-up capabilities, though, are purely software in nature and any Xcode user can take advantage of one or more of them. These features are examples of a software genre known as RAD (Rapid Application Development) tools and, in the vernacular of the '80s, they're truly "rad" tools for software developers.

- You can greatly reduce the build time using *precompiled headers*. Precompiled headers are collections of frequently included system and project headers combined in a *prefix file* (a file that #includes and #defines the items you want precompiled) and stored in an intermediate, already processed form usable by the compiler. Obviously (we hope), you aren't going to be making changes to the system headers like Carbon.h, a header that is included in virtually every source file in a Carbon application and which, in turn, includes a number of other header files. Precompiling system headers means that the compiler doesn't have to repeatedly spend processing time on them for each file that includes the headers. Similarly, if your project-specific interfaces are stable, you can precompile those as well, saving the compiler even more time. Once you have your prefix file, use a target's Info/Inspector window to change the Prefix Header and Precompile Prefix Header settings on the Build pane.

- You can employ *predictive compiling* to have Xcode sneakily make a head start on the build process before you ever tell it to build. Because of the dependency graph (which we described earlier in this chapter) and Xcode's knowledge concerning the current build state of your targets, Xcode can bring files up to date in the background as soon as all the files on which it depends are ready, while you blithely continue editing. Xcode will even start compiling the file you're editing. Now, when you initiate a build, Xcode checks to see whether the temporary files it has created during the head-start process are current — if they are, it just copies them into place; otherwise, it discards the temporary file(s) and builds things as necessary. You can turn on Predictive Compiling by selecting the Use Predictive Compilation option in Building Preferences (see Figure 11-7).

- The last RAD tool is *ZeroLink* and it is only available for development builds. ZeroLink means that Xcode creates an application stub that points to each of the unlinked object (.o) files comprising the application and then links the object file in at runtime as needed. ZeroLink is turned on for development builds by default in the Development build style. You can turn it off by opening the project's Info or Inspector window and deselecting ZeroLink in the Development build style, as shown in Figure 11-8.

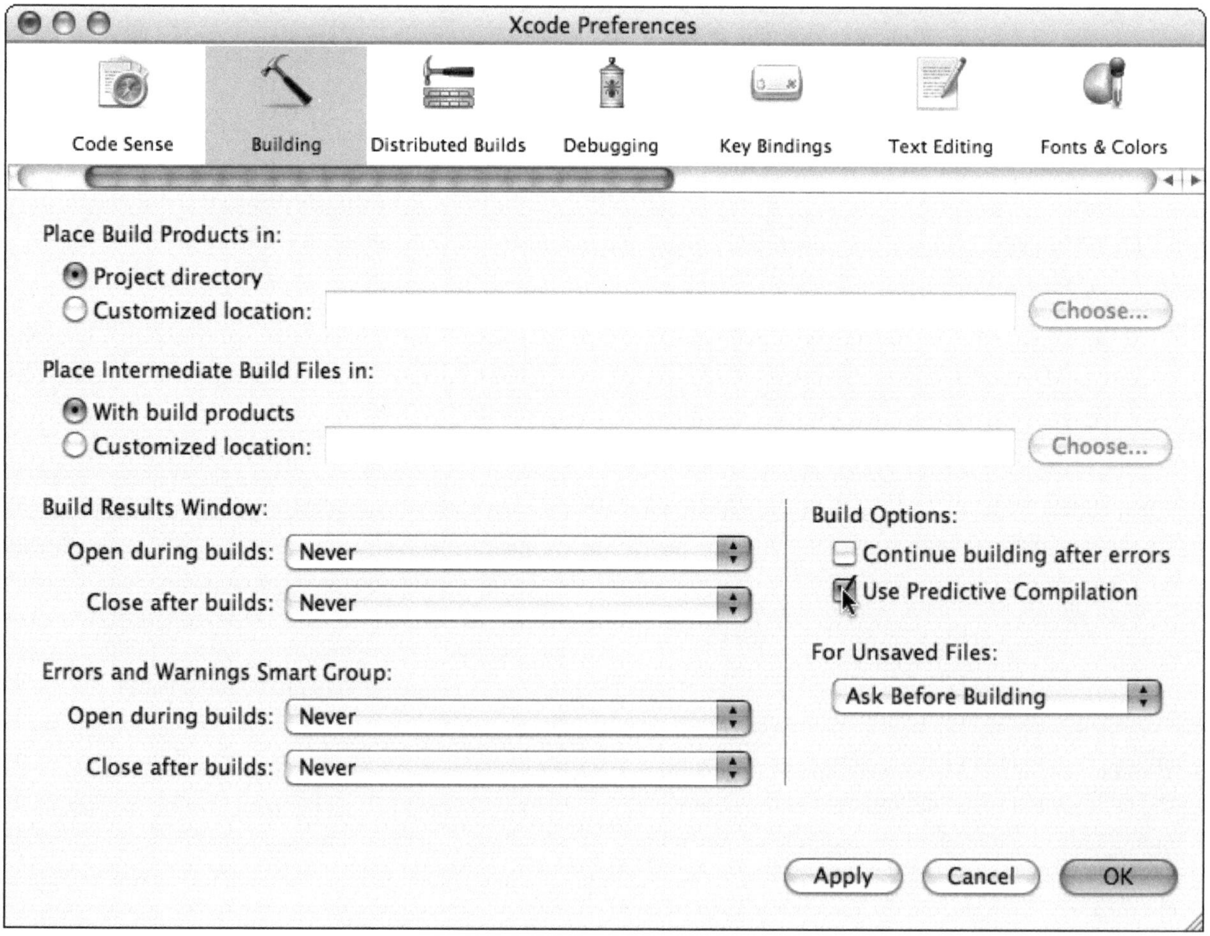

Figure 11-7
Turn Predictive Compiling on in your Building Preferences

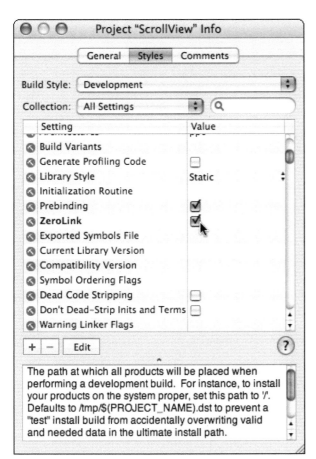

Figure 11-8
Turn ZeroLink off (or back on) in the project Info's
Development Build Style pane

BUILD LOG

In this chapter, we've looked at the origins of Carbon and
described the particular steps of the build process. We
explained how build dependencies work and how Xcode
keeps track of them. We then looked at an actual build and
showed how you can monitor the build process in the way
that seems best to you. Finally, we explored the rapid-
application-development features incorporated into Xcode
and expressed our sadness that we aren't rich enough to
afford the top-of-the-line development network of multiple dual-processor G5s that would allow us to take advantage of some of these features.

12

Cocoa Is the NeXT Big Thing

Cocoa with a Marshmallow on Top
It All Depends• Status Symbols
Totally RAD-ical Techniques
Build Log

It was the era of the Mac IIx and System 7.0.1 when we first saw one: a jet-black 12-inch cube with a black keyboard and black 17-inch grayscale monitor. The only splash of color was in its logo, which read, "NeXT." It ran a "grown-up" operating system, something called Unix, and it came with a software development tool kit that actually let you build a complete text editor just by clicking and dragging a few graphics around the screen. What made this "interface building" kit possible was the magic of "object-oriented programming" as realized in a bunch of software libraries written in a new programming language called "Objective-C."

Today's Mac OS X has more than a splash of color, but it still runs the same grown-up operating system, it still comes with a development tool kit that actually lets you build a complete text editor just by clicking and dragging a few graphics around the screen, and it still provides a powerful object-oriented programming environment made possible by a bunch of software libraries known as Cocoa, written in a venerable programming language called Objective-C. Cocoa *is* NeXT's Big Thing, living on into the 21st century as one of the core components and essential development paradigms for Mac OS X. And it's bigger than ever.

In addition to all of the cool technologies that Cocoa could offer the developer when it was NeXTStep (and if you doubt its essential coolness, remember that the early NeXTStep environment was what Tim Berners-Lee used to create a little thing called the World Wide Web), it now offers the developer all of Apple's cool Mac OS technologies, too — and more stuff is being added to it all the time. Because Cocoa is so easy to use and so powerful, and perhaps because so many of

Apple's whizziest Mac OS X technologies tend to debut in Cocoa, Apple recommends that developers who are new to the Mac start with Cocoa.

Like the sweet drink after which it is named, it can quickly become habit-forming.

In a good way.

Really.

 Note

> If you see amazing similarities between this chapter and the preceding chapter, it's probably because they *are* amazingly similar. Chapter 11 covers almost exactly the same material, using many of the same words (and even some of the same jokes), but presented from the perspective of a Carbon programmer. Turn back to Chapter 11 if the virtual life-forms you develop are Carbon-based.

COCOA WITH A MARSHMALLOW ON TOP

Remember the templates we saw in Chapter 2? They include the basic build instructions for almost any application you want to build (so, really, we don't have to write this chapter at all — oh, right, we have to, because it's in the contract). And, if you add any targets to your projects beyond what the template provides, Xcode will know how to build those as well after analyzing the dependencies (see "It All Depends," later in this chapter). Xcode sometimes seems as all-knowing as Santa: It knows what to do with your project's files and targets; it knows which compiler(s) to use, which files to copy and to where, which frameworks and libraries need to be linked, and in what order to perform its tasks; it may even know when you've been sleeping, and when you've been awake (so be *good* for goodness' sake!).

OBJECT-ION, YOUR HONOR

We'll be talking about Objective-C a lot in this chapter, but you should realize that Cocoa isn't just for Objective-C programmers: As you discover in the next couple of chapters, you can also build Cocoa applications in Java, call Cocoa methods from Carbon apps, and even write Cocoa apps that consist of a blend of Objective-C and C++ (courtesy of the Frankensteinian monster of all C languages, Objective-C++). Apple is proud of Cocoa and wants you to use it and is always finding new ways to make more and more developers Cocoa addicts.

The process of taking all your project's pieces and constructing your end product is called the *build process* and, quite unoriginally, the mechanism the build process employs is called the *build system*. Back in Chapter 3 we introduce *targets*; in the Xcode world, targets are the build process's roadmaps to creating products (in some ways, a target is kinda sorta like a traditional makefile because it specifies the make *process*). Although Xcode's build system(s) can produce many different target types, we're concerned here with Cocoa-based applications; however, keep in mind that your Cocoa application target might depend on subordinate targets, such as a proprietary framework or a Unix command-line tool. Xcode, in the process of building your application, ensures that such subordinate targets are current and available.

That targets are roadmaps (or recipes or blueprints) is an important concept, because we poor English-speaking folks are accustomed to correlating the word "target" with a goal or a physical entity. Fortunately, a target and the product are very closely related, almost like gestation and an embryo. The target organizes the build process's four inputs:

- Each target includes a list of input **files** that need to be processed (compiled, copied, and so on) to create the final product.

- The operations required to process the above-mentioned files are organized into **build phases**. Each build phase includes a list of files and a task to be performed on those files; for example, preprocessing headers (see "Totally RAD-ical Techniques," later in this chapter), compiling sources, or copying nibs.

- Just how a build phase is performed is controlled by variables called **build settings**. Compiler options are examples of build settings, as are the paths to where files are copied.

- To determine which build settings are to be employed is the province of **build rules**. The most common example of a build rule for an Objective-C/Cocoa project is that files with the .m extension are to be compiled as Objective-C sources. Build rules only apply to the Sources and Resource Management build phases.

Associated with each target is a *product type*, describing the build process's output product (for example, a development build, useful for debugging, or a deployment build, useful for, say, distributing to users). Xcode uses the product type to establish the default build settings, which build phases will take place, and how the product will be structured. It all goes something like this:

- You create a project and Xcode establishes a number of build phases for you, based on the project template you select.

- As you add your source files to the project, Xcode consults its build rules to determine in which build phases the files belong.

- Xcode examines the dependency graph (see "It All Depends," later in this chapter) that it creates for your target in order to determine the sequence in which the

build phases should be executed. This ensures that the files produced by one build phase, and that are needed by another build phase, actually exist when that subsequent phase begins. For example, if you haven't compiled your source files yet, the object files won't exist for the link phase (compare the famous Viking terms of engagement: first you pillage, and *then* you burn).

- The build progresses and, assuming that there are no errors, your product comes into being. (If there are errors, you fix them and restart the build.)

If you click a target's disclosure triangle in the Groups & Files list, you see the build phases displayed in the order in which Xcode performs them, as shown in Figure 12-1 (the figure shows the TextEdit example provided with Xcode, which you can find in the Examples folder's App-Kit folder — and, yes, that is the actual source code for Apple's TextEdit application).

You can reorder the build phases by clicking and dragging them into a different order, and you can remove a build phase by selecting it and pressing the Delete key or by choosing Edit → Delete. Xcode displays a parenthesized number to the right of each build phase (for example, the "(6)" after Copy Headers in Figure 12-1) that tells you how many files are involved in a particular build phase. Click a build phase's disclosure triangle to see a list of that phase's files (or just select the build phase and see the list appear in the detail view).

▼ Caution

You can click and drag the build phases into a different order, but be sure you know what you're doing! If you rearrange them so that a file required for a particular build phase won't be created until a subsequent phase, your build will fail and the gods will weep.

You can do more with a target's build phases than merely drag them around and delete them. For example, you may

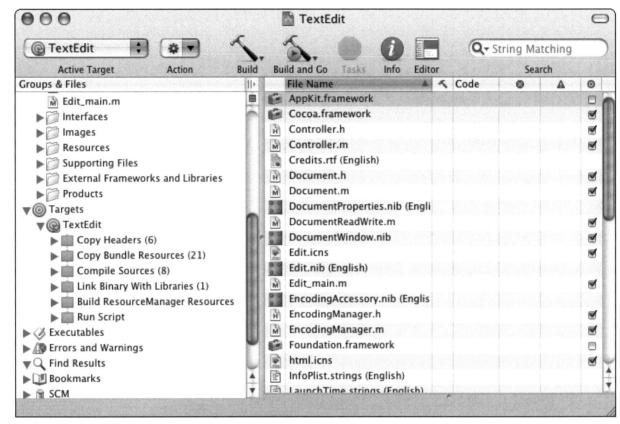

Figure 12-1
Build phases appear in order, subordinate to their target, in the Groups & Files list

need to create a build phase to run one or more shell scripts to prepare some of your files. You can add a build phase in a specific position by selecting the phase you want it to follow, and then choosing the build phase type you want from the Project ➜ New Build Phase submenu (or Control+click the phase you want the new phase to follow and choose from the contextual menu's Add ➜ New Build Phase submenu).

The two most common types of build phases you are likely to add are a Copy Files build phase and a Shell Script build phase.

 Note

Thanks to drag and drop, you don't have to decide which phase you want the new one to follow ahead of time. You can neglect to select a phase when creating the new build phase and the new phase will be added at the end. Then, when you've decided its position in the logical sequence, just drag it into place.

A Copy Files build phase is useful when your product requires some particular files included with it; for example, you may want to store a PDF version of your app's documentation in its bundle or some sample data files for a demo mode. Obviously, in addition to knowing which files Xcode is supposed to copy, a Copy Files build phase really needs to know *where* you want them copied. Adding the files is easy: Just select them and drag them to the Copy Files build phase entry in the Groups & Files list. Specifying the destination, though, requires a bit more thought. Once again, the Info/Inspector window is your specification portal. When you create the Copy Files build phase, Xcode immediately opens the window shown in Figure 12-2.

Figure 12-2
Specify where your files get copied in the Copy Files Info window

The Info window's Destination pop-up menu gives you three general destinations:

- an Absolute path in the file system that you specify in the Path text box,

- the same location as where the built target is to be placed, or

- a folder within your product's bundle (the Resources directory is the default location).

▼ **Tip**

You can specify a subdirectory within the chosen bundle directory in the Path text box.

If you don't want the files copied during development builds, select the Copy only when installing option.

The Shell Script build phase is useful when you want some task or tasks performed whenever you build. For example, notifying members of your test team that a new build is ready is easy to do by invoking a script to send mail — maybe even by executing an AppleScript (this is also how you can let your boss know that you're doing more than just playing *Starbase Defender* in your cubicle). Similarly, you could invoke a script to create a disk image that contains your build results. Figure 12-3 shows the Info window for a Shell Script build phase.

Here's how to specify a Shell Script build phase:

- Tell Xcode which Unix shell your script is written for in the Shell text box. Figure 12-3 is using the venerable sh shell.

- Type your script in the (large) Script text box. If you only want the script executed on deployment builds, select the Run script only when installing option.

- Add the input files used by your script in the Input Files list and the output files in the Output Files list (use the plus and minus buttons to add and remove items from the lists). If you don't specify any output files, the script executes every time you build; however, if there are output files specified, Xcode checks to see whether the input files were created before or after the output files to determine whether to execute the script.

Figure 12-3
Set your Shell Script build phase parameters here

You probably aren't going to want to have to type (or paste) scripts into the Script text box — Xcode's editor has surely spoiled you by this time. Besides, you probably want to debug the script before you set this phase up. So, once you have your script ready, use a `source scriptname.sh` entry in the Script text box, replacing `scriptname.sh` with your script's filename.

IT ALL DEPENDS

In every Cocoa project, you're undoubtedly going to have multiple source files, including header files that get included in one or more source files. Complex projects can have a lot of files, and might even have multiple intermediate targets. If Xcode had to recompile and rebuild everything in your project every time you made a minor change to fix a bug or add a feature, you would end up wasting a lot of time and computer cycles that you could better spend playing Knights of the Old Empire or writing your blog. Fortunately, Xcode is smart and only recompiles files that have changed or files that depend on files that changed. It performs this voodoo by creating a *dependency graph*, a structure it consults to ensure that everything downstream from your change gets rebuilt to incorporate the change. Figure 12-4 illustrates a very simple example of how Xcode knows what to do when you make a small change at a low level of your project's code. The example is, again, Apple's own TextEdit application, which is included in the AppKit examples.

▼ **Note**

Because Xcode doesn't actually provide a way to show you a dependency graph (maybe it's just shy), we've performed a "FInd in Project" for `#import` statements in all the TextEdit project's .h and .m files. Then we picked one, EncodingManager.h, that had a cascading impact to use for the example. Keep your eyes open for occurrences of ScalingScrollView.h in the figure; after all, it's what Xcode keeps an eye on when we make a change to it.

Making a change in EncodingManager.h affects Encoding-Manager.m (of course) and Preferences.m, as well as Document.m and Document.h. Xcode knows this so that when EncodingManager.h is changed, Xcode recompiles not only it but also the three .m files and the .h file before linking (or running, if you're doing a development build with ZeroLink as described later in this chapter in "Totally RAD-ical Techniques").

WE'VE COME A LONG WAY, BABY

More than 20 years ago — ancient history, in technology terms — in the BM (Before Mac) era, I (Dennis) worked at a company named Ashton·Tate that created and sold the leading database product for the IBM PC, an application named dBASE III. dBASE III was written in C, but the DOS-based compilers of the day were awkward command-line tools, the editors were horrific, and DOS wasn't a very good environment for automating a build process, so we did most of our development work on a DEC VAX minicomputer running BSD Unix because of the wealth of (also command-line) tools Unix offered. One of the most important of these was the make command because it was very easy with Unix's scripting to automate a make depend step that created and incorporated dependency lists into the makefile, allowing us to speed our edit-build-test cycle tremendously — of course, having a cross-compiler on the VAX that built Intel 8086 binaries didn't hurt. Using the DOS-based development tools of that era meant it was usually easier to just recompile and relink everything when you changed anything, lest you forgot one of the .c files that depended upon a particular .h file you just changed.

In the mid-1980s, a small Boston-based company named Think Technologies released a couple of development environments for the Mac: Lightspeed Pascal and Lightspeed C. Compared to their competition, they deserved the name because the edit-compile-test cycle was so fast. This was due, primarily, to the introduction of the *project* concept — which kept track of dependencies behind the scenes and only compiled what needed to be compiled and relinked very quickly. In very short order, these compilers became the most popular development tools for the Mac platform, easily surpassing even Apple's MPW (Macintosh Programmers' Workshop) environment, which was available for free — most developers were willing to part with cash for a fast and easy-to-use tool, even if it was somewhat less capable than the platform producer's free tool. (Actually, many developers of major projects adopted a hybrid approach, doing their development work with the Think products and then doing distribution builds with MPW to take advantage of slightly superior code optimization and linking.) A couple of years went by and Think dropped the Lightspeed name, rebranding the products as Think C and Think Pascal. Then Think Technologies was gobbled up by Symantec and the compilers' market shares rapidly dwindled: Metrowerks' CodeWarrior product became the de facto standard because Symantec was incredibly slow to get on the PowerPC bandwagon (and when they finally did so, it was with a version that had none of the polish to which Think customers were accustomed). Metrowerks provided the support and responsiveness that had originally been part of Think's success.

With development systems like Xcode and, previously, CodeWarrior and Think C, we don't even have to construct the dependency graph, table, or list (depending on how a particular system chooses to implement dependency tracking) — and a good thing, too, because today's applications are orders of magnitude larger and more complex than was dBASE III, one of the largest commercial applications of its time. After all, dBASE III fit on a single $5^1/_4$" floppy disk (or two, if you want to count the support files and examples that were on a second floppy). By contrast, database products like FileMaker Pro or Microsoft Access (Windows only) take up a couple hundred megabytes — well over 100 times the size of dBASE III.

Figure 12-4
Part of TextEdit's dependency hierarchy

STATUS SYMBOLS

Different developers have different needs and desires (and not just in terms of development systems, contrary to what *some* people may think), and so Xcode offers several, increasingly more detailed, approaches to tracking a build's status as it progresses. The simplest and least detailed feedback mechanism is the status bar at the bottom of the project window, shown in Figure 12-5. The left side of the status bar displays the step currently being performed and, when the build attempt is complete, the right side of the status bar will indicate whether the build succeeded or

failed, as well as whether there were any errors (okay, this only happens with a failure) or warnings.

If you want to see more detail, you can open the Build Results window. There are three ways to bring the Build Results window front and center:

- You can set your Building Preferences to have the Build Results window open during builds as we describe in Chapter 3.

- You can double-click the status bar's Succeeded or Failed item.

- You can choose Build → Build Results (Shift+⌘+B).

The Build Results window is shown in Figure 12-6. By default, the Build Log pane is hidden, but we're showing it here so that you can see what happens when the Show Build Log button is selected.

The Show Build Log button, by the way, is one of the four tiny buttons living on the left side of the separator between the Build Results pane and the Build Log pane. From left to right these tiny buttons are:

- **Show build steps:** When this button is selected, each step of the build process is detailed in the Build Results pane. When it is not selected, only steps that produce errors (or warnings) are shown.

- **Show warnings:** Select this button to display warnings as well as errors, or turn it off to display only errors.

- **Show build log:** Select this button to show the Build Log pane.

- **Auto-open Build Results window:** This button produces a pop-up menu that lets you override Xcode's Building Preferences (which we describe in Chapter 3) so that you can choose when the Build Results window

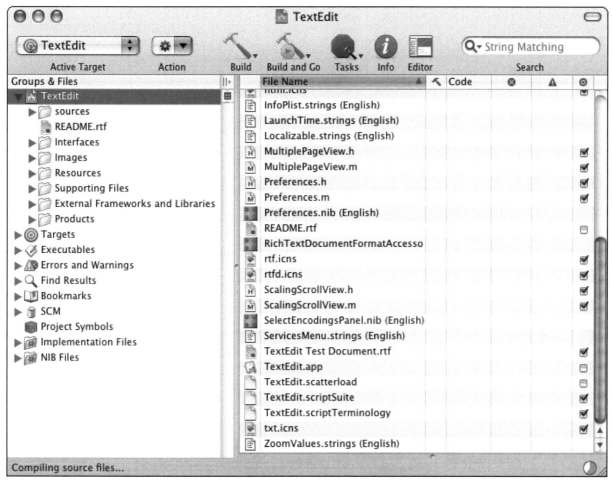

Figure 12-5
The status bar at the bottom of the Project window tells you what's going on

automatically opens and closes for this project only, regardless of how your Building Preferences are set.

▼ Tip

As we note in Chapter 3, we like to have the Build Results window open at the start of each build, so that we can see what's going on without having to track quickly flashing text in the status bar, and to have it automatically close if the build produces no errors or warnings. You might like these settings as well — if a window automatically opening and closing doesn't disturb you.

As always, you can double-click an error or warning to make Xcode obligingly display the offending file, scrolled to show the offensive line, in either an embedded editor pane or an editor window, depending upon how your Editing Preferences are set.

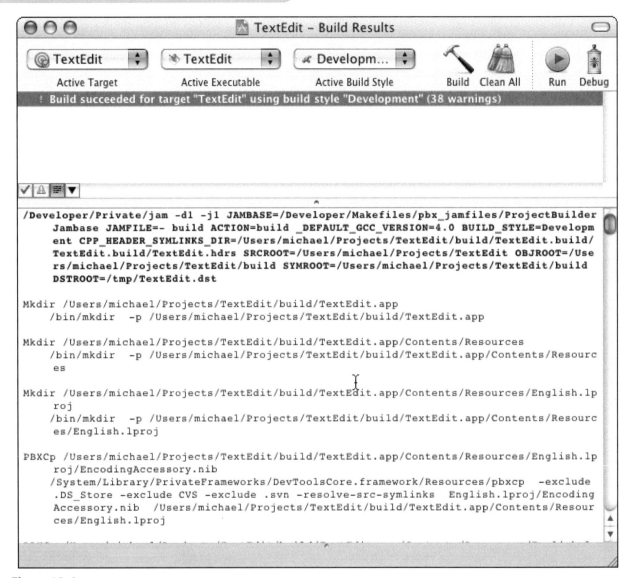

Figure 12-6
Xcode's Build Results window

TOTALLY RAD-ICAL TECHNIQUES

RAD is Rapid Application Development, and it is not so much one particular technology or one specific set of techniques as it is the Holy Grail that programmers have been seeking since the first bit was twiddled. Some backstory...

Very early in our programming careers, Michael and Dennis both worked at JPL (the Jet Propulsion Laboratory) in

La Cañada, California — we were even in the same building on the same floor, albeit in different groups, for a while. It was there that we learned from various managers that almost every good programmer is a little bit lazy — but lazy in a good way. Because our egos make us want to believe that our managers were truthful when they told us we were good programmers, we'll tell you about "good lazy" from our perspective.

Good programmers like to produce code that works and does what it is supposed to do, when it is supposed to do so; however, they really hate to go back and rework code they've already written to remove bugs or shoehorn in functionality that they omitted the first time through. Therefore, good programmers will do the upfront work to make sure that they've dotted their *i*'s and crossed their *t*'s — the Design tools described in Chapter 10 assist greatly in that effort. In other words, programmers will expend a lot of effort making tools for themselves to automate repetitive, tedious, and mind-numbing tasks down the road. Think of those tools as the products of great programmers, created for their most appreciative audience — their peers.

In one very important sense, Cocoa is in and of itself a RAD tool: The dynamic runtime system, the rich and extensible class libraries, and the intelligent power of Interface Builder make it possible to design and build very complex applications quite easily and, therefore, quickly. How quickly? Well, check out the example TextEdit project again, which is extraordinarily compact given its feature set. The number of source files is quite small — only eight implementation files, most of which are only a few hundred lines long. That's small. Most of that is because much of the app's work is done by Cocoa itself, and Cocoa is the result of years and years of applied programmerly laziness.

Programmerly laziness means that programmers not only want to reduce the amount of work that it takes to write an application, but to streamline the edit-build-debug cycle so that they spend less time twiddling their thumbs. Again, consider the TextEdit project: Building the entire app only takes a minute or so on a low-end 500 Mhz G3 iBook with 256MB of RAM. That's rapid. Much of that is due to the speed and efficiency of the GCC compilers and, again, that is the result of years and years of applied programmerly laziness.

But, beyond these, Xcode offers several additional features to help you cut down on the thumb-twiddling habit. Two of its RAD features are hardware related and won't be available to all of you.

- If you have a multiprocessor Mac (like a dual-processor G5), you can set your Building Preferences for the number of concurrent tasks you want Xcode to perform. Xcode will then allocate tasks to separate processors when and as they are available.

▼ Note

Apple obligingly sets the Building Preferences default here to "Best for this machine" for you, so if you have a dual-processor G5 (or G4), you're already set to take advantage of this feature. The only reason you might want to change the setting is if you plan to do something fairly processor-intensive concurrently with your builds and don't want Xcode hogging both processors.

- If you have multiple Macs on your network all with the same version of Xcode, you can use the Distributed Builds Preferences to have multiple networked computers operate in parallel, each building a part of the project. (We, being merely poor starving authors who spend almost all our time writing about software, rarely have the time to develop a project that's large enough to make us bemoan the fact that we can't afford multiple systems across which to distribute a build — but we will bemoan it anyway [*n.b.*: hardware donations from our devoted readership are *always* appreciated].)

Three other speed-up capabilities, though, are purely software in nature and any Xcode user can take advantage of one or more of them. These RAD tools are, in the vernacular of the '80s, truly "rad" tools for Xcoders.

- You can greatly reduce the build time using *precompiled headers*. Precompiled headers are collections of frequently included system and project headers combined in a *prefix file* (a file that #includes and #defines the items you want precompiled) and stored in an intermediate, already processed, form usable by the compiler. Obviously (we hope), you aren't going to be making changes to the system headers like Cocoa.h, a header that is included in virtually every source file in a Cocoa application and which, in turn, includes a number of other header files (such as AppKit.h, which in turn includes over 150 other headers). Precompiling system headers means that the compiler doesn't have to repeatedly spend processing time on them for each file that includes the headers. Similarly, if your project-specific interfaces are stable, you can precompile those as well, saving the compiler even more time. Once you have your prefix file, use project's Info/ Inspector window to change the Prefix Header and Precompile Prefix Header settings on the Styles pane (see Figure 12-7).

- You can employ *predictive compiling* to have Xcode sneakily make a head start on the build process before you ever tell it to build. Because of the dependency graph (which we described earlier in this chapter) and Xcode's knowledge concerning the current build state of your targets, Xcode can bring files up to date in the background as soon as all the files on which it depends are ready, while you blithely continue editing. Xcode will even start compiling the file you're editing. Now, when you initiate a build, Xcode checks to see whether the temporary files it has created during the headstart process are current — if they are, it

just copies them into place, otherwise it discards the temporary file(s) and builds things as necessary. You can turn on Predictive Compiling by selecting the Use Predictive Compilation option in Building Preferences (see Figure 12-8).

Figure 12-7
Precompiling headers can accelerate your build process

- The last RAD tool is *ZeroLink* and it is only available for development builds. ZeroLink means that Xcode creates an application stub that points to each of the unlinked object's (.o) files comprising the application and then links the object file in at runtime as needed. ZeroLink is turned on for development builds by default in the Development build style. You can turn it off by opening the project's Info or Inspector window and deselecting ZeroLink in the Development build style, as shown in Figure 12-9.

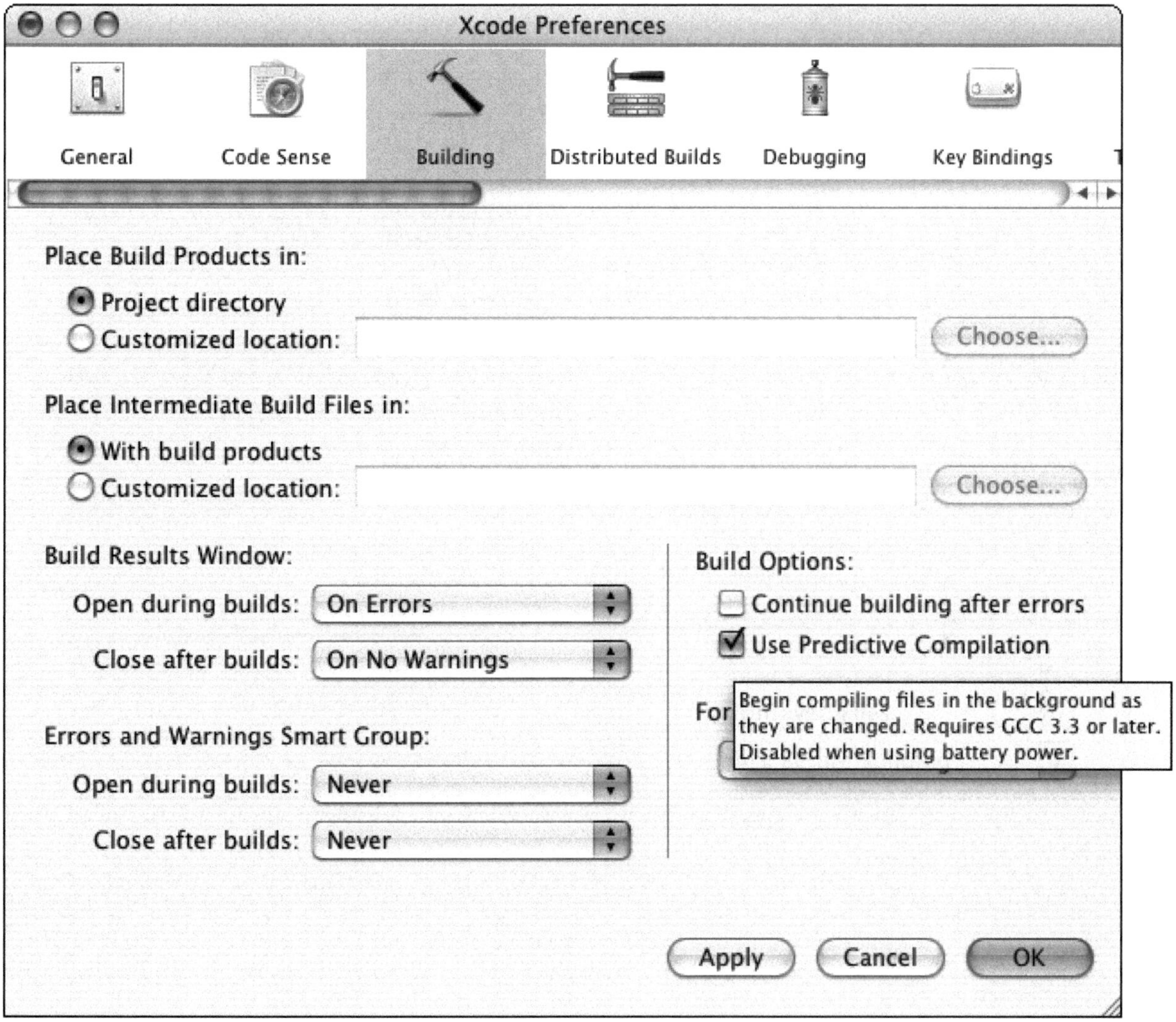

Figure 12-8
Turn Use Predictive Compilation on in your Building Preferences

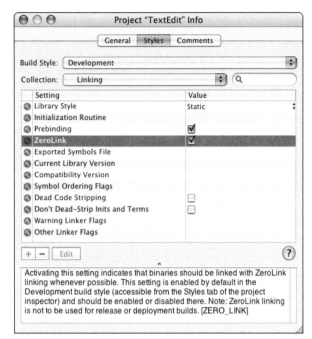

Figure 12-9
Turn ZeroLink off (or back on) in the project Info's
Development Build Style pane

BUILD LOG

In this chapter (which duplicates much of the previous chapter from a Cocoa perspective), we've looked at the origins of Cocoa and described the particular steps of the build process. We explained how build dependencies work, and how Xcode keeps track of them. We then looked at an actual build and showed how you can monitor the build process in the way that seems best to you. Finally, we explored the rapid-application-development features incorporated into Xcode, and expressed our sadness that we aren't rich enough to afford the top-of-the-line development network of multiple dual-processor G5s that would allow us to take advantage of some of these features.

13

Java Nice Day

So Many Brews
Cocoa-Covered Espresso Beans
I Take My Java Black • Ant No Big Deal
Filtering the Grounds

There was a time when Java was really, really hot — and, no, we're not talking about coffee, although one of us, at least, does enjoy a cup of coffee that's blacker'n sin and hotter'n h... oh, right, getting off-topic again. Sorry. Anyway, there was a time when Java was so hot in the information technology world that marketing people would do just about anything to link their products with the ultrahype being accorded Sun Microsystems's cross-platform object-oriented programming language (for example, that's how JavaScript, a scripting language developed at Netscape that actually has *nothing* to do with Java, came to be called JavaScript). However, before Mac OS X, Java on the Mac seemed something of an afterthought — slow, buggy, and perennially two versions behind the one the rest of world used. Poor Java support, in fact, seemed to be just one more nail in the coffin of the soon-to-be-dead Apple Computer, Inc.

Luckily, Apple woke up and (cheap pun coming!) smelled the coffee. As Mac OS X began to take shape, Apple worked closely with Sun to make Java into a first-class peer of C++ and Objective-C on Mac OS X. And it largely succeeded — so well, as we noted earlier in this book, that Power-Books running Mac OS X have become the preferred techno-arm-candy of many of Sun's Java development team members.

Even though the Java hype-storm has abated, the Java language, along with its accompanying runtime interpreter and code libraries, remains a very important tool for software developers — especially those developers attempting to craft rich, cross-platform products meant to be deployed on the Web or in enterprise environments or both. But Java on Mac OS X is not just for the cross-platform biz-app crowd: The Java language and its object-oriented methodology turns out to be a pretty good fit for one of Apple's own technologies, too, a sweet little brew that it calls Cocoa.

SO MANY BREWS

Good heavens, where to start? Java is so many things, all sort of intertwingled together: It's an object-oriented programming language; it's a virtual machine running under a variety of operating systems; it's a compiler; it's a bunch of code libraries; it's a floor wax *and* a dessert topping. Trying to figure out where and how it fits into Mac OS X and into Xcode can boggle even the most boggle-resistant of minds.

In its guise as the cross-platform, trademarked, Write Once, Run Anywhere software technology developed by Sun Microsystems, Java is supported in Mac OS X by the *Java Runtime Environment*. This environment provides the virtual machine that runs your Java binaries; the class libraries that make up the *Java 2 Platform Standard Edition* (J2SE); and the frameworks that implement Java so that, among other things, Java apps and applets can transparently employ the native Mac OS X look and feel. Mac OS X also includes various tools and utilities (such as the *javac* compiler — essential for compiling Java code) that Java developers from other platforms expect — nay, demand — to have available. And, as we'll see in more detail in the next section, Mac OS X also includes a *Java/Objective-C runtime bridge* that allows Java code to call the Mac's Cocoa APIs. What Java on Mac OS X means to you depends on what you mean to do with it: It can do a lot of different stuff.

Xcode can help you with the "what you mean to do with it" part. The New Project maitre d'ude that we met back in Chapter 2 offers you a number of choices (see Figure 13-1).

Figure 13-1
You remember the maitre d'ude, don't you? He wants to serve you Java

Some of these offerings, such as the Cocoa-Java application choices, give you a project that looks very much like any other Cocoa project (see Figure 13-2); all you have to do is write your implementation in Java instead of in Objective-C.

Other choices produce projects that don't look *quite* so familiar to Mac programmers; for example, a project meant to produce a pure cross-platform Java applet that employs Java's standard AWT comes with a rather different assortment of source files and build phases (see Figure 13-3); yet, even here, all you have to do is write your

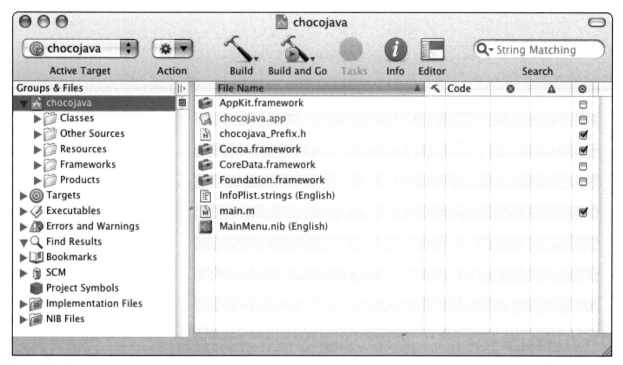

Figure 13-2
Cocoa-Java projects look surprisingly familiar

LOOK INTO THE SUN

Apple provides a lot of documentation scattered around inside of Xcode and on its developer site (http://developer.apple.com), but most of it discusses Apple-specific implementation and development details. For example, Xcode provides the comprehensive list of Cocoa-Java APIs, and Xcode's code-sense feature (described in Chapter 6) happily completes your statements for you when you're writing in Java, just as it does for Objective-C and C++ code. But when it comes to the authoritative documentation of the standard Java class libraries (which Java developers call *packages* — and isn't *that* confusing) such as Abstract Window Toolkit (AWT) or Swing, Apple suggests that you turn to Java's mother ship: Sun Microsystems (http://java.sun.com).

And that's as it should be. Apple wants to make Java developers happy and eager to work on the Mac, and that means a delicate tap dance: Apple has to make Java work as seamlessly with Mac OS X and Xcode as possible, but it also has to preserve Java's distinct identity and the essential qualities that make it so practical for cross-platform development. Those essential qualities include the Java libraries, on which only Sun can speak authoritatively... as a certain other software company eventually discovered in the course of years of litigation.

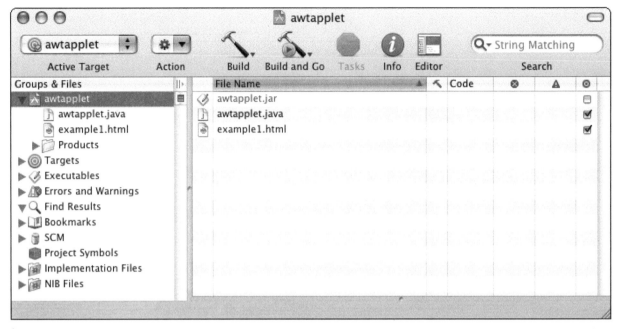

Figure 13-3
Pure Java projects may look *jar*ring

applet using Xcode's editor and then build it... Xcode knows what to do.

Some Java projects forego the typical set of build-phases that make up a target and use the popular cross-platform Ant build system (see Figure 13-4); Xcode even knows how to invoke that as well. We described Ant in Chapter 2 and we'll discuss it in more detail in "Ant No Big Deal," later in this chapter.

Over time, Xcode (and its predecessor, Project Builder) have become increasingly Java-savvy, and that trend shows no signs of abating. These days, it can brew up a mighty fine cup of coffee.

COCOA-COVERED ESPRESSO BEANS

Apple goes to great lengths to point out that Java is a "first-class citizen" (as one of its Web pages puts it) on Mac OS X. Nowhere is this more clearly seen than in the Java version of Cocoa: Just about the entire set of Objective-C Cocoa classes is also available to Java programmers who want to write Cocoa programs. Which raises two questions:

- How'd they do that?

- Why would a Java programmer want to write a Cocoa app, anyway?

Apple answers the first question this way: The "affinities" between Objective-C (Cocoa's native language) and Java "are so strong that Apple found it possible to build a runtime

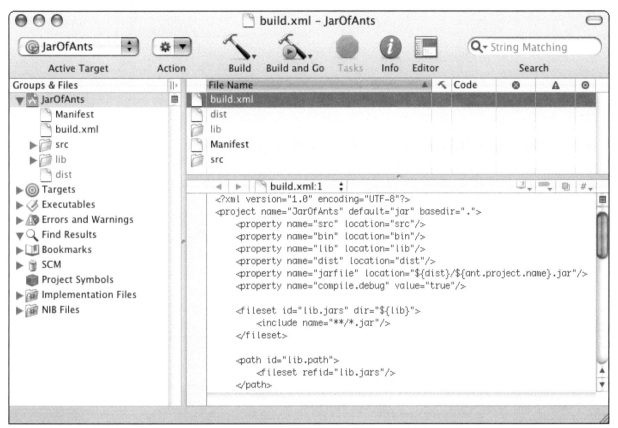

Figure 13-4
Farming out a build to an Ant

I DREAM OF JNI

Surprisingly, at least to us, Xcode doesn't have a new project template for building JNI libraries (that is, native code files that Java apps can call; JNI is Java Native Interface and is one dandy way of speeding up a Java application... if you don't need it to be cross-platform). This omission is especially surprising, given that Xcode *does* have a template for building a Java application that *calls* a JNI library. (Of course, as we're writing this, Xcode 2 is still in development, and a JNI library template *may* ship with the release version... but then again, it may not.)

There is, however, some sample code at Apple's site that contains a Project Builder project (compatible with Xcode) that builds both a JNI library and an application that calls it. You can find it at `http://developer.apple.com/samplecode/JNISample/JNISample.html`.

MULTIPLE JAVA TARGETS

As Java evolves, it means there are various versions of Java running "in the wild," any one of which you might specifically want to target. In fact, Mac OS X itself supports multiple versions of the JRE and it automatically selects the right one, based upon the Java executable. Your project can target particular versions of Java, via Xcode's target settings (see Figure 13-5), which you can view and change by double-clicking the target in the project window's Groups & Files list.

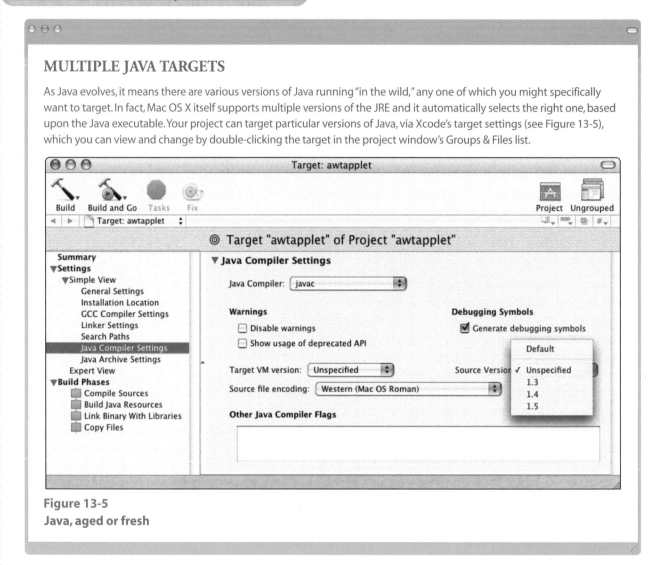

Figure 13-5
Java, aged or fresh

bridge between them for Cocoa." That is, Apple jiggered both its Cocoa runtime environment and its implementation of the Java runtime environment so that the two could communicate, using proxies to represent corresponding objects in either environment; Apple also made this bridge responsible for tracking Java objects in the Cocoa runtime

environment so that the Java garbage collector could do its work across the bridge (similarly, the bridge allows the Cocoa runtime system to engage in reference counting for Objective-C Cocoa objects that happen to have found their way onto the Java side of the bridge). They also performed a few other tricks along the way to make it all work.

THE CAFFEINATED INTERFACE BUILDER

If you took a close look at some of the screen shots in Chapter 9 — our exploration of Xcode's Interface Builder application — you might have noticed that IB's Class Inspector's Attributes pane has a set of radio buttons for choosing a language; the choices it offers are Java and Objective-C (we've repeated one of the figures here as Figure 13-6). As this set of buttons strongly implies, you can use Interface Builder for your Cocoa Java apps just as you can for your Objective-C Cocoa apps.

Apple has enhanced Interface Builder to read and write Java methods for Java classes: When you create a subclass of any of the Cocoa classes that IB knows about, you can use the Write Files command (found on IB's Classes menu — we show this in Chapter 1 and again in Chapter 9) to create the appropriate Java files in your Cocoa Java project. Put that in your mug and sip it!

▼ **Note**

You can find more gory details (actually, there is not much gore involved, even though Al Gore does sit on Apple's board of directors) about the runtime bridge by searching Xcode's Reference Library for "java version of cocoa"; the article you want is appropriately called "The Java Version of Cocoa." You may also enjoy checking out the Currency Converter tutorial, which shows how to create a Cocoa Java application, and which you can find in Xcode's Reference Library under Cocoa ➜ Java; the document is titled "Developing Cocoa Java Applications: A Tutorial."

The second question is rather harder to answer, because there are a good number of possible reasons. For example:

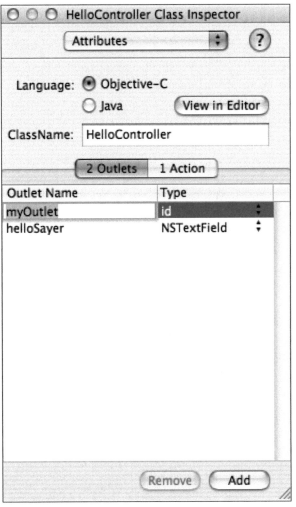

Figure 13-6
You've seen this before, in Chapter 9

- A Java programmer might find the Cocoa libraries exciting, and might wish to use them, but might not wish to learn Yet Another Language.

- A Cocoa programmer might be sick and tired of dealing with `retain` and `release` methods of memory management and simply want to rely on the tender mercies of the Java garbage collector.

- A Java developer might already have a well-factored application that has separated out its underlying data-processing engine from its user interface, and desires to implement that app on Mac OS X using all the wonderful features of Interface Builder.

There may be other reasons as well. Two of our favorites are "Because you can" and "Why not?"

However, there are some small things you should be aware of when you write a Cocoa Java app:

- Both Objective-C code and Java code incur some slight performance penalties due to the background activities of their respective runtime environments; however, Java code also incurs an additional performance penalty because it has to be interpreted by the Java Virtual Machine. Although Apple has done a wonderful job optimizing the Java VM for Mac OS X, it can't make Java bytecode run quite as fast as native PowerPC binaries. Deal with it... and if you're running on a high-end G5, you probably don't really care, anyway.

- Not all Cocoa methods and classes are available to Java. For example, Java uses the normal Java file-handling routines instead of Cocoa's NSFileManager, NSFileHandle, and NSPipe classes.

- Some Cocoa Java classes have different names than their Objective-C counterparts; for example, NSCalendarDate is NSGregorianDate in Java.

- Memory management in Java differs from that in Objective-C; in particular, Cocoa Objective-C weak linking may cause some pure Java objects associated with Cocoa Objective-C objects to vanish if not handled correctly.

Apple's documentation on Cocoa Java, available in Xcode, outlines the hidden Cocoa Java gotchas in more detail. There aren't many, though.

I TAKE MY JAVA BLACK

The whole *raison d'etre* of Java, of course, is its cross-platform development and deployment capabilities; without that, it would just be a cool C-like object-oriented programming language. As we said, Sun calls these capabilities, Write Once, Run Anywhere. But is it more than just a trademark? Is it true?

Well, yes, pretty much, it is. If you have the appropriate Java Runtime Environment installed for your operating system (and, on Mac OS X, it is built in), you can run all properly written "pure" Java applets or applications, regardless of the platform on which they were written. The hitch, of course, is in the phrase "properly written"; it is easy for a programmer to assume certain things about, say, filenaming conventions or character sets that are platform specific, and even a pure Java program that incorporates these assumptions will fail ignominiously when run in the JRE of some other platform. So watch it, bub!

Both pure Java applets (designed to run in a Web browser environment) and applications (designed to run on their own inside the JRE) tend to come packaged in *JAR* files, Sun's *Java AR*chive format that's built on top of the ancient and ubiquitous ZIP file format. Naturally, Xcode's build system creates JAR files if the project type requires it (for example, a Java AWT applet such as the one shown earlier in Figure 13-3).

 Note

> JAR file suffixes include .jar, .ear, and .war. The last two are used for Java 2 Enterprise Edition things: .ear is for Enterprise Application archives and .war is for Web Application archives. But if you're building those sorts of things, you already knew that. (We hope you note that we didn't digress into jokes about otology or the Pentagon here.)

Java applets are among the most common types of projects built with Java (after all, there's a lot of Web browsers out there, and it was the potential of cross-platform Web applets that ignited the early Java hype-storm in the first place). There's no mystery to building an applet with Xcode; just compose your applet's source using Xcode's editor and choose the Build or Build and Go tool. Xcode creates the JARs and, if you select Build and Go, launches Sun's Applet Viewer application so you can try it out (see Figure 13-7).

Figure 13-7
Build and Go brings up Applet Viewer

▼ Tip

Xcode also creates sample HTML pages with applet projects, so you can run the applet in a browser (such as Safari). Unfortunately, double-clicking the HTML file in the project opens the Xcode editor rather than launching your browser. And choosing File ➜ Open With Finder opens the HTML file in your project folder, not the one copied into your project's build folder when you built the project, so it won't see the JAR file. The solution? Control-click (or right-click) the JAR file in your project window and choose Reveal in Finder from the contextual menu. That brings up your build folder, and you can open the HTML file from there to see the applet in your browser.

SHOW ME THE WAY TO GO HOME

One question that Java developers moving to the Mac always ask is, "Where is everything?" Obviously, they don't literally mean everything, because the only answer to that is, "The universe, you silly goose." What they're usually asking is really something like, "Where is `java.home` on this machine?" Mac OS X keeps a symbolic link to the "real" Java home directory in Library/Java, and the target of that link is what `System.getProperty("java.home")` returns. (In fact, though, most of Java is in System/Library/Frameworks/JavaVM.framework but you don't want to mess directly with anything there... trust us.)

If you need to extend Java on your machine, chances are you want to put your extensions (JNI libraries, perhaps, or some additional .class files) into the directory known within Java itself as `java.ext.dir`; as implemented in Mac OS X, this directory is actually two directories: /Library/Java/Extensions and ~/Library/Java/Extensions. The second one, of course, is the current logged-in user's directory, and it is where you want to put extensions if they only apply to a single user on your machine (you may have to make the directory). Extensions in /Library/Java/Extensions are available to all user accounts on the Mac.

Pure Java applications are a little more problematic than applets... not to build, that is, but to deploy. This is because Java apps are not Mac apps, no matter how much of a "first-class citizen" that Apple claims Java is: They may, for example, contain nothing in the way of a user interface and send all of their output to Java's standard output, which might be the Terminal window (if launched from the command line), or the Console utility's window, if the app's JAR is double-clicked.

▼ Note

That's right; starting with Java 1.4 on Mac OS X, you can double-click a JAR to run it. If it's a Java application, and it has an appropriate manifest included in it, double-clicking it launches the Jar Launcher app, which actually runs the app.

Even if the Java app supplies its own GUI, double-clicking a JAR is not like double-clicking a real Mac app. For one thing, all JARs tend to look alike (and their icons *don't* look like application icons, that's for sure), and, for another, you can't really pass command-line options to a file that you double-click. There are two solutions here:

- If you are bringing a project created on another platform to the Mac, you can use the Jar Bundler app (in Developer/Applications/Java Tools) to turn the JAR into a double-clickable application bundle (see Figure 13-8). There's even a place to supply command-line options. And you can give it a custom icon.

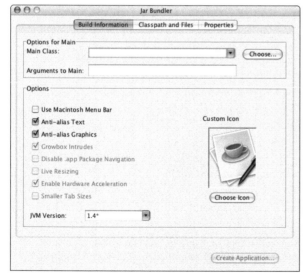

Figure 13-8
Bundling a JAR

LAF WITH ME!

LAF is look-and-feel. In Mac OS X, Java Swing applications use the Aqua LAF, which gives you those lovely lickable buttons and all the other nice Mac OS Xish bits of GUI goodness when Java presents Swing widgets. However, Aqua widgets don't always directly match up with their Swing counterparts as seen on other platforms. For example, Swing's JTabbedPanes allow for multiple rows of tabs, but Aqua only provides a single row of tabs, with a drop-down menu widget to indicate additional tabs. Also, Swing buttons and their Aqua equivalents don't completely correspond; you should consult the Apple Human Interface Guidelines (available — where else? — in your Xcode reference library) for the details about how buttons should look and act, and, for that matter, about any issues regarding interface element size and placement.

If you want to compare how your Java application looks in Aqua-fied form with how it may look in the default Swing LAF (known as "metal"), you can launch your app from the (*gasp*) Terminal command line. Pass in the flag -Dswing.defaultlaf= javax.swing.plaf.metal.MetalLookAndFeel to the java command. You'll see your app in Swing's default metal. And if you're like us, you'll be glad you have a Mac and don't have to look at things like that every day.

- You can simply use one of Xcode's new project templates that create a Java application (such as a Java AWT application template or a Java Swing application template). Xcode automagically creates an application bundle containing the JAR and related resources when you build it.

INSIDE A BUNDLED JAR

You may be wondering what special nuggets of Mac goodness are contained in the Mac OS X application package that Xcode or Jar Bundler wrap around a JAR (you might be especially interested if you have fallen into total control-freak mode and want to make your own application bundle from scratch). Here are the essentials:

- An Info.plist file that, among other things, contains setup information for the JRE when the Java app starts up. This file is a standard XML property list file that the Property List Editor (yet another of the developer tools Apple provides with Xcode) can edit. Jar Bundler and Xcode builds create this file for you. You can tweak it to change various settings; for example, you can change property values that, from the command line, you would specify with the java command's -D option (for example, changing the Swing LAF from Aqua to the default Java metal look, which we described in "LAF with Me!"). This file is stored in the bundle's Contents folder.

- A PkgInfo file, which all application bundles have, and which associates the bundle with a four-letter creator code in old-time Mac tradition (creator codes associate an application with files created by it). You'll probably use the default ???? creator code unless you want to go to the trouble of registering your unique creator code with Apple (something you might want to do if you plan to commercially distribute your app and if your app creates data files).

- Of course, the actual Java code. This can be in .jar or .class files, and is placed in the Resources/Java folder inside the bundle package's Contents folder.

- A small native app, nestled inside the Contents/MacOS folder, that exists merely to launch the Java VM.

- In the package's Contents/Resources folder, the application's icon, so the Finder and the Dock have something to display other than the default application icon. Various image file formats work; the Info.plist file has an entry that specifies which image file in that folder is the icon file. Xcode comes with the Icon Composer utility (/Developer/Applications/Utilities/), which can make a standard .icns icon file from other image files if you want to use that format for your icon (check it out; the .icns format is custom made for icons... literally).

- Various optional folders inside the Resources folder that contain localized language resources; for example, English.lproj for the English language strings and resources. The Xcode Java application templates provide some basic .lproj folders.

▼ Note

If you use an Xcode template to build a Java app, the bundle it creates will run just great on the Mac. On other platforms? Not so great. If your Java app is intended for non-Mac distribution, you might want to try the Ant-based Application Jar project template, which produces more "vanilla" output.

ANT NO BIG DEAL

When we first heard that Apple was providing "Ant support" in Xcode, we went "hootchie-mama!" and danced our little geekjoy dance, thinking, "Cool! A hip Apple GUI front end to Apache's Ant build system!"

Unfortunately, we were engaging in premature terpsichorean behavior: By "support," Apple meant merely that

- Xcode would now be able to build Java products using Ant-compatible build.xml files;

- the open-source Ant tool would be installed automatically when the Developer tools were installed;

- Xcode's Build and Clean commands would be smart enough to call upon their Ant equivalents in an Ant-based project; and

- Xcode would now include some Java project templates that employ Ant instead of Xcode's native build facilities.

Color us disappointed; we wanted a space cruiser and Apple delivered a bicycle. Still, for a bicycle, it's not bad. And, like a bicycle, you may have to do some work, but it will get you where you want to go.

Note

In fact, the Ant developers themselves are working on a GUI for Ant, known as Antidote. The project is in its "early stages." You can read more about it at `http://ant.apache.org/manual/Integration/Antidote.html`.

Even the (in our humble opinions) limited Ant support in Xcode is quite useful. After all, Ant is a very popular build system used by developers all over the Javascape, which, Mac partisans though we are, we have to admit is much bigger than the Mac-based Java development community. And Ant *is* cool; unlike old-school Unix makefiles and make facilities, Ant is not limited to any particular platform because it is (tada!) written in Java. There's something appealing about a Java build system written in Java, especially to Java fans (who can be quite as vociferously dedicated to their platform as Mac fans are to theirs).

In Figure 13-4 (see "So Many Brews"), we show a typical Ant-based JAR project as created from an Xcode template. There are two important things to note in that figure:

- One of the files created by the template is build.xml. The figure shows an embedded editor displaying part of that file. This is the file that Ant will use to build the project. And we have to say that it is somewhat more understandable than a typical Unix makefile tends to be.

- The target has precisely zero build stages in it. This should not surprise you, because it is Ant, and not Xcode, that is going to do the building: The actual build stages (or the Ant equivalents of such things) exist in the form of XML statements in the build.xml file.

Figure 13-9 shows the complete target summary for our JarOfAnts project, which is Xcode's Ant-based Application Jar template just as it came from the New Project dude. As you can see, Ant is implemented as an *external target* in Xcode, which means that Xcode simply passes along your project's name to the custom build tool it is calling. In this case, as shown in the figure's Custom Build Command setting, the custom build tool is the ant tool that Xcode has stashed in the depths of Developer/Java/Ant/bin.

Tip

You should sneak a peak in the docs subdirectory of the Developer/Java/Ant folder. It contains local copies of most of Apache's Ant Project Web site, which provides a good starting point for learning more about Ant and its capabilities.

So what's Ant good for in the Mac corner of the Javascape? Actually, quite a bit if you're into Java:

- If you are participating in any sort of large Java development project with colleagues who are working on a variety of platforms, it allows you to use Xcode to

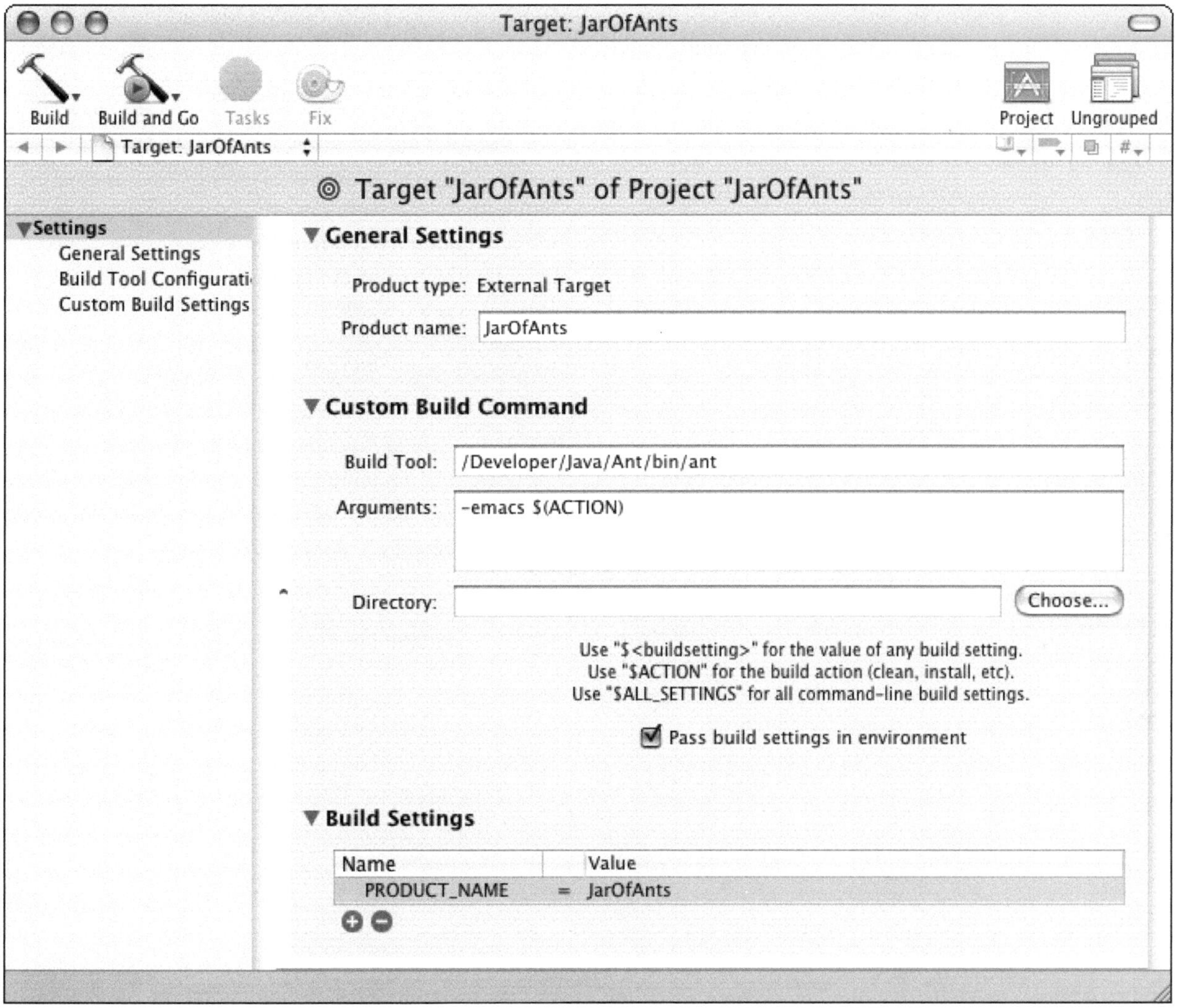

Figure 13-9
An Ant-infested target

create your contributions to that project. Your sources and build files will be compatible with the ones your colleagues create. And vice versa.

○ It easily allows you to import Java projects that you may find scattered around the (virtual) world; if

you're a Java newbie and want to teach yourself the old-fashioned way (that is, by examining and using code developed and made available by others), you won't have to do a lot of reconfiguring of these examples just to get them to compile in Xcode.

- Conversely, it allows you to distribute your Java sources to any struggling newbies out there who want to see How a Real Programmer Does It.

- It allows you to make use of an ever-growing assortment of extensions to Ant. After all, as a Java app, Ant can incorporate additional classes to add to its bag of tricks.

▼ Tip

A good place to find Ant extensions is at the Home of the Ant, apache.org: `http://ant.apache.org/external.html`.

Hmmm... looking back over this portion of the chapter, we wonder why we were disappointed with Apple's Ant support in the first place. Ant rocks!

FILTERING THE GROUNDS

In this chapter, we presented another broad overview of the State of Java in Xcode. We discovered that Objective-C and Java are apparently long-lost cousins, making it possible for Apple to provide just about all of its Cocoa APIs in Java form, which in turn makes possible full-fledged Mac OS X applications written entirely in Java. We looked more closely at some of the more popular kinds of pure Java projects for which Xcode provides templates, and checked out some of the interesting implementation decisions Apple made in the course of incorporating Java into Mac OS X as a first-class citizen. We also explained how you can disguise a Java application as a native Mac app by wrapping it in a bundle. Finally, we looked at how Xcode supports Apache's Ant build tool in order to make Xcode into a first-class peer of other Java IDEs.

Then we had a cup of herbal tea.

The Studio System: Building an AppleScript Application

An Obvious Example: Hello, World, in AppleScript

Beyond Ask and Answer

Cocoa-Flavored AppleScript

Wrap Party

Once upon a time, there was a DOS command line. Ordinary folk hated it, because it was nonintuitive, unforgiving, and hard to master. Geeks loved it because it was nonintuitive, unforgiving, and hard-to-master... and when it *was* mastered, it offered a great deal of power and control (and what geek doesn't love power and control?). Someone using a PC running DOS could write *batch files* — text files consisting of PC-DOS command-line statements and some other syntactic elements — to do things that a Mac user simply couldn't, such as automatically renaming a bunch of files, or formatting a floppy disk and then copying every file on the machine's hard disk that was created after a certain date and whose name started with the letter *q* to the floppy. The Mac may have been elegant, friendly, and technologically cool, but it just didn't do batch. Well, eventually it did, but not out of the box: You had to acquire and install MPW (Macintosh Programmer's Workshop), which didn't show up until 1985, required a hard disk system, and involved lots of funny option-key characters (like § for the current selection, ∞ for a wildcard match-anything character, and the like).

It took Bill Atkinson's crazy WildCard project to bring batch to the Mac mainstream. Renamed *HyperCard*, it was included with every Mac and came with a friendly, easy-to-learn programming language called *HyperTalk* that could do much the same sorts of things that batch files could do on the DOS-running PCs. Apple quickly discovered that scripting was just as cool to some people as an elegant graphical user interface was to others, and it began work on a system-level scripting technology that would allow programs to communicate with one another, that could automate certain mundane-but-crucial processes, and that would be easy to learn and easy to expand. And thus was born AppleScript.

HyperCard is now consigned to the same dark regions of the computer history catacombs as the "classic" Mac OS, at least as far as Apple is concerned, but AppleScript not only lives on in Mac OS X, it has gotten even more powerful with each new OS version. Where once only a minority of programs were AppleScriptable, it is now a rare program that can't be scripted, and the tools for creating Apple-Script scripts have evolved from the simple HyperCard-like scripting window of AppleScript's first incarnations to a complete set of developer tools incorporated into Xcode.

This Xcode toolkit is called AppleScript Studio. It's batch made bitchin'. In fact, it is so cool that Andy wrote a paean to it in his MacObserver column in June 2004 (www.macobserver.com/columns/ihnatko/2004/20040618.shtml).

 Note

> Like most programmers (and other people), we're a little bit lazy. One aspect of that laziness exhibits itself as a tendency to abbreviate or create acronyms for long terms and phrases that we repeatedly employ. Unfortunately, decorum precludes our indulging that urge when it comes to the name "AppleScript Studio" (for fairly obvious reasons). Most states wouldn't let us use the acronym for a person-alized license plate, either.

AN OBVIOUS EXAMPLE: HELLO, WORLD, IN APPLESCRIPT

In keeping with our tradition of presenting the most trivial and universal example first, we're going to run through the process of creating an AppleScript Studio *Hello World*

application. Follow the numbered steps to construct your AppleScript-based *Hello World* application.

1. **Choose File → New Project.** The New Project Assistant (see Figure 14-1) appears.

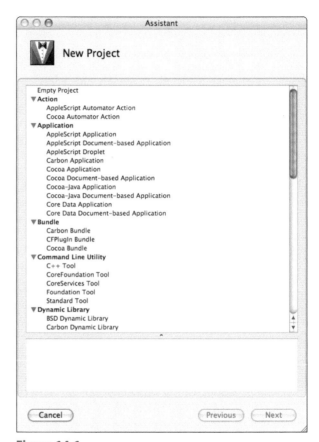

Figure 14-1
Your old friend, the New Project Assistant

2. **Select the AppleScript Application template, and click Next.**

 Note

> We chose AppleScript Application here rather than the AppleScript Document-based Application or the AppleScript Droplet template because our Hello

World application isn't going to be creating or otherwise processing document files. If you intend to create documents with your AppleScript Studio application, select the AppleScript Document-based Application template. If your application is going to process documents dropped onto it (something like StuffIt Expander does), use the AppleScript Droplet template.

The Assistant asks you to name and specify a location for your project. Do so (we're naming ours "Hello World" — sans quotes), and then click Finish. Xcode presents the project window shown in Figure 14-2.

 Note

When you create an AppleScript application, you get the Cocoa and Foundation frameworks, a MainMenu.nib file, and a main.m file, written in Objective-C. In short, an AppleScript Studio application **is** a Cocoa application with some additional frameworks thrown in.

3. **Choose File → Save so that you have the project's inception saved to disk.** (*Save early, save often* is a very good motto for anyone using a computer to create anything, and an especially good motto for a developer.)

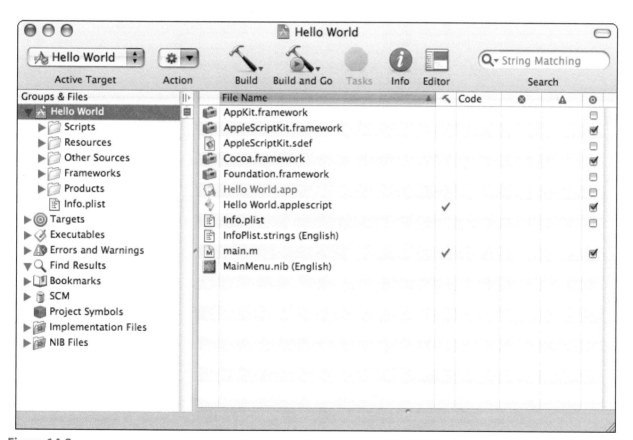

Figure 14-2
Your project window, all set up for you to be creative

4. **Double-click MainMenu.nib (English).** Interface Builder (see Chapter 9) opens, turning your screen into something resembling Figure 14-3 (the size and location of the Dock and windows will vary depending on your screen, preferences, and what else you have running).

5. **If the palette isn't showing the Cocoa-Controls pane (ours was showing the Cocoa-AppleScript** pane in Figure 14-3), click the Cocoa Controls and Indicators icon in the palette's toolbar (the icon's default location is second from the left) to make sure the window shown in Figure 14-4 is available.

6. **Click and drag a button from the Cocoa-Controls palette into the Window window; the result should look something like Figure 14-5.**

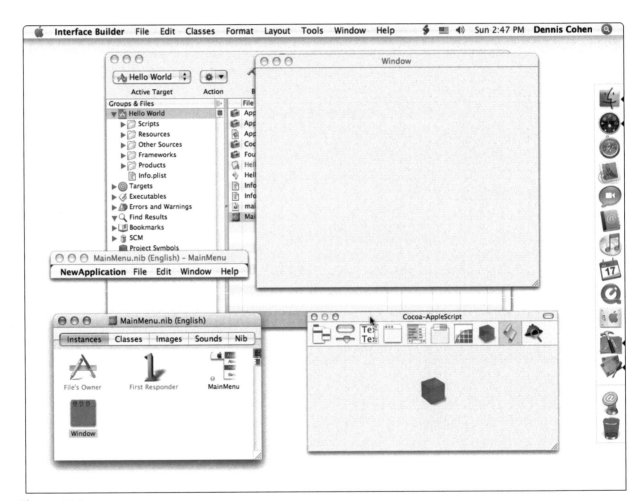

Figure 14-3

Interface Builder launches, presenting you with a few windows

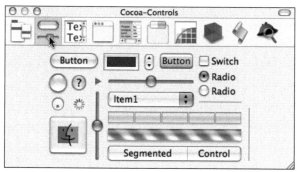

Figure 14-4
You need the Cocoa-Controls palette pane

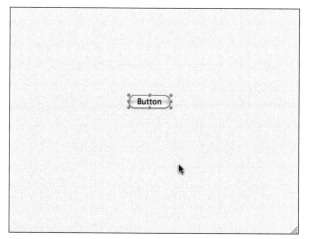

Figure 14-5
Click and drag a button into the center of your window

7. **Double-click the button's text to select it and type "Hello, World", and then press Return to set the button's new title, as shown in Figure 14-6.**

8. **With the button still selected (notice the attractive blue dots surrounding it), either choose Tools → Show Inspector or use the keyboard shortcut Shift+ ⌘+I.** The NSButton Inspector window appears, as shown in Figure 14-7.

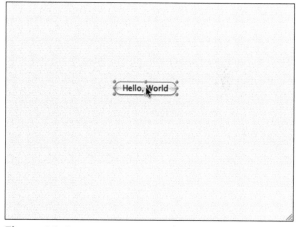

Figure 14-6
Give your button a meaningful name

9. **Choose AppleScript from the pop-up menu at the top of the window (or press ⌘+8) to display the AppleScript pane, shown in Figure 14-8.**

10. **Select the clicked option beneath Action (click the disclosure triangle beside Action if necessary to display the checkbox).** Selecting the clicked action tells Xcode that the Hello, World button should have a clicked event handler, called when the user clicks the button. Also, enabling this action causes an Apple-Script Info item to appear in the MainMenu.nib's Instances pane.

11. **In the NSButton Inspector's AppleScript pane, select the checkbox next to Hello World.applescript (down in the Script section of the Inspector).** You've now identified Hello World.applescript as the clicked handler.

12. **Click the Edit button at the bottom of the NSButton Inspector window.** You'll be returned to your project window in Xcode, which now stands ready for you to write your AppleScript handler — as you can see in Figure 14-9, Xcode has already built the handler's skeleton for you and selected the comment that you're going to replace with your code.

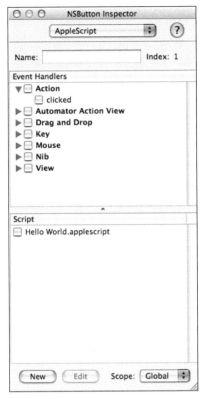

Figure 14-8
We need the Button Inspector's AppleScript pane

13. **Type display dialog "Hello World!"** (Obviously, you could add other AppleScript code here, but then you wouldn't be creating the archetypal Hello World application.) Your project window should now look something like Figure 14-10.

14. **Choose Build → Build, press ⌘+B, or press the toolbar's Build icon to build your Hello World application.** Xcode will prompt you to save your project and its files first, if you've neglected that step or don't have your preferences set to save your work automatically.

Figure 14-7
The Button Inspector appears

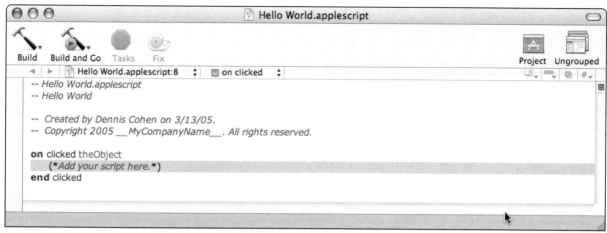

Figure 14-9
Back in the project window, you're ready to insert your handler's code

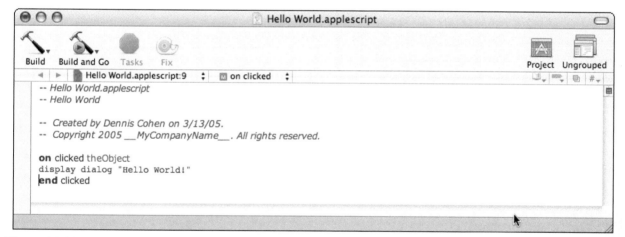

Figure 14-10
Your handler is now ready

When you build the application, Xcode not only compiles Hello World.applescript, but also the Objective-C main routine; in addition, it prepares the resources, links the application, and copies everything necessary into the application bundle for you.

Now, if you run the application from where you told Xcode to build it, or if you click Build and Go, you'll see the result shown in Figure 14-11 when you click your application window's Hello World button.

If you happen to look at main.m, you'll see that very little Objective-C code is required to build an AppleScript Studio application, and Xcode's template already wrote that basic code for you. Without your having to add a single line of Objective-C code, you can build very complicated and powerful applications — browse through the AppleScript examples that accompany Xcode and you'll see that very few of them add any Objective-C code. But, remember, every AppleScript Studio application *is* a Cocoa application and it

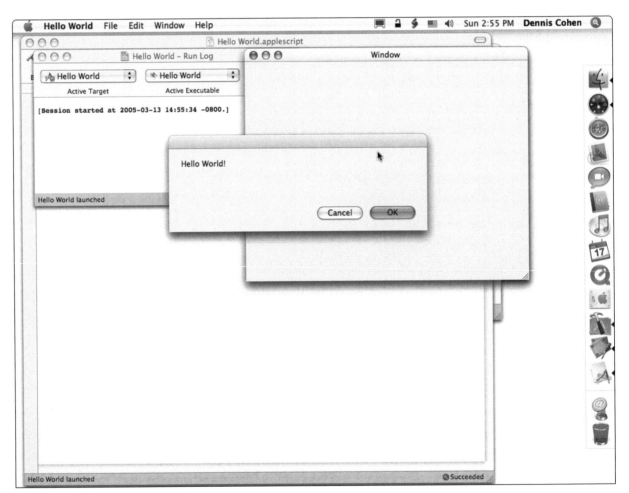

Figure 14-11
Hello World rides again

is the Cocoa framework that does all the heavy lifting. In "Cocoa-Flavored AppleScript," later in this chapter, we delve into what you can do to combine your own Objective-C code and AppleScripts to create even more complex applications.

BEYOND ASK AND ANSWER

If all you could use AppleScript Studio to create were simplistic applications like Hello World or a value converter where you feed in a number or string and the application processes that datum, it would hardly be worth Apple's effort to include AppleScript Studio in Xcode nor our time to tell you about AppleScript Studio. So it should come as no surprise that we've barely touched the top of the visible portion of AppleScript's iceberg.

AppleScript is a rich programming environment. With it, you can create:

- simple value converters, like the Currency Converter example program included with Xcode;

- more complex applications, such as the Browser example program that mimics Finder's column view;

- tools to access data across the Internet, such as the Daily Dilbert example that retrieves Scott Adams' Dilbert comic strip or the Language Translator that processes input strings using BabelFISH's SOAP translators (SOAP stands for Simple Object Access Protocol); and

- applications that provide a GUI interface to Unix command-line tools, such as the Archive Maker example that creates tar archives and, optionally, employs the gz compression tool.

But, integral to creating a user interface is Xcode's favorite interface design tool, Interface Builder. We describe the IB basics in Chapter 9, but there are additional features that

become available when AppleScript is added to the mix, and these are found in the AppleScript palette and the Inspector's AppleScript pane (which you saw briefly in the Hello World example earlier in this chapter).

When you create an AppleScript Studio application, IB's palette window includes an extra palette in the toolbar, the AppleScript palette shown in Figure 14-12. The one object you see in the AppleScript palette is a *data source object*, an item that supplies the data for a table view or other row and column view.

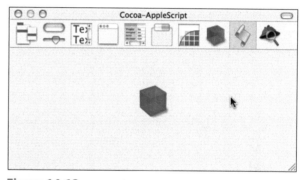

Figure 14-12
The AppleScript palette's only item is a data source object

▼ **Note**

Interface Builder's palette collection is extensible — you'll find the supplied add-on palettes (Sherlock and ASKPalette, for AppleScriptKit) in the Palettes folder inside your Developer folder.

What you're going to use the most when implementing an interface, though, is the Inspector's AppleScript pane. This is where you specify the AppleScript handlers for the various interface objects: for example, the buttons, checkboxes, radio buttons, and text boxes. Figure 14-8 showed the handlers that can be attached to a button. You also set the initial state (enabled or disabled, selected or deselected, initial text, and so forth).

Making life as easy as possible for you, all you have to do is select the handler(s) you want to add in the Inspector's AppleScript pane and select the AppleScript file to which you want them (or specify a new file by clicking the New button) in the Script section at the bottom of the pane. Then click Edit. Poof, you're back in Xcode's project window with the file open and the cursor positioned for you to start coding your handler. The only thing that really surprises us is that Apple didn't add some sort of "whoosh" sound effect as the switch is made.

 Tip

While most of the example AppleScript Studio applications that ship with Xcode are so simple that they contain just one .applescript file and one .nib file, you'll see that some of the larger ones include multiple files of one or both types. As your projects grow, you'll find it a lot easier to maintain and debug your application if you follow the latter example. Create multiple nib files, maybe one for each window, dialog, sheet, or drawer. Similarly, create separate script files when it reduces script complexity. For example, every button is going to have a clicked handler and if you have just one script file, the if test to determine which button was theObject is going to get really messy (and possibly even degrade performance). Modularity is a good thing.

COCOA-FLAVORED APPLESCRIPT

Because every AppleScript Studio application is a Cocoa application, some Cocoa terminology has migrated into AppleScript. One consequence of this migration is that a whole new group of handlers has been added to AppleScript that you can employ. The following are a few examples:

- You can employ a should close handler to perform validation checks when an attempt is made to close a window, and have it return false and not close the window when something is amiss. should handlers are equivalent to Cocoa's should phrase.

- Alternatively, if a Cancel button is clicked, you aren't going to need to validate anything, so you would employ a will close handler. This corresponds to Cocoa's will phrase.

- Finally, in line with Cocoa's did phrase, which reacts to an event that has already occurred, AppleScript Studio has past tense verbs, such as activated and zoomed, that allow you to respond to completed operations.

Not only does Cocoa enrich AppleScript Studio's handler vocabulary, AppleScript Studio can invoke Objective-C object methods in your application through the AppleScript call method command. Because Objective-C methods can invoke code written in other languages, invoking an Objective-C method gives you access to code written in other languages as well — all you need is a simple Objective-C method that calls the code (in other words, a wrapper).

The iPhoto Tour example project, downloadable from Apple's Web page at www.apple.com/applescript/ studio (in the Example Projects area on the right side of the page), includes examples of calling methods added to your program. For example, the ASKit Dictionary for QuickTime movies doesn't include all the methods you might want to use — after all, QuickTime is h-u-g-e! Check out Figure 14-13 to see how easy it is to add Objective-C methods to your AppleScript Studio project and call them from an AppleScript handler.

 Caution

For those AppleScript developers amongst you who are accustomed to AppleScript applications saving their properties back into the AppleScript application, be forewarned that AppleScript Studio applications do not work this way.

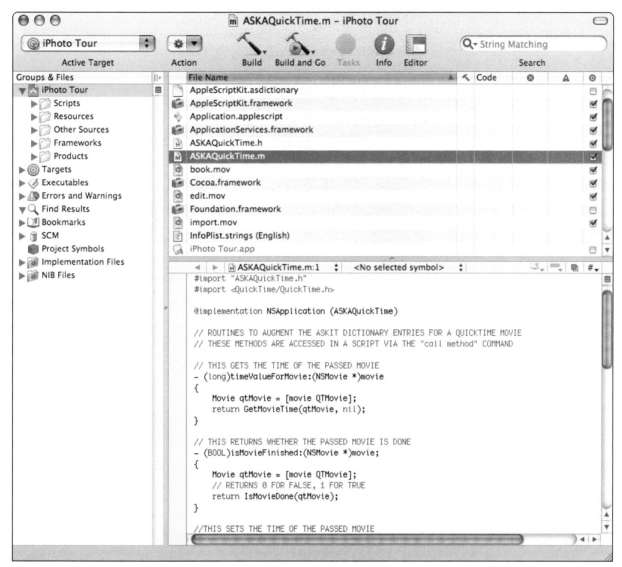

Figure 14-13
Add Objective-C methods when you need to — your AppleScripts can call them

Because AppleScript Studio applications are full Cocoa citizens in the land of OS X, the standard user `defaults` system is available. So, to achieve persistent value storage, you would write the values to a .plist (preferences) file before quitting and load them in upon launch. You can find out all about accessing defaults in Apple's handy AppleScript Studio Terminology Reference's discussion of the `user-defaults` class and the `default entry` class.

In a like vein, one script cannot access another script's global variables unless you include a `load script` command, and even then, all you'll find are read-only versions of the variables' current values. So, back to `user-defaults` and `default entry` if you want multiple scripts to reference and update the same variables.

Another dash of Cocoa is the AppleScript Studio version of the `display dialog` scripting addition. Because you're creating a full-blooded Cocoa application, you need to be able to manage all the standard interface elements, and dialogs that appear as sheets (that is, dialogs attached to a window) are a major interface element. The AppleScript Studio version of `display dialog` includes the `attached to window "foo"` terminology to indicate that the dialog should be displayed as a sheet. You can find a very clear example of this in the aptly named Display Dialog program included with the AppleScript Studio examples that come with your Xcode 2 distribution. Figure 14-14 shows the relevant section of the example's AppleScript code.

 Tip

You can designate an icon via the `with icon` term. That term's argument can be a string enclosed in quotes, such as `"Spenser"`. All you need to do is include a .tiff file with the matching name among your application's resources.

Your argument to `with icon` can also be a number chosen from 0, 1, and 2 for the `stop`, `note`, and `caution` icons, respectively, because AppleScript's `stop`, `note`, and `caution` constants aren't recognized. Apple recommends against using these icons, but they're available in numeric form in case you feel a compulsion to employ deprecated interface elements.

EXAMPLES ARE FOOD TO A DEVELOPER

For those of you who are interested in getting really involved with AppleScript Studio, we're going to recommend that you check out www.apple.com/applescript/studio. In addition to all the links, tips, documentation, and so forth that you'd expect to find there, you'll also see a link to subscribe to Apple's AppleScript Studio mailing list, where you can get involved in discussions about how to use AppleScript Studio (or just lurk and learn). You'll also find a number of links to example projects, expanding on the collection that ships with Xcode.

We firmly believe that perusing, tweaking, and extending code that already exists and functions is the quickest and easiest way to hone your programming skills. A great repository of AppleScript source code, including a lot of AppleScript Studio examples, is located at www.scriptbuilders.net. (Hint: Do a search for AppleScript Studio to narrow it down to example projects.)

That said, one of the better single example projects we've come across is iDVD Companion. The source is available for download from Apple's Web site at www.apple.com/applescript/idvd/companion.html.

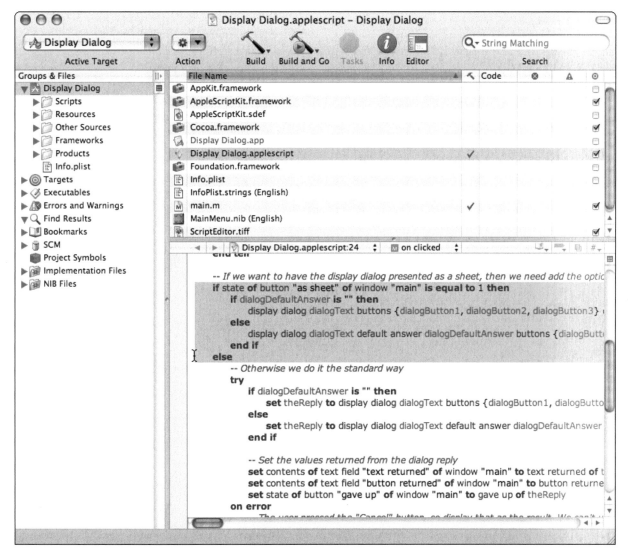

Figure 14-14
You can display a dialog either as a sheet or in the normal manner

Apple has a very informative, if somewhat soporific and dense, PDF file almost as large as this entire book entitled *Building Applications with AppleScript Studio*. It goes into excruciating detail, and if what we've shown you about AppleScript Studio here whets your appetite, we encourage you to download and peruse it. You can find the PDF at `http://developer.apple.com`.

WRAP PARTY

We once again built a Hello World application, this time using AppleScript Studio, which is Xcode's way of creating a Cocoa application using AppleScript. In the process, we discovered that Interface Builder provides AppleScript support, allowing you to link interface elements to AppleScript handlers. Then we looked at the ways AppleScript applications may be used, and took a closer look at some of Interface Builder's AppleScript support capabilities. We revealed how an AppleScript Studio application can incorporate additional Cocoa methods, opening up all sorts of strange and wonderful hybrid application possibilities. And, finally, we encouraged you to consult Apple's copious documentation and support resources for AppleScript (and AppleScript Studio) development.

15

Mixing Languages in Crossover Country

Drinking Cocoa by the C++ Side
Who Put Carbon in My Cocoa?
The Eight-Dollar Question
The Final Mix

An ancient engineering axiom goes something like this: If the only tool you have is a hammer, everything looks like a nail. (This, by the way, may be related to the ancient definition of a hacker: someone who makes furniture with an ax.)

When we find a tool that we like to use (or, at least, have finally figured out *how* to use), we often find ourselves thinking about the problems we have to solve, or the tasks we need to complete, in terms of that tool and only that tool. It's a form of tunnel vision (toolnel vision?) that can afflict even the most open-minded of us, whether the tool in question is a two-horsepower, four-speed band saw (with an included miter gauge!), or the C++ programming language: Give us a project and we immediately look to our favorite tool to help us complete it. And why not? We spent the time (and the money) to acquire and master the tool in the first place; it would be a shame not to use it.

Except, of course, that some tools are better than others, depending on the job you want to do... a pitchfork is great for throwing hay, but it does not make a particularly good rake, and, though you can probably drive a nail with an ax if you have to, a hammer does a much better job of it.

Xcode comes with a bunch of useful tools: programming languages, compilers, frameworks, editors. And all of them are useful. However, not one of them is the be-all and end-all of development tools — in fact, Xcode itself is not the be-all and end-all of Mac OS X development tools, either, and not even

Apple claims that it is. Sometimes we have to put down that classic hickory-handle claw hammer and pick up a six-bit screwdriver with a ratcheting handle (or a six-ounce screwdriver made with a fine vodka). Sometimes it pays to be a jack-of-all-trades instead of the master of only one.

In this chapter, we look at how to mix and match some of the programming tools and techniques that Apple and others have provided to make your programming efforts more productive... and, maybe, to help you widen your vision. You can climb back into your tunnel later.

DRINKING COCOA BY THE C++ SIDE

As we've mentioned previously, and more than once, Carbon and Cocoa were initially separate (and not particularly equal) OS X development strategies. As time has passed, the acolytes for each religion have become less strident in asserting that its approach is the only path to Mac programming heaven. They're each still saying that theirs is the better approach, but are now admitting that, at least occasionally, the opposition has something of value to offer.

Because earlier OS X releases implemented new functionality in the Cocoa APIs well before the Carbon APIs, it is little wonder that Carbon developers sought ways to leverage this Cocoa-specific functionality without having to reengineer tens of thousands of lines of functional, debugged code into another language in order to add one more feature. Another old programming axiom is, "If it ain't broke, don't fix it!"

LET ME GET MY WRAP

When we first started writing this section, we were going to assume that you all knew what *wrapper functions* are — after all, we're assuming that you all know how to program, already. But we decided that a little discussion is probably in order because not all of you are professional or even highly experienced programmers.

Wrapper functions are small functions callable by C (or some other language) that, well, wrap a method invocation within some housekeeping code. They're written in the language used for the method (in our case, Objective-C).

Because Cocoa manages memory dynamically (and differently) from Carbon, any Cocoa method you call requires the housekeeping code to allocate an `NSautoReleasePool` before the method call and release the pool on return. These wrapper functions should be C-callable with a parameter list that matches those parameters required by the Objective-C method. Additionally, the wrapper function must return the data returned by the Cocoa method it wraps.

As we've said elsewhere in this sparkling tome, working example code is one of the best and easiest ways to learn new programming techniques, and Apple provides a lot of useful sample code on its ADC Web site. A useful example that demonstrates Cocoa from Carbon is a spell-checking application that you can find at `http://developer.apple.com/samplecode/SpellingChecker-CarbonCocoa/SpellingChecker-CarbonCocoa.html`.

(Parenthetically [see them around this sentence?], Apple's convention is to lowercase the first character of Cocoa method calls, which leaves capitalizing the first character as a convenient convention for the wrapper name — if you don't find that confusing.)

▼ Note

In point of fact, because the frameworks that Cocoa development makes available to the Xcode programmer are implemented atop the same procedural APIs available to Carbon developers, the temporal discontinuity between when a feature became available in one framework versus the other was more a function of which development team first had the people, time, and interest to implement support within the framework. For a long time Cocoa was the "more equal pig" when it came to internal resources — and it still is, but to a lesser extent.

Taken directly from Apple's SpellChecker sample program that we tell you about in "Let Me Get My Wrap," the code shown in Figure 15-1 exemplifies typical wrapper functions.

Once you have all your wrapper functions written, including the Cocoa framework initialization code that you'll see in the SpellCheck example (copy-and-paste is your friend), you have two ways to go. You could just build a private framework bundle that you'll load into your various Carbon projects where you wish to leverage the Cocoa functionality. Figure 15-2 shows the project window for the Carbon SpellingChecker project that employs a private bundle, SpellCheck.bundle, in the details list.

If you are only going to require the functionality in one Xcode project, your easy route is to proceed as follows:

1. **With your Carbon Xcode project open, choose File → New File.** The New File window opens.

2. **Select Empty File In Project and click the Next button.** The New Empty File In Project sheet appears.

3. **Name the file, giving it the .m extension that tells Xcode the file is an Objective-C file.**

UP A LAZY RIVER

Apple refers to building and including a private bundle for the Cocoa wrapper functions as *lazy initialization*. Lazy initialization requires Mac OS X 10.1 or later. Because this technique doesn't require linking your project against the Cocoa framework, Cocoa is only loaded by OS X's dynamic loader (dyld) when needed. This can reduce launch time at the expense of a performance hit when the user initiates an action requiring Cocoa to be loaded.

One time you might want to use lazy initialization is when the Cocoa functionality is fairly isolated and might not be used by all your customers or in many application runs. An example might be an archival function in an accounting application — you only invoke the archival functionality once a month, once a quarter, or once a year.

The main thing to remember is that you create an Xcode project that's based on the Cocoa Bundle template (you can find that template in the New Project window's Bundle category). Make sure to give the main file a descriptive name with an .m suffix and that it includes directives to import the Carbon.h and Cocoa.h header files.

After that, you just create your Carbon application as usual, with the single exception of adding your private framework to the project.

One downside of using a private bundle is that calling the C wrapper functions is no longer transparent. You now need to load the Cocoa bundle and obtain function pointers to your C wrapper functions. And, of course, you still have to initialize Cocoa. Apple's SpellChecker example that we've been citing demonstrates all the niggling details.

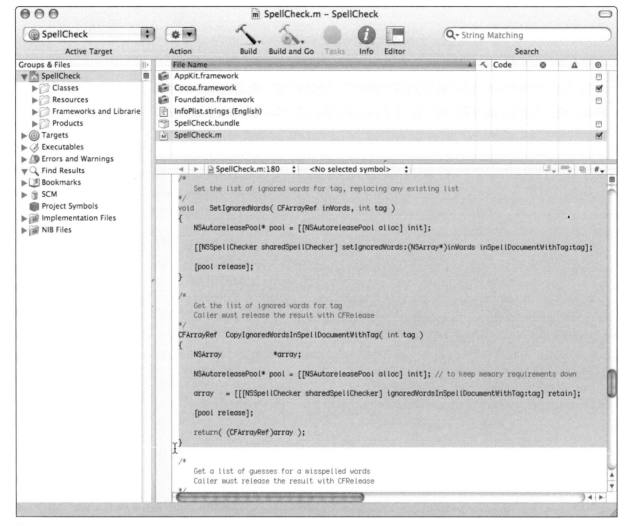

Figure 15-1
C-callable wrapper functions are straightforward to write

4. **Click Finish.** Xcode opens an editor pane for the new file.

5. **Add the following statements to your new file:**

```
#include <Carbon/Carbon.h>
#include <Cocoa/Cocoa.h>
```

Now, add your wrapper functions and you're good to go.

WHO PUT CARBON IN MY COCOA?

Cocoa developers using Objective-C have matters even easier than Carbon developers using C++ or C when they want to leverage functionality from the other framework. After all, Objective-C is a superset of ANSI C and Objective-C code calls C functions routinely — no fuss, no muss. And, because the Application Services framework

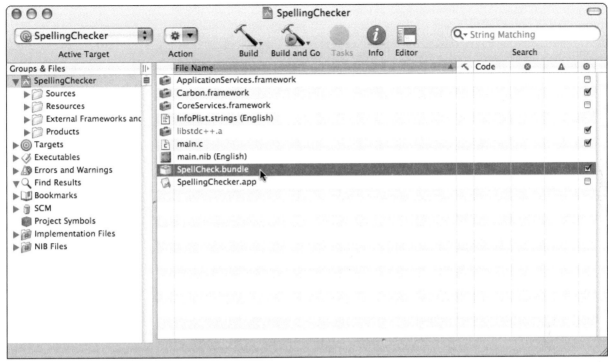

Figure 15-2
Include the private bundle in your Carbon project and just call the wrappers as necessary

THE E-POSTMAN COMETH

You aren't limited to Apple's ADC Web site (`http://developer.apple.com`), the documentation that comes with Xcode 2, and the various other Web pages you might find through a Google search when it comes to tackling issues like mixing languages and frameworks. Apple also maintains a number of mailing lists (yeah, we've mentioned this before), two of which are particularly useful in dealing with framework issues: carbon-dev and cocoa-dev. Hie thee on over to `http://lists.apple.com/mailman/listinfo` and sign up for all the lists that you find of interest, or at least as many of them as you can deal with filling your e-mailbox.

You can get digests that contain each day's mail exchanges, which is great if you want to keep your In box slimmer — you can change your subscription options on the same page on which you subscribed... look near the bottom for the button that says "unsubscribe or edit options." You can also search the archives for discussions that took place before you subscribed. And, of course, be a good netizen and read the FAQs for the lists.

is already included by the Cocoa framework, all the low-level functions are already defined and accessible. Calling Carbon user interface functions is almost as easy — just add `import Carbon.h` and include the Carbon framework in your Xcode project to link against.

Utilizing QuickTime is probably one of the most common reasons for a Cocoa application to call Carbon functions, so we're going to use it to talk about some common Carbon-in-Cocoa issues. QuickTime is easily one of Apple's crown jewels, which we guess makes it a diamond (diamonds are carbon, after all, as most anyone who took science in school or read *Superman* comics is well aware). Moreover, although Cocoa offers access to QuickTime through NSMovieView, there are a lot of QuickTime functions that aren't in the Cocoa APIs. Some of the more notably absent functions include `GetMovieTrackCount` (find out how many tracks make up the movie), `GetMovieIndTrack` (retrieve a track's index number), and `SetMovieLanguage` (specify which audio track to play when a movie has multiple language tracks).

All you have to do in a Cocoa app to use the Carbon Quick-Time library is call the QuickTime function, `EnterMovies`, which initializes the QuickTime Movie toolbox so the rest of your code can access any or all of the QuickTime functions that Cocoa doesn't make immediately available.

Remember that QuickTime, like many Carbon routines that migrated over the Great OS Divide from the old Mac toolbox, uses so-called *Pascal strings* (`Str255`) for most strings. The first (zero index) byte gives the string's length, the actual string content starts at byte 1, and strings aren't null-terminated. This means that when your Cocoa method calls require an `NSString`, you need to specify `&stringVar[1]` as the `stringWithCString` parameter value and `stringVar[0]` as the length parameter (where `stringVar` is your `Str255` variable).

QuickTime, being Carbon, also uses the `FSSpec`-based File Manager. As a consequence, many QuickTime calls will

WHAT ABOUT THIRD-PARTY COMPILERS?

Yeah, what about them? This *is* a bit of a dicey problem when it comes to calling Apple's frameworks from languages (such as Pascal or Fortran) supplied by third-party developers. We're going to have to punt here: The fact is, it all depends on how well the third-party developers did their jobs. Some do it well; for example, a group of enterprising open-sourcerers have developed a Python-Objective-C bridge that enables Python coders to get at the Cocoa frameworks (you can see the details at `http://pyobjc.source forge.net/`). And the Free Pascal compiler can support Carbon applications if you use the integration kit at `http://instantware.bei.t-online.de/ Xcode-FreePascal/`. Chances are, if the compiler can be used with Xcode, it probably provides some access to the Apple frameworks.

Even if the compiler doesn't support Carbon or Cocoa directly, though, you might be able to use some of the techniques for 64-bit applications described later in this chapter (see "The Eight-Dollar Question") with languages that don't directly support Apple's frameworks. You may end up building a sort of hybrid collection of interacting apps but, heck, that's the Unix way!

require `FSSpec` parameters. Apple sample code (blatantly reproduced here as Listing 15-1) shows how easy it is to obtain an `FSSpec`, given a path:

Listing 15-1: Obtaining an FSSpec

```
- (BOOL) myMakeFSSpec (FSSpec *) myFSSpecPtr
fromPath: (NSString *) inPath
{
FSRef myFSRef;
// Call the FileManager to convert a path to an
// FSRef structure
OSStatus status = FSPathMakeRef ([inPath
  fileSystemRepresentation],
```

```
  &myFSRef,, NULL);
// if there's no error, call the FileManager to
// map the FSRef to an FSSpec, without any
// catalog information
if (status == noErr)
  status = FSGetCatalogInfo(
    &myFSRef, kFSCatInforNone,
    NULL, NULL, myFSSpecPtr,
    NULL);
return (status == noErr);
}
```

THE EIGHT-DOLLAR QUESTION

"Two bits, four bits, six bits, a dollar..." goes the doggerel. We're talking about 64-bit computing here, so if the sequence kept going, we'd be at $8 when we got to 64 bits. Of course, we could have titled this "The Eight-Byte Question" because a byte contains 8 bits, but that wouldn't have been as funny or obscure, and we're nothing if not obscure (one of us in his misspent youth actually read *Finnegans Wake* for fun).

Apple knew that the G5 was coming when it released Panther, so the hooks were there for Mac OS X to utilize more than 4GB of RAM when running on a G5, but that didn't help you, the application developer. Your applications were still constrained by the 32-bit address space and the 4GB limitation that results. Historically, whenever a system architecture has evolved to support larger address spaces, applications written for the older architecture suffered in performance as a "compatibility mode" kicked in (some of us will remember the days of Windows 3.1 and the headaches that came with the move from an 8-bit to a 16-bit model, one of the more cumbersome transitions). But the PowerPC processor, versions of which Apple has been using for more than a decade, was designed from the beginning as a 64-bit architecture with a 32-bit subset and this design decision makes a compatibility mode unnecessary and eliminates the performance bottlenecks. (The PowerPC is a chip that Thinks Different.)

What does 64-bit addressing really mean, though? The first thing it means is that the theoretical limitation to

memory on a 64-bit processor is 16 *exabytes* — that's 4GB *squared*, or more than 4 billion times the 4GB address space that we've been limited to with 32-bit addressing. That's the contents of almost 4 billion DVDs!

 Note

The currently blessed statement of Moore's Law (which we've always thought of as Moore's Extrapolation) says that data density doubles approximately every 18 months. If this "Law" were to continue to hold true (and there's some doubt whether it does, much less will), moving from 32-bit to 64-bit addressing gives us 32 "doublings"... or 48 years before we need to be concerned with a transition to 128-bit addressing.

SOFTWARE CENTAURS AND MINOTAURS

Greek mythology gave us centaurs (men's torsos on a horse's body) and minotaurs (a bull's head on a man's body). The symbol for the constellation Sagittarius is a centaur. While we never saw much sense in these creatures, man-beast hybrids were not uncommon in myth and fable — whether it was Greek, Roman, Norse, Egyptian, or you name it.

With software, though, such hybrids start to make sense. You can create applications that place a pretty Cocoa user interface on an existing, sturdy Carbon application or even put a Carbon UI on a Cocoa application. Apple provides simple examples of both on the ADC Web site. Check out `http://developer.apple.com/samplecode/CocoaInCarbon/CocoaInCarbon.html` and `http://developer.apple.com/samplecode/CarbonInCocoa/CarbonInCocoa.html` for the Xcode projects and source files.

JUST DON'T WANNA FACE IT

If you have a Unix background, you're familiar with the concept of *daemons*, background processes that run without user interaction. This is a *faceless app*. Background processes, such as background printing, are probably more familiar to Mac users as examples of faceless apps.

FBAs (our shorthand for *Faceless Background Applications*) perform tasks behind the scenes, generally without any user interaction. iCal's Alarms feature, for example, is an FBA that gets launched (this is called *spawning a process*) by iCal and runs in the background, periodically checking the system clock, waiting to notify you of your impending appointment or event. iCal doesn't even have to be running for the notification to occur.

OS X's Unix heart runs a great many FBA daemons. If you don't believe us, just launch your Mac's Activity Monitor and set it to show All Processes. You'll find an impressively long list of tasks such as `cron`, `update`, `netinfod`, and `lookupd` running, just waiting to do their jobs without any direct input from you, as shown in Figure 15-3.

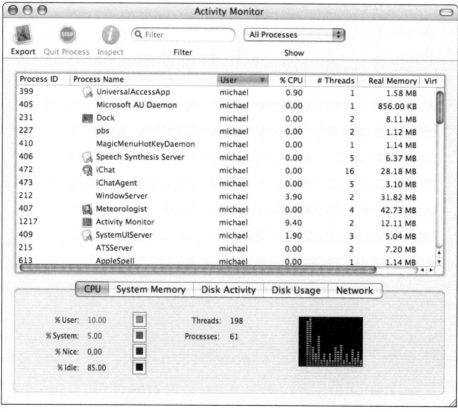

Figure 15-3
Michael's iMac runs quite a few FBAs

Tiger provides much broader support for 64-bit addressing than Panther. Before you get all excited, though, there are some limitations to Tiger's 64-bit support, the main one being that 64-bit addressing is only available to non-GUI processes, such as command-line tools and *faceless apps* (see the sidebar "Just Don't Wanna Face It" for a brief discourse on faceless apps). But, that's not such a big deal because, as we've seen earlier (such as in Chapter 14's AppleScript Studio coverage), Xcode makes it easy to call a command-line tool from a GUI application. Apple also provides four messaging methods to let your 32-bit GUI app communicate with your 64-bit command-line tool:

- it can employ the command-line task's stdin and stdout pipes;

- it can use Unix domain sockets to pass messages;

- it can use Mach-based IPC messaging; and

- it can use shared memory.

▼ **Tip**

Apple recommends using the simplest strategy (one of the first two, as appropriate) to preserve flexibility in case you might want to migrate to a client-server model. One example would be running the command-line process on a G5-based Xserve while your GUI client ran on any Mac networked to the Xserve. This would allow your client applications to run on non-G5 systems and still benefit from the Xserve's 64-bit addressing while it runs the command-line process. (This approach also helps Apple sell more Xserves to the enterprise. We're just saying....)

THE FINAL MIX

In this chapter we finally broke down and talked about actual coding techniques instead of just talking about Xcoding techniques. We looked at some of the issues involved with calling Cocoa from Carbon apps and introduced the concepts of *lazy initialization* and *wrapper functions*. We suggested some Apple mailing lists that could help you. Then we went to the flip side and talked about calling Carbon from Cocoa, using QuickTime as our focus because it is a really popular Carbon API, and discussed such esoterica as how to deal with FSSpecs and Str255s. Finally, we looked at what Tiger's new 64-bit addressing capabilities do, and don't do, for Carbon and Cocoa developers, and came face-to-non-face with faceless background applications.

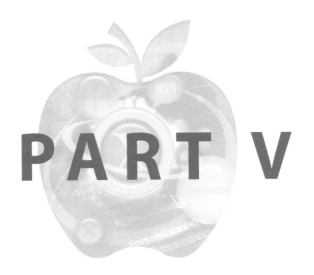

PART V

Of Cat Herding
and Flea Baths:
Debugging, Optimizing,
and Version Control

16

Avoiding Falling Anvils
and Other Crashes

GDB, or, I GNU a Debugger Once, Too

The Fix (and Continue) Is In

How Not to Lose Your Memory

Debugging at a Distance

Debugging Debriefing

Big bugs have little bugs
Upon their backs to bite them.
And little bugs have littler bugs.
And so, *ad infinitum*!

Jonathan Swift apparently knew something about the software development cycle. Although we all like to think we are perfect, and that the code we write is perfect, and that this is the best of all possible worlds (as Swift's contemporary, Voltaire, wrote... though we suspect he may have been kidding), we aren't, we don't, and this isn't.

In the course of software development, stuff happens (substitute your own favorite word beginning with an *s* here — we bet you can think of one). We get tired. We get confused. We don't think things out completely. And even if our code *were* perfect, it's not the only dancer in the dance hall doing the digital do-si-do: Our Macs host many other dancers at any given moment, and each of them is capable of inadvertent toe-tromping. It used to be truism that a successful compile was the first stage of a major system crash. In Tiger and its OS Xish predecessors, major system crashes are rare, but application crashes are still all too common. In short, bugs are inevitable. If you don't believe it, you are definitely in the wrong line of work.

Xcode comes with a pleasing plethora of debugging tools to help you answer the essential question of debugging: What went wrong? From setting breakpoints to monitoring memory allocation, Xcode can help you turn your app from a Two-Left-Feet Larry into a Bulletproof Baryshnikov.

So get ready to make with the *tour jete!*

GDB, OR, I GNU A DEBUGGER ONCE, TOO

Seeing as how the standard compilers for Xcode 2 come from the Free Software Foundation's GNU project, it should come as no surprise to anyone with more than a neuron or two to rub together that the standard source-level debugger throbbing under Xcode's glossy Aqua-tinted hood is the GNU Project debugger, GDB (biologists take note: this GDB is not the same GDB as the human Genome DataBase).

The GDB that ships with Xcode 2, like all the GDBs before it, is quite capable of being run from the Unix command line as has been done since days of yore, and there are some old-school Unix jockeys that wouldn't have it any other way. But, as with the various compilers in the GCC, Xcode wraps GDB in GUI goodness that is not only more attractive than the command line but also more convenient and practical (see Figure 16-1).

What this figure shows you is Apple's TextEdit application stopped at a breakpoint that we set so we could show you what the Debugger window looks like when it *is* stopped at a breakpoint... which is one of the most common ways you are apt to see the Debugger window (now isn't that worthy of a picture?). And, because we have the window, let's take a look at its main components.

OK, I'M A TOTAL NOOB... WHAT'S A DEBUGGER?

Ah, Noob, we won't laugh; we were all newbies once, too. A debugger, contrary to what its name rather strongly implies, does not remove the bugs in a program. That's your job. A debugger is a standard tool that helps you do that. It does this in several ways.

- It lets you set "breakpoints" that halt your program at specified lines of code, or in specific situations.

- It allows you to peer inside your program while it is stopped so you can examine the program's variables.

- It lets you step, line by line, through the program so you can get the ultimate slo-mo picture of how your program is functioning.

- It can, in some situations, let you actually alter the program's code or variables while it is halted, and then resume the program's execution so you can see what those changes do.

- It can make your hair shiny and more manageable.

All, right, it doesn't do that last thing. But it might keep you from tearing your hair out.

The Debug window

Along the top is the window's toolbar. The figure shows the standard toolbar for the window:

- **Build and Debug** lets you rebuild the program and start the debugger on it again; useful when you've been making changes in a debugging session.

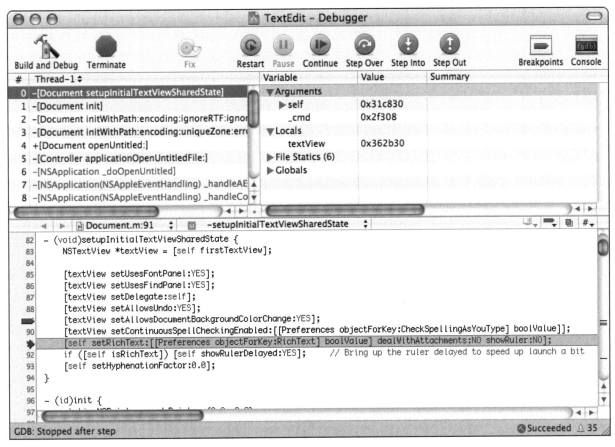

Figure 16-1
GDB in Xcode's clothing

- **Terminate** either phones the governor of California or forces your program to quit. We think it's the latter. If there is nothing running to be debugged, this becomes the Debug button, which, when clicked, launches your project's executable for debugging.

- **Fix** lets you use Xcode's Fix and Continue feature, described later in this chapter.

- **Restart, Pause,** and **Continue** let you, respectively, restart the program (which is much like terminating the program and then starting the debug session up again), pause the program's execution wherever it

happens to be (which often leaves you deep inside a low-level PowerPC assembly-language routine), and resume execution after you've paused the program manually or stopped it on a breakpoint.

- **Step Over, Step Into,** and **Step Out** let you step through the program, line by line:

  - Step Over executes the current program line and halts at the next line; if the current line is a function call, it completes the function call (unless, of course, there's a breakpoint in that function).

Step Into executes the current line; if that line calls a function, the debugger stops at the first line of the called function.

 Step Out causes the program to complete whichever function it is currently in, and then stops execution when that function returns to its calling function.

▼ Tip

You'll use these commands so often that you may wish to know their keyboard equivalents: Step Over is Shift+⌘+O, Step Into is Shift+⌘+I, and Step Out is Shift+⌘+T. Learn them. Live them. Love them.

● **Breakpoints** shows you the Breakpoints window, which, as you might expect, shows you the breakpoints that are currently set in the program (it also lets you set them, but that's another story, which we tell later in this section).

● **Console** shows you the debugger's Console window, where messages that GDB generates are recorded and displayed. It also allows you to type commands to control the debugger just as you would do from the traditional Unix command line.

You can modify the toolbar of the Debug window much as you can other Xcode windows by choosing View ➜ Customize Toolbar, which gives you the plethora of icons shown in Figure 16-2.

Below the toolbar are three panes that give you debugging details.

○ The pane on the Debug window's top left shows you the **thread view,** which presents the current thread's *call stack* (the function calls that have led to the currently running function in the current thread of execution). You can choose to view a different thread's

call stack by picking it from the Thread pop-up above the pane. If your application is not multithreaded, this menu won't be of much use to you.

○ The pane on the top right is the **variable view.** It shows you all the variables that are currently available to the current function of the current thread, along with their values. If you happen to be viewing some gnarly assembly code, this panel shows you the gnarly contents of the CPU registers.

○ And below these two panes is the **editor,** which shows you your code. You can see the current breakpoint, if any, in the margin. The line about to be executed is indicated by a red arrow in the margin; the line itself is shaded as well.

▼ Note

If you are viewing your source code and want to see both it *and* the equivalent assembly code, choose Debug ➜ Toggle Disassembly Display; the Editor pane splits to show you the disassembled binary code as well as your source code.

Finally, at the bottom of the Debug window, is the usual Xcode status area, with which you should be more than familiar at this point.

▼ Note

If you prefer a somewhat different layout for the Debug window, choose Debug ➜ Toggle Debugger Layout. This places the thread and variable views on the left and the editor on the right.

The Debug menu

Because we've brought up the Debug menu a few times already, you may be wondering what wonders it contains. Figure 16-4 reveals its hidden splendor.

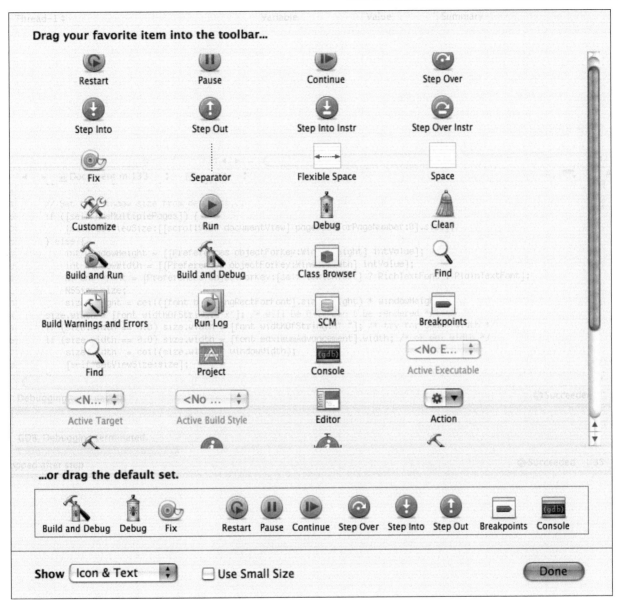

Figure 16-2
Tools... we got tools...

EXECUTABLE ENVIRONMENTALISM

In most cases — for example, when you are building applications based on Xcode's templates — the debugger knows how to present you with meaningful information because the templates automatically create a Development build style that generates all the good stuff the debugger needs in order to associate your source with the compiled code (see "How Do I Build Thee?" in Chapter 3).

What the Development build style, and other build styles, are doing is creating an *executable environment*, and ordinarily you never worry about it. Sometimes, though, you have to. For example, if you are building an application that depends on the value of a particular environment variable (as some ported Unix tools might), or if you are building a command-line tool or a framework, you will need to customize the executable environment. This is where the Executable Inspector comes in (see Figure 16-3).

You can bring up the Inspector by selecting the executable in your project's Groups & Files list and choosing File ➡ Get Info (or you can click the Project Window's Info icon in the toolbar). The Inspector has four tabs that let you customize the execution environment:

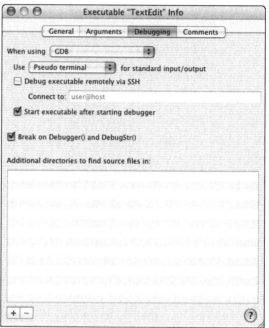

Figure 16-3
The Executable Inspector is a committed environmentalist

- The **General** tab lets you specify the path to the executable, set the working directory, select where standard input/output comes from and goes to (useful for command-line tools), and specifiy which suffix to use when loading frameworks (for example, Apple provides `.profile` and `.debug` versions of its frameworks that you may wish to load).

- The **Arguments** tab is where you go when you want to pass arguments to your executable (such as arguments that a command-line tool may require) or if you need to set environment variables for your executable.

- The **Debugging** tab (shown in Figure 16-3) lets you pick how Xcode's different debuggers use standard input/output (Xcode provides not only GDB, but AppleScript and Java debuggers), set up remote debugging (described later in this chapter), and some other useful options you can probably figure out on your own.

- The **Comments** tab lets you associate comments with your customized executable environment, so you can understand the next morning the settings you set the night before.

So, if you're a framework-writing, tool-crafting, plug-in-producing kind of developer, you definitely want to learn to control your executable environment with the Executable Inspector. And if you're not, the Inspector's still instructive to peruse and use.

Figure 16-4
The extensive offerings of the Debug menu

The Debug menu is divided into several sections.

- The first section lets you open the Debug and Breakpoints windows.

- The second section lets you open and manipulate various log windows; which ones you use depend on your particular situation. For example, the Standard I/O Log comes in handy when you're writing tools that send output to standard I/O.

- The third section lets you control the debugger and the executable being debugged. The Launch using Performance Tool submenu in this section is used with the performance tools, some of which are described later in this chapter, and some of which are described in the next chapter.

- The fourth section deals with stuff you can see. The Tools submenu gives you windows for looking at global variables, shared libraries, and memory; the

Variables submenu contains commands that let you tailor how the variables view presents its wares.

- The fifth section controls the executable's activities; many of the commands here replicate the command icons in the Debug window's standard toolbar.

- The sixth itty-bitty section lets you set or remove breakpoints, which we explain a bit further on in this chapter... in fact, right after the very next bullet point.

- The seventh and final section lets you set what happens when the executable being debugged runs into an exception; it also lets you control what happens when it hits a special debug statement in your code and whether or not to run the executable with Guard Malloc active. We deal with Guard Malloc when we tell you "How Not to Lose Your Memory" later in this chapter.

Breakpoints

We've also nattered on a bit about breakpoints, and if you are new to the debugging world, you may be wondering just what they are and how they are created.

 Note

Breakpoints have *nothing* to do with the 1991 surfing thriller, *Point Break*, although Keanu Reeves *was* pretty good as Johnny Utah.

Breakpoints are places in your code where you want the debugger to stop program execution so you can see what's going on. Because they are so fundamental to debugging, Xcode makes them quite easy to set, and it provides a number of ways to set them.

- In an editing window, you can click the gutter beside the line where you want a breakpoint set. A small arrow appears in the gutter to indicate the existence of the breakpoint.

- You can click anywhere in a line of code in an editing window and choose Debug ➜ Add Breakpoint at Current Line — or you can press ⌘+\.

- You can open the Breakpoints window (choose Debug ➜ Breakpoints or press Option+⌘+B) and then click the New Symbolic Breakpoint button (see Figure 16-5). The window offers a text field in which you can type the name of a function in your code; every time the function is called, the symbolic breakpoint halts execution so you can check things out in the debugger.

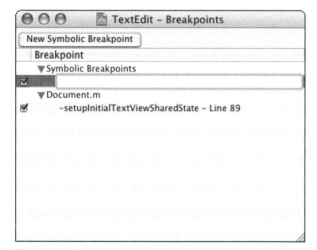

Figure 16-5
Breakpoints window lets you set symbolic breakpoints

 Note

In C and C++ code, the name of a function suffices to set a symbolic breakpoint. For Objective-C methods, you also need to provide the brackets and a plus or a minus; for example, - [EncodingPopUpButton awakeFromNib].

Removing breakpoints is simple, too. Simply click an existing breakpoint arrow in the editing window, and the break-point vanishes. Or, if the editor's cursor is on a line that has a breakpoint, you can choose Debug ➜ Remove Breakpoint at Current Line (⌘+\). Or, if the Breakpoints window is open, you can click to select the breakpoint and just press the Delete key.

 Tip

Xcode allows you to disable breakpoints so that they remain in place but the debugger ignores them. To disable breakpoints, ⌘+click them in an editor window; the breakpoint arrow changes to light gray to indicate it is disabled. You can also uncheck the box by a breakpoint's name in the Breakpoints window to disable it. You can activate disabled breakpoints by a second ⌘+click, or you can check the box in the Breakpoints window.

SING, YOU SINNERS!

GDB is apparently well loved by its community of users... at least, judging by the fact that they've written songs about it (see http://www.gnu.org/software/gdb/song/).

For example, Joel Bion, Mark Baushke, and Lynn Slater of the Free Software Movement seem to have created *The GDB Song* (based on a little ditty from *The Sound of Music*), which begins, "Let's start at the very beginning, a very good place to start, / When you're learning to sing, its Do, Re, Mi; / When you're learning to code, it's G, D, B...."

Then there's Waider's song, *GDB!* (based on *Tragedy* by Barry, Robin, and Maurice Gibb), which starts, "Here's vi / In a lost and lonely part of code / Held in time / In a world of bugs my head explodes...."

See what can happen when you spend too much time in the debugger?

THE FIX (AND CONTINUE) IS IN

Some apps are big and take way too much time to compile and link (especially by the impatient standards of today's caffeine nation), but even the smallest app often seems to take more time to rebuild than you'd like, especially when you are in the throes of a debugging frenzy. That intense need to just hurry up and get on with it already is what Fix and Continue was made for.

Fix and Continue performs the seemingly impossible task of letting you pause in the middle of debugging, fix a line

or two or ten of code, recompile and link just those changes, and continue the same debugging session, using the changed code... *right from where you paused!* Wow! Okay, it does come with some hidden gotchas, and we'll get to those. First, here's how it works.

1. **In a debugging session, pause the debuggee, either manually or with a breakpoint.** If you are debugging, you probably have a few of these doorstops sprinkled through your code.

2. **Edit the source file, making the fixes you think are necessary.** Figure 16-6 shows a Debugger window

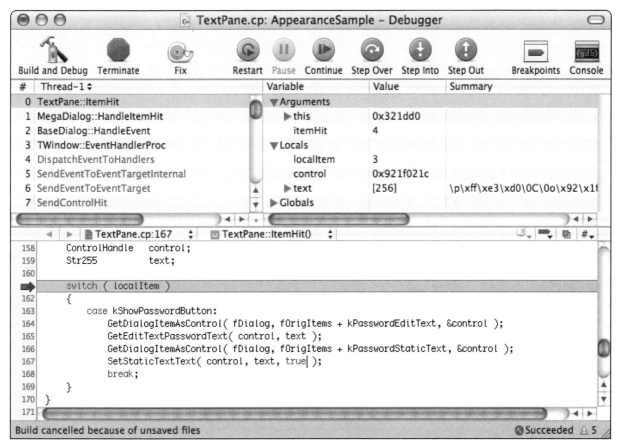

Figure 16-6
Ready to fix

with a file in the editor view to which we've made changes while the debugger was paused.

3. **Click the Fix button in the Debugger window's toolbar, or choose Debug → Fix.** Xcode asks you to save the file.

 Note

You can only fix one file at a time. That is, if you change the contents of, say, three files, you have to click the Fix button for each of them. And you have to wait for the fix process to complete before getting on with your debugging session.

4. **Save the file.** Xcode compiles and links the file, which only takes a few seconds.

5. **Resume the debugging session.** Marvel at the utter coolness of this technological wonder.

And that's all there is to it.

 Note

Changes made with Fix and Continue do not affect the compiled object files on your hard drive, because the process patches the object code in memory only. You must rebuild your project to update your project's object files.

Of course, this power all comes at a price. You can't Fix and Continue with just any project, for starters. You have to ensure that the following steps have been taken.

- You must compile your code with GCC 3.3 or a later version. This means that you can't target the oldest, hoariest versions of Mac OS X.

- If you're writing in C++, you have to make sure that your build uses Zero Link. You can find this setting by editing your project settings (Project → Edit Project Settings) and clicking the Styles tab in the project settings information window. The Zero Link setting is in the Style tab's Linking collection.

HOW'D IT DO THAT?

GDB maintains a lot of information about your app while it is running. When you patch a file with Fix and Continue, the patch is loaded into memory with the rest of the executable code; GDB compares the patch to the original, makes sure that the patches are not the sort that would cause the whole house of cards that GDB has created to come crashing down, and then, if everything checks out, executes the patch instead of the original binary code.

GDB also makes sure that any functions that call or otherwise refer to any of the replaced code are redirected to refer to the replacement, and that any global variables that refer to the patched code are updated.

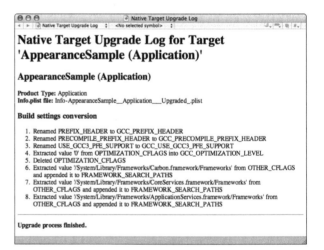

Figure 16-7
A target upgrade

- You have to be debugging a *native target*. If you've begun a new project using Xcode's application templates, you probably already are using a native target, but you will have to convert older projects. To do that, select the target and choose Project ➔ Upgrade to Native Target. This command duplicates your target and makes a number of changes to it (see Figure 16-7).

○ You have to build your project *without* optimizations and *with* debugging symbols enabled; these can be set in your target's compiler settings (select the target and choose Project ➔ Edit Active Target or press Option+⌘+E). Figure 16-8 shows the appropriate settings.

HOW NOT TO LOSE YOUR MEMORY

So many program bugs are related to memory, either leaking it or touching it where it doesn't like to be touched. We'll deal with the last problem first.

Whenever we encounter memory access errors, we keep hearing a revised version of *The Way We Were* rattling around in our heads: "Memory may be beautiful and yet /

Figure 16-8
Fix and Continue wants settings like these

SOME THINGS YOU JUST CAN'T FIX

GDB will tell you if it decides that the changes you make can't be incorporated into a Fix and Continue patch, and it gives you the option of continuing the debugging without the patch. However, there are some things it *won't* warn you about, but which could cause your app to crash and burn anyway. Here's a list of *don't*s.

- Do not change any nib files. GDB doesn't know nuthin' about nib files.

- Do not add a new Objective-C class as part of a fix.

- Do not try adding any methods, either to a class or a category.

- Do not remove methods from classes or categories.

- Do not add or remove class instance variables.

- Do not add try blocks.

- Do not add catch handlers to existing blocks.

- Do not add a C++ class specialization.

- Do not change how you've defined any structs or unions.

- Do not add static variables to multiple patches (GDB can get confused).

- Do not add a function to a file called from a different file that you patched in the same session; this way lies madness.

- Do not refer to any external variables or functions if those references are unresolved.

- Do not change functions that, in order to resolve symbol conflicts, require two-level namespaces during linking (and do not try to understand this sentence unless you are a rather advanced programmer).

- Do not taunt Happy Fun Ball.

When your pointers pass an array's end / Your app does more than just forget...."

Such errors are all too common in C, which can be a dangerous language, encouraging you to engage in all sorts of fun and games with pointer arithmetic. Sure, such games can give you great power and help speed program execution, but they make it very easy to blunder and let a pointer go just a little too far, tromping on memory it shouldn't touch. (Pop quiz: How many of the last few years' viruses and worms rely on executing code reached by way of a buffer overflow?)

Xcode provides a way for you to catch such oversights in your own code: *Guard Malloc*.

Guard Malloc (which you can enable in your development work by choosing Debug ➜ Enable Guard Malloc), is a dynamic library that goes by the command-line name of `libgmalloc.dylib`, and that handles all your code's `malloc` calls. With Guard Malloc enabled, spotting a bug related to accessing memory beyond the bounds allocated to a variable through `malloc()` is extraordinarily easy: Your application immediately crashes with a bus error. Simple. Elegant. Annoying. And essential.

▼ Tip

You can find out all about Guard Malloc by consulting the Unix `man` page for `libgmalloc.dylib` (remember, the Xcode Help menu has an Open man page command for just such occasions). There, you can also learn the various environment variable options it offers, and, if one or more of them look useful to you, you can use the Argument tab in your executable's Inspector window to set these up.

Memory leaks are also pernicious, if not quite as dangerous as access errors. Leaks occur when you don't release memory that you are no longer using, which means that your program keeps requesting more and more memory over time and eventually grinds to a slow painful halt.

One tool that helps you with such bugs is *MallocDebug*. MallocDebug is a separate application that Xcode can launch from the Debug menu: Debug ➔ Launch Using Performance Tools ➔ MallocDebug.

When you issue this command, Xcode launches MallocDebug, all primed and ready to examine your application (see Figure 16-9). Click MallocDebug's Launch button, your app launches, and the leak-hunt begins.

What the program does is keep an eye on all memory allocations created with `malloc()` (sound familiar?). It cruises through your app's memory looking for pointers to these allocated blocks; if it doesn't find any such pointers, it calls it a leak and marks it as such.

Using the program is simple. Launch your app with it. Play with your app, trying out various features. When you

get tired of that, choose Leaks from the analysis pop-up menu (see Figure 16-10).

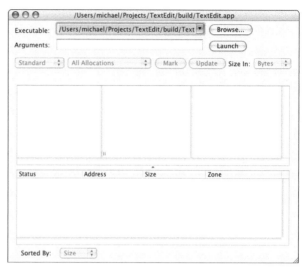

Figure 16-9
MallocDebug before things get interesting

Figure 16-10
Check your app for leaks

THE AGGRESSIVE GUARD MALLOC

Guard Malloc performs its magic through a very simple trick related to virtual memory. Every time you call `malloc()`, Guard Malloc allocates the memory at the end of a separate virtual memory page, and snuggles it up against an empty, unallocated page. So, if your code tries to access anything beyond what was allocated, kaboom! You get a bus error and your app crashes.

Guard Malloc also deals with the related problem of trying to access memory that has been deallocated. Each call to free memory deallocates the virtual memory page that Guard Malloc previously allocated. Attempts to access that missing memory give you a bus error. Once again, kaboom!

Obviously, a crash is a pretty severe way to detect memory trespasses, which is why you should have GDB running when Guard Malloc is enabled. That way, you can see where your program was when the hammer came down.

MallocDebug will provide a wealth of information, showing you a list of possible leaks, which you can click to see. Various menu choices let you tailor the display so that it makes sense to you.

Tip

MallocDebug has a Help menu that is quite helpful. Use it to find out all the features and displays of which this program is capable.

You can also use MallocDebug to check a particular feature of your program to see if it is leaking. Click the window's Mark button, play with that feature, and then click the Update button. MallocDebug shows you allocations made since you clicked Mark, which may be leaks.

Note

MallocDebug likes to keep its main window open until the app it is examining quits. In other words, don't try to close the MallocDebug window while your app is still open or you'll be told off, politely but firmly.

Another way to find leaks, one that is especially useful for Objective-C programmers, is *ObjectAlloc*. Like MallocDebug, it is a separate program that you launch from the Debug menu: Debug → Launch using Performance Tools → ObjectAlloc.

ObjectAlloc is designed to work with object-oriented programs, and it keeps track of which objects were created, rather than where they were created, presenting them in histogram format (see Figure 16-11).

ObjectAlloc likes to think it is a media player, so it presents its controls as playback buttons along the top of its window; from left to right they are:

- **Start/Stop Task,** which causes the program being examined to quit (the button changes appearance accordingly);

- **Pause/Continue Task,** which either pauses execution of the app or allows it to continue (this button changes appearance accordingly, too);

- **Step Backward** and **Step Forward,** two buttons which, when the app is paused, let you move backward and forward in time, watching allocations as they happen/unhappen; and

- **Mark,** which lets you start keeping track of allocations from the current time only. You use it in conjunction with the Show since mark option to switch between allocations since the mark and all allocations since the world began... that is, since your app was fired up.

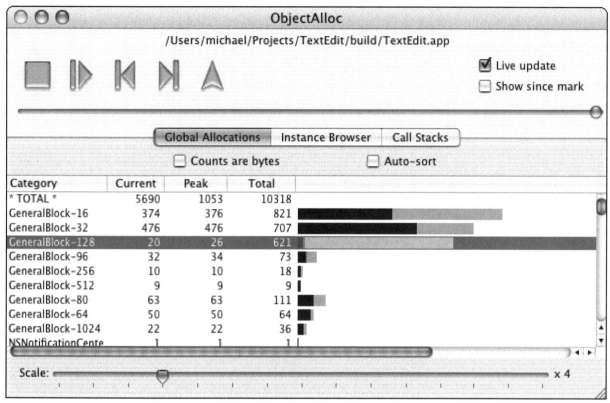

Figure 16-11
So, a bunch of objects walk into a bar chart...

▼ **Tip**

The slider above the display also lets you move backward and forward in time so you can scoot around watching the history of your app's object allocations unfold.

ObjectAlloc's Global Allocations tab shows you all the object allocations:

● The **Category** column shows you the type of object; types that ObjectAlloc can't figure out are marked *GeneralBlock*.

● The **Current** column shows how many of each kind of object is currently around and unreleased.

● The **Peak** column shows you the maximum number of objects of each type that existed at any one time.

● The **Total** column shows you how many objects of each type there ever were.

● The histogram shows you a bar that combines the current, peak, and total counts for each object graphically; you can use the Scale slider beneath the display to adjust the size of the bars for easy viewing pleasure.

The program also offers an Instance Browser tab that shows you a three-column view (see Figure 16-12) that shows you each type of object that has been allocated in the left column, their addresses in the central column, and the allocation events related to the object in the right column. Beneath is a pane that will show you the contents of the selected object, if possible.

And let us not forget the Call Stacks tab, which is designed to show you the function calls that led to the object allocations (see Figure 16-13), so you can trace your allocations back to your code (or to code that called code that called code that called code that lives somewhere in the bowels of some framework somewhere).

With ObjectAlloc you can see if you are creating too many objects of a particular kind, or if certain objects are not being created when they should be, or if certain objects are being created when they shouldn't be.

Sure, with its Aqua sparkly buttons and dancing bar graphs, ObjectAlloc does not look like the typical utilitarian memory debugging tool, but who said debugging couldn't be pretty?

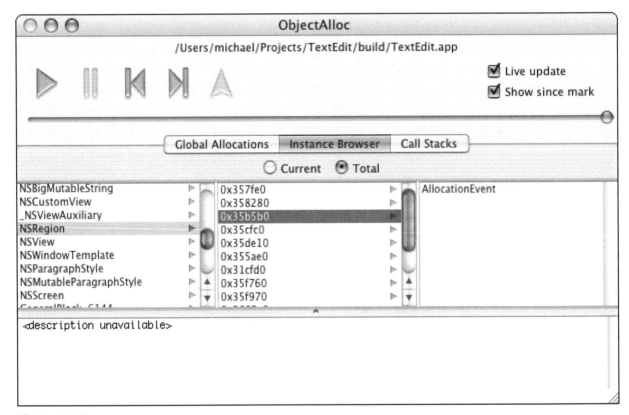

Figure 16-12
For instance, take a look at these objects...

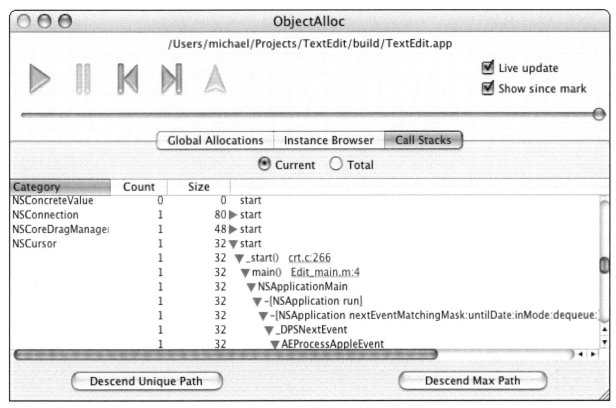

Figure 16-13
Little object, who made thee?

DEBUGGING AT A DISTANCE

Not all applications can be debugged successfully on a single computer. Take games, for example. They like to take over your screen... all of your screen... and whatever else they can take up, leaving no place for a debugger to present its findings, and few resources with which to do its work.

Xcode allows you to run an app on one machine and debug it on another, as long as you've set things up right.

First, you need a network, so the two machines involved can talk to each other. Apple's docs call the machine running Xcode the *local* machine, and the other machine, the one running the app to be debugged, the *remote host,* so we'll do the same. These two machines communicate using SSH public key authentication; Xcode integrates with `ssh-agent` to provide remote debugging services so that you don't have to enter a password every time the machines establish a connection.

Second, you have to set the machines up to use SSH for remote login. We're not going to go into how to do that here; it can require a bunch of command-line statements involving generating keys and concatenating key files and setting permissions, and all of this can vary from setup to setup. Xcode's documentation provides an example of how to set this up (look for "Remote debugging in Xcode" in the Documentation Viewer), and if you can't follow that, we suggest you find a Unix guru to help you. Seriously.

Third, the project files have to be available through the same path on both the local machine and the remote host. The best way to do this is to have the project files available through a network home directory that both machines use. Furthermore, if it is a GUI app you are debugging, you must be logged in to the remote machine with the same user account as the user connecting through SSH, and this user account has to have sufficient permissions to build stuff (so you can't use your six-year-old daughter's login account unless she has those kinds of user privileges).

Fourth, you have to set your app up for remote debugging:

1. **Select the executable to be debugged in the Project window.**

2. **Bring up the executable's Inspector window (a click of the toolbar's Info button should do the trick).**

3. **Click the Debugging tab (see Figure 16-14).**

4. **Click the Debug executable remotely via SSH option.**

5. **Choose Pipe from the Use for standard input/output pop-up menu.**

6. **Type the user name and the name of the remote host in the Connect to: field.** Put it in the form of *user@host*; for example, andyi@minimac.

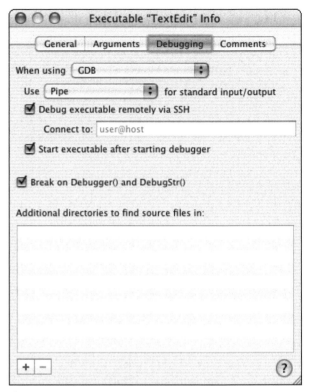

Figure 16-14
Getting ready to go remote

7. **On the local machine, build and debug the application as you ordinarily would.** Xcode may show you an authentication dialog the first time.

And that's it. You're now in two places at once, burning twice as many machine cycles.

DEBUGGING DEBRIEFING

We discovered that beneath Xcode's debugging abilities is GDB, the open-source debugger that has its own song. We illustrated how Xcode wraps this command-line tool in a rich GUI shell that shows you code, variables, and threads, and that has all sorts of nice debugging controls for pausing and stepping through your code. We then pointed out how Xcode gives you various ways to set, remove, enable, and disable breakpoints so you can quickly stop right where you want and examine why things aren't working (or why they are working so well). We also discovered what an executable environment is and why you might want to care about it. Next we looked at the seriously splendid Fix and Continue capabilities that Xcode provides to let you fix your code as it runs, and listed some of the reasons why you sometimes can't use it. We looked at three of Xcode's tools for debugging memory problems — Guard Malloc, MallocDebug, and ObjectAlloc — while humming a tune from a 1974 movie. Finally, we outlined how to run a program on one machine and debug it on another. After all of which, we crashed.

Shave and a Haircut, 64 Bits: Optimization Tools

Free Samples • What's Going On Right Now?
CHUD for the Defense
Performance Monitoring, or, Are You Going to Be in There Long?
Curtain Call

You've compiled your program with no errors... aaaand it runs without crashing! Woohoo! Now the real work begins: making it fast like a bullet, sleek like an otter. Welcome to the world of optimizing (or, as Homer Simpson might call it, "optimazizing").

Few things are more disappointing for users than finally getting a new program that does exactly what they want, but that moves more slowly than the Malaspina Glacier. And even fewer things are more exasperating than a Mac program that tosses rainbow pizzas more often than the sole pizzeria in a college town. Such programs may be programmatically flawless, but they're still practically useless.

Xcode comes with a passel of programs and a truckload of tools to help you figure out what your program is doing at any given time. These tools go by a number of unlikely names, such as Saturn and Shark, MONster and BigTop, CacheBasher and Skidmarks. With them, you can dive into the heart of the CPU itself to change registers, or get the big picture that shows you where your program is spending most of its time. You can see a color-coded timeline of all the executable threads in your app, examine what Quartz is doing when it draws your app's display, and monitor just what is going on when the spinning rainbow pizza is delivered to your Desktop. Sound interesting? Sound geeky? You don't know the half of it, pardner...

... but with Xcode's performance optimizing tools, you will.

FREE SAMPLES

One approach to program optimization is to find where your application is spending its time and concentrate on speeding up those routines. Two performance utilities, Sampler and Spin Control, team up to help you locate bottlenecks in your program — those operations that take longer than they should and those that present your customers with a rainbow-hued pizza.

Before you resort to performance-monitoring tools, though, Apple recommends running through the following checklist and fixing any problems the list brings to light:

- If your application is a mach-o executable (it almost always will be), make sure it is prebound in your Build Settings.

- Ensure that you have compiler optimization settings turned on.

- Run the `top` command-line utility or another activity monitor to make sure that it is your application and not some other process that's bogging things down.

Once you've checked everything off the above checklist, you need to find out where your application is spending its time. That's where tools like *Sampler*, *Spin Control*, and *Shark* (we write about Shark later in this chapter in "Performance Monitoring, or, Are You Going to Be in There Long?") come into play.

Sampler

You can't really use `gdb` (or other debugging tools you encounter in Chapter 16) to accurately gauge performance bottlenecks. After all, if you're stopping and starting the application and stepping through the code, you're not experiencing the full, mind-numbing boredom of waiting for the computer to finally do something — anything — in response to your last action or command.

Periodic *sampling* (checking what code is executing) is the primary method for gathering data on what's going on without recompiling your code. Sampling takes periodic snapshots of your application's execution stack and converts that information into a call graph of your code's functions.

You can launch Sampler before your application launches if you want to sample launch time code execution instead of, or in addition to, normal operation. To sample launch time execution, choose File ➜ New (⌘+N); however, to sample a currently running application, choose File ➜ Attach (⌘+T). If you choose to attach Sampler to an already executing application, you'll see the Attach dialog shown in Figure 17-1, listing the currently running processes and their *pid*s (Process IDs). In either case, you'll see the window shown in Figure 17-2 (some of the expository text will change depending on which application you're sampling).

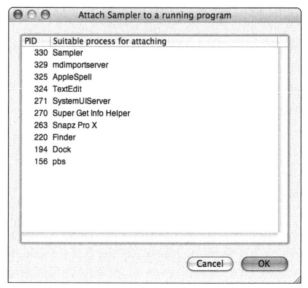

Figure 17-1
Let's form an attachment

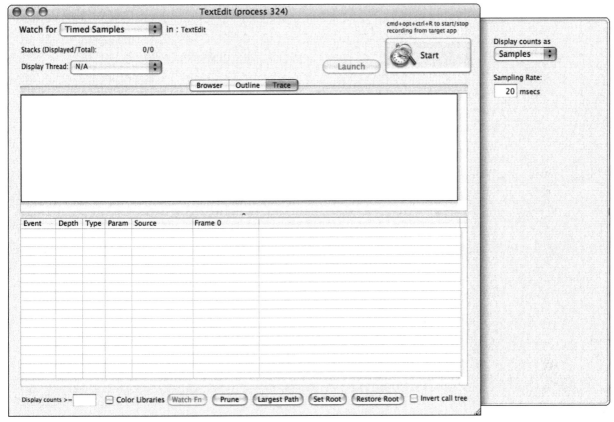

Figure 17-2
Step up to Xcode's sample counter

▼ Note

If you choose File ➜ New, the Start button will be labeled Launch & Probe.

Sampler's default is to take timed samples (see that up in Figure 17-2's Watch for pop-up menu?) and display them in the Trace pane, as shown in Figure 17-3. You can also view execution threads in outline form (see Figure 17-4) or in a browser column view (see Figure 17-5).

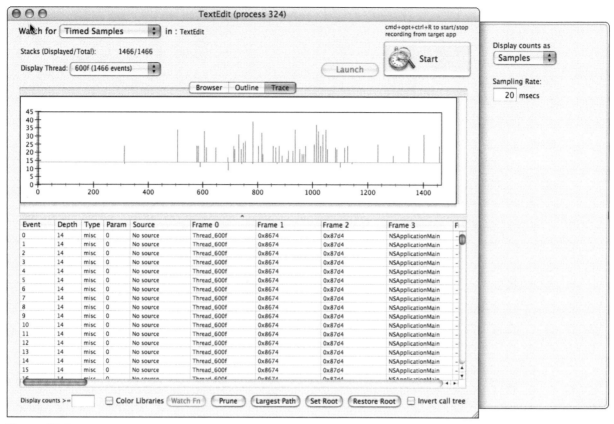

Figure 17-3

The trace view presents a histogram and a scrolling display of sampled data

▼ Note

The trace view chart is live, meaning that if you click in it, the table at the bottom of the view will scroll to the corresponding sample. The trace view's downside is that you frequently have to scroll a long way, horizontally, to explore an event's stack frame.

As you peruse the output from Timed Samples, you can determine which functions are being executed the most often (that is, where your program spends the bulk of its time). The places in which your application spends the most time are obviously the best candidates for you to try and optimize.

Figure 17-4

Hark back to beginning composition courses and work from an outline

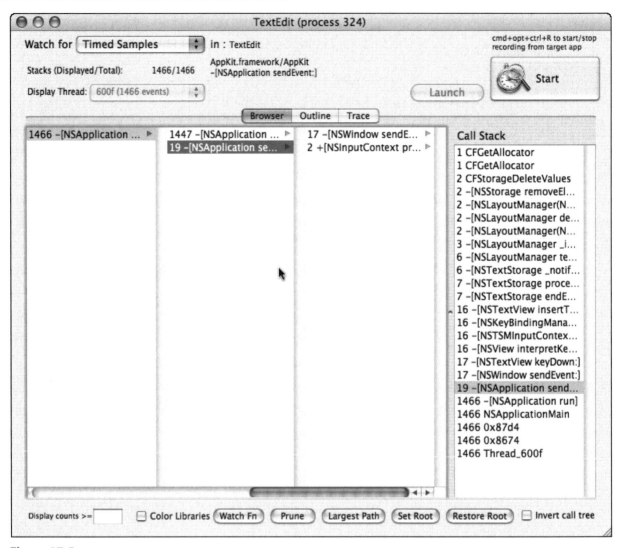

Figure 17-5
Browse your sampled thread in a column view with accompanying call stack

Timed samples are all well and good, but you might be more concerned with a particular function (or group of functions/methods) or with memory allocations. Sampler also lets you watch for these activities. The main Sampler window remains the same, but Sampler's drawer changes to let you specify which functions to monitor (see Figure 17-6) or to sample when a memory allocation takes place (see Figure 17-7).

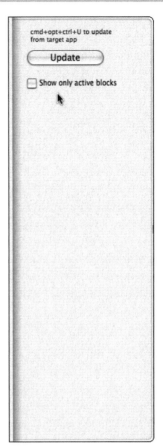

Figure 17-7
... or just sample when memory allocations occur

Sampling function calls is a lot like setting a breakpoint in the debugger and looking at the call stack. But, and this is a very large "but" (we'll pause briefly to let the eight-year-olds out there stop giggling... got that out of your systems? fine...), sampling lets you collect all the information in one view concerning how often the function is called and from where it is called, automatically. This automatic collection and presentation saves you lots of time and manual

Figure 17-6
You can sample based on specific function calls...

effort — do you really want to manually record the call stack and repeat the process *ad nauseum* and then collate all that data? Sampler even provides preset collections of functions, such as File I/O, to load into the watch list, and, best of all, it lets you save your own collections as presets and then load them later, after you've made some changes to your code and rebuilt.

Sampling memory allocations is really just a special case of function call sampling, collecting data on calls to memory allocation primitives like `malloc` and `NewHandle`. When you know which parts of your program are allocating memory, you have a leg up on adjusting your code to reduce the memory requirements. Besides, having this information is a handy adjunct to GuardMalloc (see Chapter 16), tracking down memory leaks, and determining what memory blocks are no longer necessary but not yet released.

Spin Control

Spin Control's name is more than a slight exaggeration. Spin Control does nothing directly to reduce or eliminate the spin cursor's appearance or duration. What it does do, however, is sit there in the background and, every time your application tosses the pizza, sample your application so that you can find out what code your application is executing when the spinning pizza appears. The data that Spin Control gathers is essentially the same as that collected by Sampler, but rather than being triggered at periodic intervals, Spin Control only collects samples while the spinning wheel turns. When the spinning rainbow brightens your screen, Spin Control starts recording a sample, and when the rainbow disappears, Spin Control lists the offender, the time, and duration of the hang in the Detected Hangs window (see Figure 17-8).

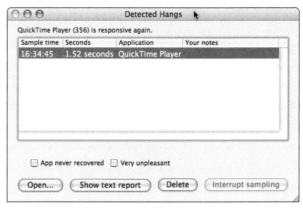

Figure 17-8
The hangman's waiting list?

▼ Note

The spinning rainbow is actually displayed whenever the Window Server thinks an application has become unresponsive. So now you know.

Select the line in which you're interested and click Open (or just double-click the line) to present the Sample Report window for the application in question (see Figure 17-9). You can also click the Show text report button to create a text file of the sample information (see Figure 17-10).

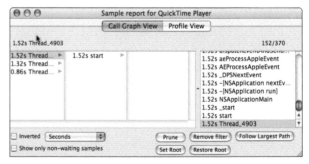

Figure 17-9
Spin Control has a mini-version of Sampler built in

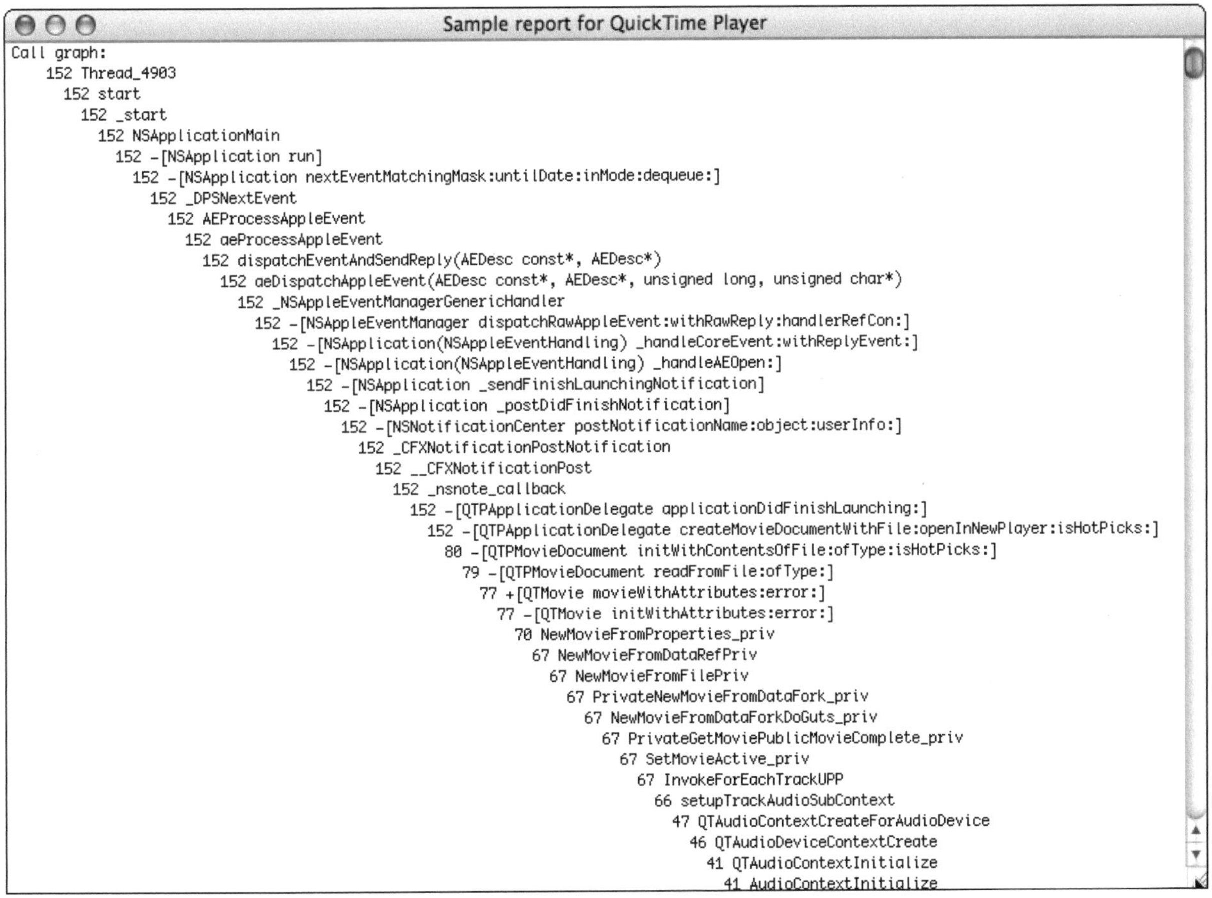

```
●○○                    Sample report for QuickTime Player
Call graph:
    152 Thread_4903
      152 start
        152 _start
          152 NSApplicationMain
            152 -[NSApplication run]
              152 -[NSApplication nextEventMatchingMask:untilDate:inMode:dequeue:]
                152 _DPSNextEvent
                  152 AEProcessAppleEvent
                    152 aeProcessAppleEvent
                      152 dispatchEventAndSendReply(AEDesc const*, AEDesc*)
                        152 aeDispatchAppleEvent(AEDesc const*, AEDesc*, unsigned long, unsigned char*)
                          152 _NSAppleEventManagerGenericHandler
                            152 -[NSAppleEventManager dispatchRawAppleEvent:withRawReply:handlerRefCon:]
                              152 -[NSApplication(NSAppleEventHandling) _handleCoreEvent:withReplyEvent:]
                                152 -[NSApplication(NSAppleEventHandling) _handleAEOpen:]
                                  152 -[NSApplication _sendFinishLaunchingNotification]
                                    152 -[NSApplication _postDidFinishNotification]
                                      152 -[NSNotificationCenter postNotificationName:object:userInfo:]
                                        152 _CFXNotificationPostNotification
                                          152 __CFXNotificationPost
                                            152 _nsnote_callback
                                              152 -[QTPApplicationDelegate applicationDidFinishLaunching:]
                                                152 -[QTPApplicationDelegate createMovieDocumentWithFile:openInNewPlayer:isHotPicks:]
                                                  80 -[QTPMovieDocument initWithContentsOfFile:ofType:isHotPicks:]
                                                    79 -[QTPMovieDocument readFromFile:ofType:]
                                                      77 +[QTMovie movieWithAttributes:error:]
                                                        77 -[QTMovie initWithAttributes:error:]
                                                          70 NewMovieFromProperties_priv
                                                            67 NewMovieFromDataRefPriv
                                                              67 NewMovieFromFilePriv
                                                                67 PrivateNewMovieFromDataFork_priv
                                                                  67 NewMovieFromDataForkDoGuts_priv
                                                                    67 PrivateGetMoviePublicMovieComplete_priv
                                                                      67 SetMovieActive_priv
                                                                        67 InvokeForEachTrackUPP
                                                                          66 setupTrackAudioSubContext
                                                                            47 QTAudioContextCreateForAudioDevice
                                                                              46 QTAudioDeviceContextCreate
                                                                                41 QTAudioContextInitialize
                                                                                41 AudioContextInitialize
```

Figure 17-10
This report illustrates how one picture can be worth more than 1,000 words

WHAT'S GOING ON RIGHT NOW?

Sometimes, you might want to know how your execution threads are spending their time. *Thread Viewer* gives you a graphical representation of what your threads are doing at sample time. The main window that appears when you launch Thread Viewer (see Figure 17-11) describes Thread Viewer's *raison d'être* while providing buttons allowing you to launch and examine a program's threads or to attach Thread Viewer to an already running process. When you click Launch, you are presented with a dialog allowing you to specify the application or command-line tool you wish to launch (and specify a working directory and arguments for command-line tools). Clicking Attach presents the scrolling table of icons shown in Figure 17-12. Select one and click OK to get started.

Figure 17-11
Simple and straightforward, Thread Viewer tells you its mission statement

Figure 17-12
Pick the process you want to monitor

Using a color-coded timeline (see Figure 17-13), Thread Viewer lets you watch as your thread moves from active to inactive and back. You can click the timeline to see the call stack at the point where you clicked, as we have done in Figure 17-13.

▼ Note

Because this book isn't in color, you might be having trouble differentiating among the various colors in the drawer's color code legend and matching up what's in the displayed timeline. The three colors in the top section are green, yellow, and dark green, respectively — the narrow blocks in the timeline are all yellow except for the selected block, which is green. The next group of four colors consists of gray, pale green (everything in the figure's timeline other than the yellow and green blocks), pink (but Apple calls it "pale red"), and lavender ("pale blue" according to Apple). The last two items are red and black.

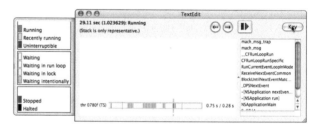

Figure 17-13
The timeline is color-coded for your convenience (or inconvenience if you're color-blind)

The annotation to the left of the timeline presents the thread's mach port number (in hexadecimal), with the thread's scheduling policy in parentheses (see the sidebar "It's All About Scheduling" for a brief description of the various scheduling policies possible).

IT'S ALL ABOUT SCHEDULING

There are three types of threads, as follows:

* TS is the most common and stands for *time-shared*, which has nothing to do with a vacation retreat. Time-shared thread priorities fluctuate depending on the percentage of CPU time they consume.

* RR indicates a *round-robin* thread — one that demands execution time at regular, fixed intervals (for example, every 20 ms). Device drivers, for example, are good candidates for RR threads.

* FIFO threads are *first-in, first-out* scheduled threads. They should be employed only when real-time response may be necessary. When a FIFO thread gets control of the CPU, it retains control until it decides to surrender the CPU (or until the thread, eventually, has used too much time and the scheduler terminates it). Because a FIFO thread monopolizes the CPU, other threads can be denied time and overall system performance can seriously degrade. Very few threads should be FIFO.

CHUD FOR THE DEFENSE

In Xcode's land of acronyms lives a group entity named *CHUD* (Computer Hardware Understanding Development) tools. At the time we're writing this, CHUD consists of nine applications and six command-line tools (check out Table 17-1, "Just CHUDing Along," for the current inventory of applications), up from the eight applications and three command-line tools present when we started this tome — Apple's always adding new weapons to their performance arsenal, so the count might be even higher by the time you read this.

▼ **Note**

Those of you who love old, bad horror films might recall another *C.H.U.D.*: 1984's film about Cannibalistic Humanoid Underground Dwellers who were created by toxic waste. Perhaps Apple's developers called their tool collection CHUD because it lives "underground," or because it has something to do with waste (wasted cycles, wasted memory). Or maybe it's because Apple's developers just have a soft spot for radioactive mutants with glowing eyes and a taste for human flesh.

A plurality of CHUD's components are *profiling* tools, helping you build a picture of when and how often your software's pieces are in play. Just as FBI profilers paint a picture of a suspect based upon the evidence and behavioral science, profiling tools paint a picture of your application based upon results from hardware and operating system performance counters.

Table 17-1: Just CHUDing Along

Icon	Tool	Description
	Big Top	Creates a graph from the output generated by the `top` and `vm_stat` command-line tools. We devote more space to Big Top later in this chapter in "Performance Monitoring, or, Are You Going to Be in There Long?"
	MONster	Creates spreadsheets and charts from the data it retrieves from hardware and operating system performance counters. You can find a large (over 50 page) PDF document about MONster by accessing its Help command. We tell you a little more about MONster in "Performance Monitoring, or, Are You Going to Be in There Long?"
	PMC Index	Searches for PMC (performance monitor counter) events designated by the user.
	Saturn	Used to analyze a program's function-calling structure, generating metrics detailing how much time is spent in each function. We spend a little more paper and ink on Saturn in "Performance Monitoring, or, Are You Going to Be in There Long?"
	Shark	Profiles the entire system while your application runs, determining which operations are getting time and cycles — it even makes suggestions toward improving your code's performance. Shark is another tool we cover in more depth in "Performance Monitoring, or, Are You Going to Be in There Long?"
	CacheBuster	This tool measures memory performance and how it interacts with the cache.
	Skidmarks GT	Probably not of use to application developers, Skidmarks benchmarks a processor's integer, floating point, and vector operations.
	Reggie SE	A hardware performance tool that allows you to manipulate and examine SPRs (Supervisor state registers) and PCI device configuration registers.
	Spindown HD	Another hardware performance tool that monitors the state of a system's connected drives.

PERFORMANCE MONITORING, OR, ARE YOU GOING TO BE IN THERE LONG?

Four of the CHUD applications are of particular interest to application developers, which is what we assume most of you to be. Of course, we all know that assumptions are the mother of all foul-ups (insert your choice of f-word, if you wish), but that's our position and we're sticking to it.

Leading off for CHUD is *Big Top*. Figure 17-14 shows the Big Top window, graphing the Finder's CPU Usage at 1-second intervals (on a relatively quiescent system). Figure 17-15 shows Big Top's window with the process drop-down list expanded. Choose a process (or All) from the drop-down list, select the metrics you want plotted from the scrolling list at the left of the window, and specify a sampling duration (if you don't want the default 1-second sampling) and how long a duration you want plotted (Unlimited displays all the data, compressing the horizontal axis as necessary; Window allows you to specify a set interval to display).

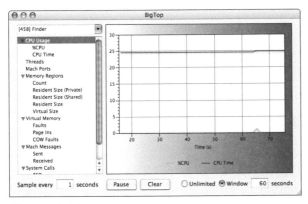

Figure 17-14
Big Top is, in many ways, a graphical `top` **display**

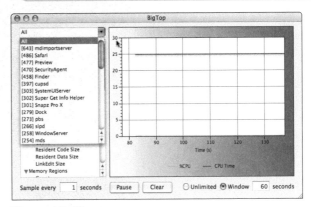

Figure 17-15
You can specify a process to graph through the drop-down list

MONster, through the CHUD framework, accesses the hardware PMCs (performance monitor counters) built into PowerPC processors and Apple system controllers, as well as the virtual PMCs in OS X. PMCs count performance events, ranging from simple operations like register `load` instructions through complex operations such as virtual memory page allocations or deallocations. MONster, though, only collects the data and presents it in a spreadsheet-like form or in a chart derived from the spreadsheet data. It is up to you to draw conclusions from that data.

Figure 17-16 displays the results of choosing the CPI (cycles per instruction) preset from the Config drop-down list across two runs (the measurements were made on an 800 MHz G4 iMac with 768MB RAM). You can chart the data in the display box at the bottom of the Results pane and can click the Config tab to define your own metric collection configuration in the Config pane. Apple provides a sizable (50-plus page) PDF MONster User Guide in the ADC Reference Library, detailing all the snoozeriffic details.

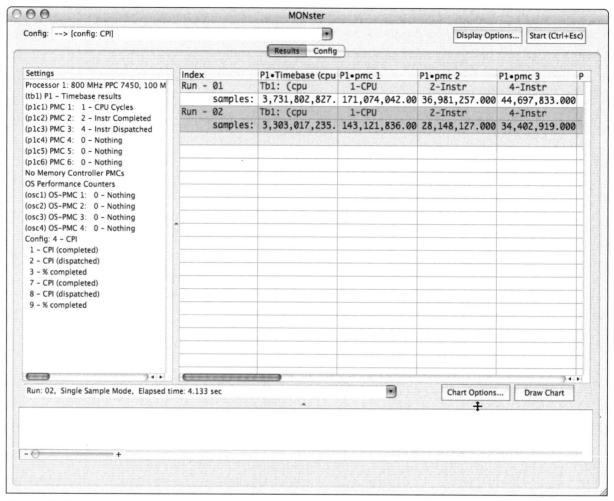

Figure 17-16
MONster collects performance event data in a spreadsheet-like table

Saturn is an optimization tool that illustrates your program's call tree and tells you how much time is spent in each function. To perform these feats of legerdemain, Saturn requires that you build your code with instrumentation prologues (and optional epilogues). These prologues can be either the standard `gprof`-compatible ones resulting from using the `-pg` compiler option or user-defined routines specified by `-finstrument-functions`. To get

Saturn's lowdown on the down-low, check out the SaturnUserGuide.pdf file in the /Developer/ADC Reference Library/documentation/CHUD directory. It's small (about 16 pages) and clearly written.

CHUD's Big Kahuna, though, appears to be *Shark* — if we're drawing the correct conclusions from Apple's copious documentation (a large User Guide PDF and two Tutorial

PDFs) and the hyperbole used in naming and describing Shark. According to Apple's Shark documentation, Shark got its name because performance tuning requires a hunter's mentality and the shark is nature's purest predator, employing all its resources in pursuit of its prey.

 Tip

Shark requires your build to include the symbol information generated by compiling with debug symbols turned on for the active target. In Xcode, you ensure that debug symbols are generated by choosing Project ➜ Edit Active Target, selecting the GNU C/C++ Compiler panel, and selecting the Generate Debug Symbols option and the Unstripped Product option. If the COPY_PHASE_STRIP variable is defined, it must be set to NO.

The active target should be a deployment build, because you want all the compiler optimizations in play. Profiling an unoptimized build (such as a development build) is almost pointless because it will not reflect the performance optimizations or bottlenecks of your deployment build.

When you launch Shark, you're presented with a fairly simple window in which you specify the type of profile you want to create and whether you want to profile everything, a single process, or a file. When you profile a process, the window expands to the right and a third pop-up menu appears, allowing you to specify the process, as shown in Figure 17-17.

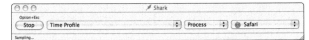

Figure 17-17
Tell Shark what to profile and what kind of profile you desire

Click Start (or press Option+Escape) and start using your target process. When you feel that it's been exercised

sufficiently to provide a decent sample set, press Option+Escape or click Shark's Stop button. You'll now see a Session window similar to the one shown in Figure 17-18.

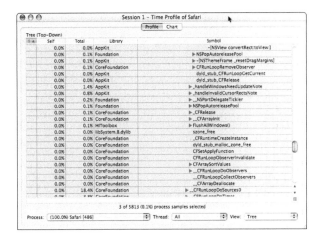

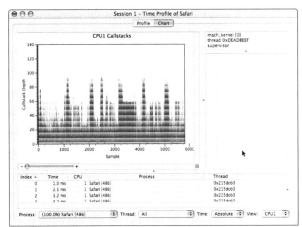

Figure 17-18
Shark presents you with first a tabular profile and then an activity chart for your sample session

 Tip

You can double-click an entry in the table to open a new tab displaying the code for the function being executed.

PERFORMANCE PROFILING AT YOUR COMMAND

In addition to the nice GUI tools, Apple provides a number of command-line tools for performance sampling and profiling. Many of these are just command-line versions of one of the GUI tools mentioned in this chapter, such as `monster` for MONster, without the pretty presentation. All of the command-line tools have associated man pages.

One command-line tool, `chudRemoteCtrl`, is kind of special — it allows you to launch MONster or Shark from a shell script or remote connection (such as through `ssh`).

Two other tools are G4 and G5 processor simulators: `simg4` for the Motorola 7400 and `simg5` for the IBM970 CPUs. You can read all about them in /Developer/ADC Reference Library/documentation/CHUD files SimG4_Users_Guide.pdf and SimG5_ReadMe.txt.

We sincerely believe that all these tools provided by Apple should be more than sufficient to alleviate any performance anxiety you might be experiencing; however, if they don't engender a mite of acronym and jargon overload, we'll be a little bit impressed.

CURTAIN CALL

We opened our performance-enhancing performance with a little duet featuring Sampler, a tool that lets you take periodic samples of your executing code, and Spin Control, which takes samples whenever the spinning rainbow pizza cursor appears. Next we showcased the work of our wardrobe department by presenting Thread Viewer, a tool that lets you shuffle through your program's threads of execution and see how and when they become active. In a sparkling intermezzo, we presented the ensemble work of CHUD, the Computer Hardware Understanding Development tools, featuring nine applications and six command-line tools designed to help you gather various kinds of execution profiles. Our grand finale spotlighted four of CHUD's soloists: Big Top, who graphically performs in the style of top; MONster, who plays the CPU's performance monitor counters with grace and style; Saturn, who presents a stunning re-creation of your program's function-calling behavior; and the famous Shark, who cruises across the stage of your system, dancing and singing with everybody, in order to give you a complete depiction of almost everything that's going on in your system, from function calls to cache misses to instruction dependency stalls. Bravo! Encore!

Eliminating Version Perversion

The Cure for Versionitis
Subversive Behavior • What's the Diff?
Making Commitments • We Check Out

We wrote the opening for this chapter a few times.

The first attempt was dull and technical. The second was strange and wacky, and we rather liked it. Then we woke up inspired in the middle of the night and wrote a new introduction. The next morning we read our nocturnal inspiration and realized that it was drivel... but, by then, the strange and wacky second version that we kind of liked was gone, and we couldn't quite remember what it was that we'd said.

As T. S. Eliot put it in *The Love Song of J. Alfred Prufrock*, "In a minute there is time / For decisions and revisions that a minute will reverse." If we'd been using a version control system, such as one of those supported by Xcode, we would have been able to reverse our decisions and revisions.

Instead, we ended up Prufrocked.

THE CURE FOR VERSIONITIS

There's only one menu in Xcode's menu bar that is an acronym: *SCM*. All the others are either real, honest nouns or verbs that give some clue as to their contents, or they're iconically familiar and need no explanation (like the Apple or Scripts menu). But SCM? What's that? It's the sort of menu that screams, "If you don't know what I am, don't mess with me." Even more frustrating, if you pull it down, all that you usually see is the stern, "No soup for you!" menu shown in Figure 18-1.

SCM Unavailable

Figure 18-1
If you don't know what SCM is, this menu won't help much

And such a pity, too, for when the mysterious SCM *is* available, you suddenly have at your cursor-tip a wonderful tool for dealing with all the false starts and wrong turns that a programming project can take, as well as a real aid for those times when you are not out riding the range on your lonesome but instead must, as our elementary school report cards put it, work and play well with others.

SCM, to spell it out, is *source code management*. And, when Xcode detects that SCM is available, the eponymous menu contains the commands that let Xcode coordinate the source files in your project with those stored inside of a source code management system (also known as a *version control system*).

▼ **Note**

Just to be completely clear on the matter: Xcode does *not* implement its own source code management system. What it does do is work with several existing and popular source code management systems.

Some SCM terms

There are a number of version control systems out there in the software development world, and each of them has proponents and detractors, but most of them share common features and concepts. Here are some terms we're going to be tossing around a whole lot in the next few pages.

● **Repository.** This is where the source code files, in their various versions, repose, along with revision tracking information for each file. Usually, the repository resides on some server somewhere, far, far away from you — across the room, down the hall, in another building — but it is also possible to set up a repository on your Mac. The repository is maintained by the versioning control software running on the server.

● **Workspace.** These are copies of the files from the repository on your machine, the ones you actually tinker with and edit. The files listed in your Xcode Project window are in your workspace. When you use SCM in Xcode, you always work with the file copies in your workspace.

● **Check out.** This is the act of copying a file from the repository to your workspace. In the process, the repository keeps track of the fact that you have copied the file; other users of the same repository can also tell that you have checked the file out, which is more convenient than shouting, "Hey, Deidre, I just copied GrafixFoon.h to my disk so I can add some new declarations!" — especially if Deidre's cubicle is in another time zone. Many SCMs allow the same file to be checked out to several different users at the same time.

▼ **Note**

Xcode 2 currently provides no check-out facilities; by the time you see the files in your Project window, they've already been checked out to you. The check-out operation is usually done with the SCM's client software, which you have to have installed in order to use the SCM system with Xcode in the first place.

● **Commit** (also known as **check in**). This is the act of copying a file back to the repository, which updates the repository's version tracking information. The file being copied back does not replace the version you checked out; rather, it is added to the repository with a new version number, which allows you to obtain a copy of a previous version if you need it.

- **Merge.** When two (or more) different users check out the same file from a repository and then, eventually, commit their changed versions, differences between the files being committed can often be made automatically by the SCM software. Merging is the automatic blending of these several sets of changes, and works best when the changes in the files don't overlap each other.

- **Resolve.** This is the nonautomatic act of dealing with incompatible or overlapping changes in multiple copies of a file that are being committed to the repository. In other words, you (in your day job as a real live sentient being) have to look at the differences and choose which changes to keep and which to discard.

Setting SCM up in Xcode

Before you can use SCM in an Xcode project, someone (you, a project manager, or some other dedicated data wrangler) must first create the repository. How this is done depends on the SCM involved, and we're not going to talk about that here because it *will* depend upon your SCM and there's a high likelihood that it isn't one we're using.

Next, the files used in the Xcode project have to be checked out of the repository and put into your workspace (for example, a project directory on your hard drive). Again, this happens before Xcode actually gets involved; exactly how it's done depends on the SCM involved (often it involves some command-line work) and we're not going to talk about that here, either.

Finally, you have to open the project with Xcode and tell Xcode that the project uses SCM. And *that's* what we're going to talk about here.

1. **Select the project in your Project window's Groups & Files list and choose File → Get Info.** The project's Inspector window appears.

2. **Click the Inspector's General tab (if it isn't already selected).**

3. **Near the bottom of the Inspector window, choose the SCM system you wish to use from the SCM System pop-up menu (see Figure 18-2).**

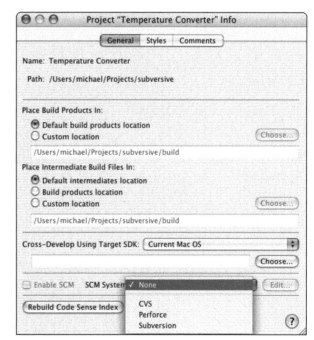

Figure 18-2
Pick an SCM and join the code-sharing party

4. **Click the Edit button beside the pop-up menu.**
Xcode presents a sheet of settings you can edit for the
SCM system you have chosen (see Figure 18-3).

Figure 18-3
You can edit your SCM system's settings

5. **Select the Enable SCM option in the Inspector
window.** If your SCM settings are in order, Xcode
contacts your chosen SCM system's server, compares
your project's files with those in the repository, and
enables the SCM menu in Xcode's menu bar.

▼ Note

In this chapter we use the Subversion SCM system in
the examples and figures; however, the other SCM
systems with which Xcode works offer similar functionality... at least, within the Xcode environment.

SUBVERSIVE BEHAVIOR

Once you have enabled SCM for your project, the SCM
menu becomes useful, and a series of subtle changes occur
in your Project window (see Figure 18-5). Specifically, a
new column, headed by a tiny canister-shaped icon,
appears in both the detail view and the Groups & Files list.
This column displays the SCM status of your project's
files.

▼ Tip

If these columns don't appear, choose View ➔ Detail
View Columns ➔ SCM to show it in the detail view,
and choose View ➔ Groups & Files Columns ➔ SCM
to show it in the Groups & Files list.

MY THREE SCMS

Xcode 2.0 supports three popular source code management systems: CVS, Subversion, and Perforce.

- **CVS** — The Concurrent Versions System is one of the oldest source code management systems, first seeing the light of day as a series of shell scripts written by Dick Grune back in 1986, though it's changed a bit since then. Implementations of CVS are available for Mac OS X, Linux, Windows, and other operating systems. CVS is open source, and can be obtained from `https://www.cvshome.org`.

- **Subversion** — According to its developers, "Subversion is meant to be a better CVS," and the developers' Web site at `http://subversion.tigris.org/` lists a variety of ways in which Subversion improves upon CVS; the arguments must be compelling, because Apple lately seems to prefer Subversion over CVS. Like CVS, Subversion is open source software. In addition, a free, downloadable manual, *Version Control with Subversion,* can be obtained from `http://svnbook.red-bean.com`.

- **Perforce** — This is a commercial version control system that's available for a wide variety of platforms and suitable for a wide variety of uses. Like Subversion, it provides more advanced features than the venerable CVS. Perforce client software is free, but the downloadable free server only supports two users and two workspaces, and additional licenses for commercial development projects cost roughly $750 for the first 20 users (though extensive telephone support is included in the license fee). However, open source development projects may be eligible for free Perforce licensing. Perforce is available from `www.perforce.com`.

In order to use any of these systems with Xcode, you must install the appropriate client software. Figure 18-3 shows the Xcode settings you need to specify to use Subversion with your project, which for Subversion consists simply of specifying the path to the installed Subversion client binary (a command-line tool called `svn`). Figure 18-4 shows the equivalent CVS and Perforce settings sheets; note that Perforce refers to its repositories as "depots."

Figure 18-4
Xcode settings for the CVS and Perforce SCM systems

An extensive comparison of the various features, capabilities, and limitations of these three SCM systems (as well as of several others) can be found at `http://better-scm.berlios.de/comparison/comparison.html`.

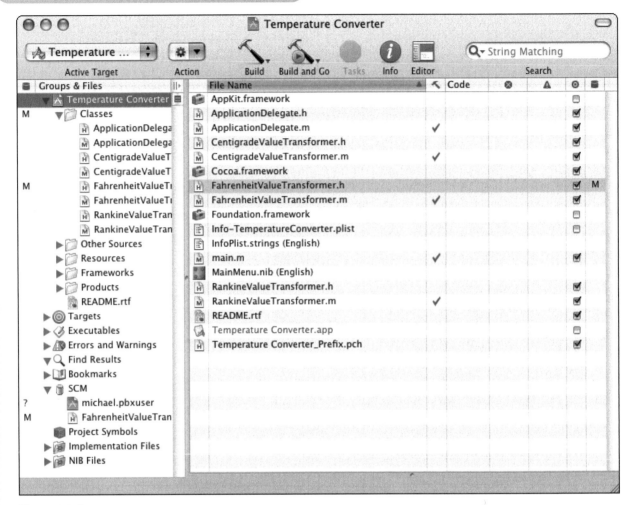

Figure 18-5
The canister columns appear

And here's what those status labels mean:

- [space] — Everything's up to date in Kansas City: Your copy of the file matches the most current version in the SCM repository.

- **C** — This means your changes conflict with the changes in the repository's latest version.

▼ **Note**
We describe comparing differences between versions in "What's the Diff?"

- **?** — This file does not appear in the repository.

▼ **Note**

You can add files to the repository from Xcode, as we describe in "Making Commitments," later in this chapter.

○ **U** — The file in the repository is newer than your copy and you might want to update your copy.

▼ **Note**

We also describe updating files in "Making Commitments." In fact, we discuss updating, adding, and removing files in that section. We tell you this now so we don't have to add a note like this to each of the next three items, because we're lazy.

○ **M** — The file has been modified and, the next time you commit changes to the repository, your copy of the file will wing its way to the SCM system's server.

○ **A** — This indicates a file that will be added to the repository the next time you commit changes.

○ **R** — This indicates a file you have marked to be removed from the repository the next time you commit changes.

▼ **Note**

When a file is marked as removed, it also can't be opened by you any longer; it appears in gray in your Project window and is really, to all intents and purposes, gone.

○ **- [hyphen]** — This appears when the file resides in a directory that's not in the repository; the hyphen can also appear beside a directory that's not itself in the repository.

▼ **Note**

You can't add a directory to a repository from Xcode; you'll have to use the SCM system's client software for that task.

One other subtle change occurs in the Project window when SCM is enabled: The SCM Smart Group in the Groups & Files view becomes useful, dynamically listing all the files and folders in your project that have a status other than up to date in the repository, as Figure 18-5 shows.

As we noted earlier, when SCM is enabled for a project, the SCM menu finally sprouts some actual commands and becomes useful (see Figure 18-6).

Figure 18-6
SCM on the menu

The first command on the menu, SCM Results, presents the window shown in Figure 18-7. This window has two faces: The first, the file list pane, lists the same files that appear in the SCM Smart Group, along with their statuses and their paths relative to the project's root directory. The second pane (which you open by clicking the little page icon below the scrollbar) displays the commands Xcode has sent to the SCM client your project uses, and the client's response. The window also has an editor pane, which you can access by dragging the separator bar up from the window's bottom.

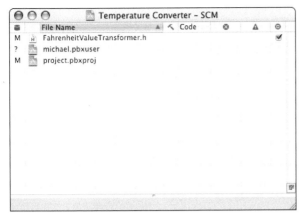

Figure 18-7
The two faces of the SCM Results window

▼ **Tip**

Beneath the second pane is yet another pane that you can drag open: an embedded editor pane that displays the file selected in the top pane.

The second command on the SCM menu, Get SCM Info, is a shortcut that's equivalent to choosing File ➜ Get Info for a selected file in the detail view and then clicking the SCM tab in the file's Inspector window; Figure 18-8 shows this window.

- At the top of the Inspector appears a summary of the file's state (if you haven't memorized what all the symbols in the Project window's SCM status column mean, the State field spells it out for you).

- The Inspector's top pane lists the file's revision history, including the message that the person who committed the revision supplied when that version was committed.

- The bottom pane provides the detailed history of the revision selected in the top pane.

- The search field at the bottom lets you search among the listed revisions for those whose commitment messages contain the search terms.

Figure 18-8
Revisionist history of a file

We'll describe the buttons along the bottom of the window, which are shortcuts for commands on the SCM menu, later in the chapter. In fact, we'll describe the remaining commands on the SCM menu later in this chapter as well. We're done with this section. Move along.

WHAT'S THE DIFF?

When you and your programming buddies are swapping files back and forth from the repository to your workspaces as you frantically try to make your product's ship date, there will be times when you end up having a file in your workspace that doesn't incorporate the changes that are in the latest version, but which does contain changes that *you've* made and that you probably want to keep. What to do?

Compare

Well, one thing you can do is compare the two versions. Xcode's SCM menu provides a Compare With submenu that let's you compare the file in your workspace with

- the **Latest** version in the repository (Option+Shift+⌘+L is the four-finger salute that produces the same result);

- the **Base** version (that is, the version you first checked out) in the repository;

- a **Revision** that's in the repository (this presents you with a sheet that lets you choose the revision in the repository to which you want to compare your local version);

- a **Specific Revision** in the repository (you get a sheet that lets you specify a revision number — it helps if you know the revision number to use this command); or

- any arbitrary **File** (you get a standard file sheet that lets you pick a file when you choose this command).

 Tip

The Compare button in the SCM Inspector (take a look back at Figure 18-8) lets you compare your file with the revision selected in the Inspector's top pane; it's equivalent to choosing SCM ➜ Compare With ➜ Specific Revision.

And what does the Compare With command do? It opens both files in a program that comes with Xcode called FileMerge (located in Developer/Applications/Utilities) that lets you compare the two files by highlighting their differences (see Figure 18-9). In fact, FileMerge does more than that; it lets you select which of the changes to accept and which to ignore and then lets you save the combined version as a new file. Of course, that new file won't be in the repository.

 Tip

You can use a different program, such as BBEdit, to perform the comparison by choosing it from the View comparisons using pop-up menu in Xcode's SCM preferences (see Figure 18-10); choose Xcode ➜ Preferences and click SCM in the Preferences toolbar.

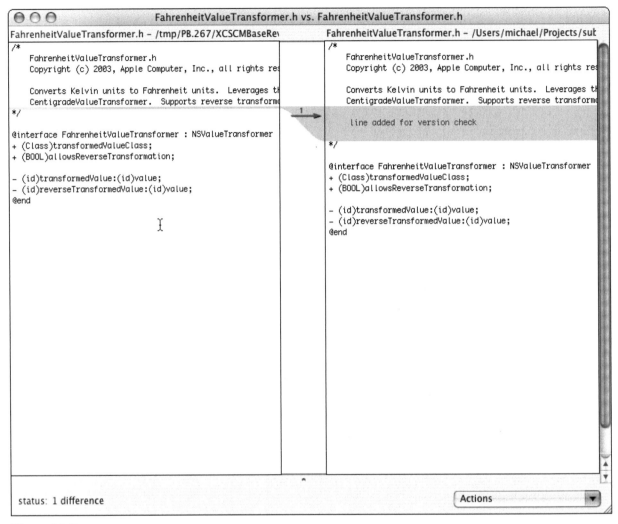

Figure 18-9

Comparing versions, courtesy of FileMerge

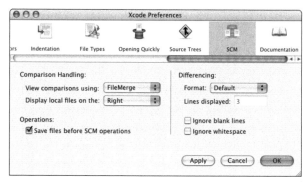

Figure 18-10
SCM preferences

Diff

For those old-school programmers who cut their teeth with the traditional command-line tool, diff, Xcode provides the SCM ➔ Diff With submenu. The choices on this submenu are the same as those on the Compare With submenu, except that the File command is not available. The Diff With command runs the diff command-line tool for the specified file versions and presents the tool's output in a separate editor window (see Figure 18-11).

▼ **Tip**

Similar to the Compare button, the Diff button in the SCM Inspector (again, see Figure 18-8) lets you diff your file against the revision selected in the Inspector's top pane; it's equivalent to choosing SCM ➔ Diff With ➔ Specific Revision.

Rather than show you the entire file, diff simply shows you the changes. You can set exactly how diff arranges its output in Xcode's SCM preferences (refer back to Figure 18-10), which provides a GUI front end to diff's command-line options (for example, choosing Side by Side from the Format pop-up menu is equivalent to using the --side-by-side command-line option).

Annotate

There are times when you just have to know in which version a specific change entered a file and who it was that committed the change. Some SCM systems let you find out just that, and, if the one you are using does, Xcode's SCM ➔ Get Annotations For submenu has commands that provide you with the annotation output from the SCM system you're using. The commands on this submenu are the same as those on the Compare With submenu, and, like the Compare command, their output is displayed in a separate editor window (see Figure 18-12).

▼ **Tip**

Similar to the Compare button, the Annotate button in the SCM Inspector (and, once again, please refer to Figure 18-8) shows you the annotations for the revision selected in the Inspector's top pane; it's equivalent to choosing SCM ➔ Get Annotations For ➔ Specific Revision.

▼ **Note**

Early releases of Subversion did not include an Annotation command, so if you are using one of those, the Get Annotations For commands are pretty much irrelevant. You might also be interested in knowing that the name of the Annotation command in the releases of Subversion that offer annotations is blame — which more or less sums up the reason this command is often used.

MAKING COMMITMENTS

Once you're done comparing file versions and looking at how they differ — and deciding whom to blame for what — you'll eventually want to use Xcode's SCM capabilities to change your own files so that you can benefit from the work of others... or to change the repository so that others can benefit from your own splendid wonderfulness.

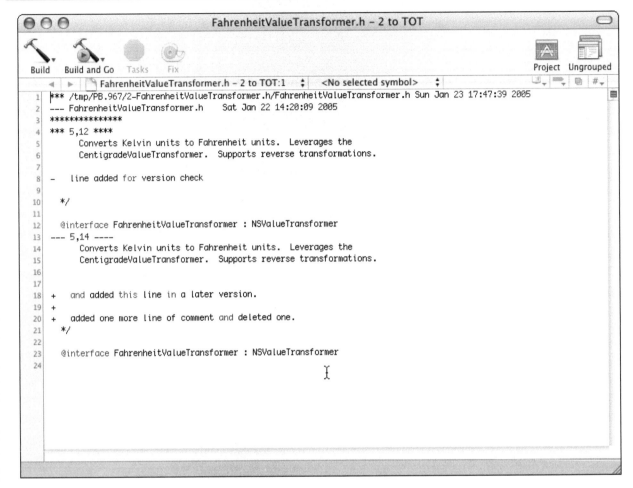

Figure 18-11
We all have our `diff`-erences

Update

You use the Update command in one of two situations:

- The version of the file in the repository is a later version than the one you have, and you want to incorporate that version's changes into your copy.

▼ **Note**

You can tell if the repository's version is later than yours if the file in your Project window's detail view has a U in the SCM status column (that's the column headed by a canister icon).

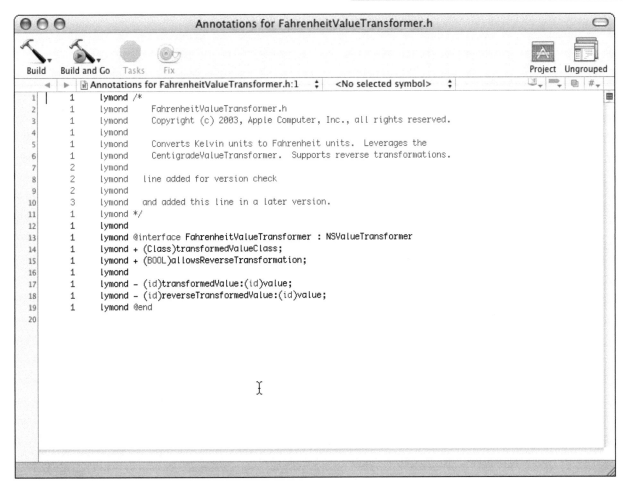

```
       1     lymond /*
       1     lymond      FahrenheitValueTransformer.h
       1     lymond      Copyright (c) 2003, Apple Computer, Inc., all rights reserved.
       1     lymond
       1     lymond      Converts Kelvin units to Fahrenheit units.  Leverages the
       1     lymond      CentigradeValueTransformer.  Supports reverse transformations.
       2     lymond
       2     lymond    line added for version check
       2     lymond
       3     lymond   and added this line in a later version.
       1     lymond */
       1     lymond
       1     lymond @interface FahrenheitValueTransformer : NSValueTransformer
       1     lymond + (Class)transformedValueClass;
       1     lymond + (BOOL)allowsReverseTransformation;
       1     lymond
       1     lymond - (id)transformedValue:(id)value;
       1     lymond - (id)reverseTransformedValue:(id)value;
       1     lymond @end
```

Figure 18-12
Annotations show who did what, when, and where

- You want to change the file in your workspace to match either the latest, or one of the previous, versions in the repository, discarding any changes you may have made.

When the repository's version is later than your workspace copy, the SCM ➜ Update To ➜ Latest command (Shift+⌘+L) attempts to merge the repository's version with your copy.

▼ **Note**

If Xcode finds a conflict between the repository's version and your version, the conflicting changes appear as comments in your file, and you see a C in the SCM status column. Once you edit the file to fix the conflict, choose SCM ➜ Resolved to let the SCM system know you've worked out your differences.

If your copy is later than the repository's version, the SCM ➔ Update To ➔ Latest command discards your changes and replaces your version with the repository's version; this is exactly the same thing that happens when you choose the SCM ➔ Discard Changes command. Xcode does warn you that you're about to discard all your hard work (see Figure 18-13).

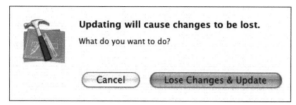

Figure 18-13
Updating to a previous version has its cost

The SCM ➔ Update To ➔ Revision command lets you pick a specific revision to which you want to update, which, we suppose, is really more of a downdate than an update, but we don't create the nomenclature, we just write about it (see Figure 18-14).

Figure 18-14
Pick a revision to up(down)date

And the SCM ➔ Update To ➔ Specific Revision, as you might expect, lets you directly specify the version number to which you want to update (see Figure 18-15).

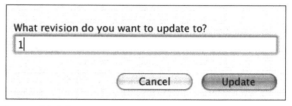

Figure 18-15
What's your number?

▼ Tip

In the SCM Inspector, the Update button (shown in Figure 18-8) updates your file to the revision selected in the Inspector's top pane; it's equivalent to choosing SCM ➔ Update To ➔ Specific Revision. You probably figured that out by this time.

Commit

You've worked hard, made a bunch of changes, tested things out, debugged till the debugger is all sweaty, and you are ready to let others share the fruits of your labors. In other words, you want to commit your changes to the repository so that the latest version is your version. Here's how you do that.

1. **Click the SCM Smart Group in the Project window's Groups & Files view.** All the files that don't match the repository's version appear in the detail view.

2. **Select the file or files you wish to commit and the** `project.pbxproj` **file.**

▼ **Note**

> The `project.pbxproj` file contains your project's inventory of files and their revision information, and you want the repository to have that information as well, so you need to commit it, too.

3. **Choose SCM ➜ Commit Changes.** A sheet appears (see Figure 18-16) asking you to describe your changes. This description should tell other users of the repository what changes you made.

Figure 18-16
Describe the nature of your commitment

4. **Type your description in the sheet's field and then click Commit.** Simply saying something like "Changes made" in your description is guaranteed to tick off your fellow developers, so try to say something substantive.

Xcode sends your version, with the description, to the repository. Now other people can blame you for their problems.

Add

Sometimes you need to add a file to your project (with, for example, the Project ➜ Add to Project command). However, even after the file is in your project, it's not in the

repository. You need to add it. There are two stages to this process: marking the file as being ready to add, and then committing it.

1. **Select the file in your project and choose SCM ➜ Add to Repository.** The file is awarded an A in the SCM status column.

2. **Click the SCM Smart Group in the Project window's Groups & Files view.**

3. **Select the file and the** `project.pbxproj` **file.**

4. **Choose SCM ➜ Commit Changes.**

5. **Fill out the commitment description and click Commit.**

Xcode puts the new file in the repository so that others can check it out and play with it.

Remove

There are also times when you wish to remove a file from your project (if for no other reason than to conceal the evidence of your coding crimes). If the file is part of the repository, you have to remove it from there as well, again through the act of committing your changes.

1. **Select the file in your project, and press Delete.** You are asked, as usual, to confirm the file deletion (see Figure 18-17).

Figure 18-17
Do you really want to go through with removing the file?

2. **Click either Delete References or Delete References & Files.** A sheet appears asking if you want to remove the file from the repository (see Figure 18-18).

Figure 18-18
Do you really REALLY want to go through with it?

 Note

At this point, you can't do much with the file in your project anyway because it's gone. However, if you don't remove it from the repository (as shown in the next step), you can still get it back by checking it out with your SCM system's client software.

3. **Click Remove.**

4. **The file is awarded an R in the SCM status column and becomes gray.**

Now you need to commit the changes so the file is truly deleted from the repository. You should know the moves by now:

1. **Click the SCM Smart Group in the Project window's Groups & Files view.**

2. **Select the file and the** `project.pbxproj` **file.**

3. **Choose SCM → Commit Changes.**

4. **Fill out the commitment description and click Commit.**

Xcode removes the file from the repository. You've committed the perfect crime. (Or *have* you? Only the SCM system's administrator knows for sure....)

WE CHECK OUT

In this chapter we described what a *source code management* (SCM) system is and provided a few basic terms. We explained how to set up an Xcode project to use SCM technology and described the SCM systems that Xcode supports. We took a look at a project that uses SCM and discussed the subtle but oh-so-important changes that appear in the Project window, listing the special SCM status symbols that can appear beside project files. We also presented the SCM menu in all its beauty and majesty. We used that menu to bring up the SCM Results window, which lets you see the commands Xcode actually sends to the SCM system (as well as what the SCM system sends back), and then showed the SCM Info window for one of the project's files. We showed how to compare files between the copies on your system and those in the SCM system's *repository* (which is a server on which copies of all the versions of the files in your project reside) so you can see their differences, using both the Compare and the Diff commands. We told you about *annotations*, which list all the changes, and who made them, for a file. We demonstrated to you how to update your files so that they match those in the repository, and how to update the files in the repository with your changes (which the jargon meisters call *committing* your changes). And, finally, we fulfilled our commitments to you, dear reader, by describing how to remove files from, and add files to, the repository.

PART VI

Appendixes

Appendix: The Xcode Developer's Diet

The Basic SDKs • Specialized SDKs • New to Tiger

Apple's collection of SDKs (Software Development Kits) is an evergrowing and mutating entity. SDKs come, they evolve, and they go (onto life support, as they're supplanted by newer technologies). As such, any attempt at "complete" coverage and enumeration today is doomed to failure on the morrow. What we list here are just some of the more critical kits and a sampling of the others to give you a taste of what's available. You can find out more about these SDKs and others, as well as how to obtain them, at Apple's developer site, `http://developer.apple.com/sdk`.

THE BASIC SDKS

QuickTime

A big honking collection of interactive media capture and display routines, semi-integrated into the very guts of the OS, and yet independent enough to have been ported to Windows. The SDK is Carbon-based, but it also includes both a Cocoa and a Java set of libraries that provide some (though not all) of the Carbon QuickTime library's functionality. Why the mess? QuickTime is really old, cross-platform, and strives for backward compatibility whenever possible, and the forces of software evolution have made it quite the platypus.

Core Audio

Apple produced this collection of services in order to avoid an incompatible morass of application-specific access to Mac's audio hardware. Using this SDK, hardware developers can develop high-quality audio and MIDI devices and drivers accessible to software developers through a common set of C and Java APIs.

Installer

As software packages became more complex, encompassing myriad files, software developers and users clamored for a consistent interface to make sure that their software got installed properly — that is, with all the pieces in all the right places and, now in the Unixy world of Mac OS X, with the appropriate permissions assigned. Similarly, as the need for bug-fix and enhancement updates increases, sending out tens or hundreds of megabytes for a small change is cost ineffective. The Apple Installer includes both install and upgrade capabilities, while providing a simple-to-use, consistent interface to the customer.

Address Book

OS X's Address Book is a central repository for contact and personal information. Using this SDK allows your application to access Address Book data, just like Mail, iChat, and iCal do.

Web Kit

You see this kit in action whenever you use the Xcode Documentation Viewer. Using Web Kit, your application's windows can access and display Web content and, by including multiple views in a window, you can display multiple frames, each with their own scrollbars (if necessary).

SPECIALIZED SDKS

AppleLoops

With programs like GarageBand, you and your Mac can make beautiful music together. This SDK lets your application create the audio loops that Garage-Band uses.

ColorSync

Scanners, printers, and monitors all employ different color technologies. If achieving color consistency isn't the Holy Grail for publishing (and publishing includes individuals wanting to print their digital photos), it is certainly in contention for the role. ColorSync is Apple's color-management system, and the ColorSync SDK lets device makers register a profile for the hardware they sell and lets application developers go beyond the basics in supporting high-end publishing customers.

iTunes Visual Plug-In

This API collection lets you write Visualizer plug-ins for iTunes (version 1.1 or later). We don't know about you, but one of us finds the built-in Visualizer strangely, and uncomfortably, reminiscent of "acid trip" scenes from 1960s movies (another of us, however, will happily spend hours staring at it instead of working on things like, oh, this book, for example).

iMovie Plug-In

If you want to write your own transitions, titles, and special effects for use with iMovie, this kit gets you onto the studio lot.

Image Capture

This API collection lets you write scanner and camera capture modules and TWAIN data sources.

FireWire

A thoroughly geeky collection of FireWire APIs, development and debugging utilities, and source code.

NEW TO TIGER

Core Image

Put the pedal to the metal when rendering graphics. Core Image harnesses the GPU's power to let you process graphic data faster than ever before.

Spotlight

Tiger's Spotlight search technology makes it easy for users to search their files for anything their little hearts (and minds) desire. This kit puts all of Spotlight's power at your application's beck and call. Additionally, if your application uses a proprietary storage format, you can use this kit's APIs to write your own `.mdimporter` plug-ins (meta-data importer — Apple ships two, for AppleWorks and Keynote, with Tiger).

VoiceOver

Hook into the power of Tiger's VoiceOver technology with this kit, at least for English-language applications (at this time). Make your applications readily accessible to users relying on Universal Access.

Appendix: Avoiding Migrate Headaches

Migrating from CodeWarrior
Migrating Other Kinds of Projects

At certain times of the year, the descendents of dinosaurs take flight and cover vast distances, seeking warmth and an ample food supply. Ornithologists call this process "migration."

At certain times in the life cycle of software, source code takes flight and covers vast conceptual spaces, seeking a new set of tools and a welcoming software environment. Software engineers call this process "migration," too.

Have we pushed the migrating metaphor farther than we should? Of course we have. We simply could have said that this appendix covers how to move your software project from other development environments into Xcode. But where would be the fun in that?

MIGRATING FROM CODEWARRIOR

We both spent part of our youth living in Las Vegas (Dennis much longer than Michael) and we feel comfortable laying heavy odds that if you're moving from another OS X–based integrated development environment into Xcode, that older environment is going to be CodeWarrior. We won't win every bet, but we'll have a larger edge than the house does on the Big Six Wheel or the slots.

Moving your CodeWarrior project into an Xcode project is, essentially, a three-step program (we don't need no steenkin' 12 steps); however, each of those three steps has its own phases.

1. **Prepare your CodeWarrior project for importing.** Depending upon which CodeWarrior version you're using, there are as many as five things you need to do (and as few as none):

   - If you aren't using CodeWarrior Pro 8.3, update your CodeWarrior installation and let it update your project. Importing projects from earlier versions is quite problematic. (The last version we used was CodeWarrior 6 and our four CodeWarrior 6 projects *all* failed to import until we updated.)

   - If you aren't already using Carbon, convert your code to use Carbon rather than the traditional Mac APIs.

   - If you aren't using the Application Package project type in CodeWarrior, choose Application Package from the CodeWarrior PPC Target pane's Project Type pop-up menu. You'll also need to create an Info.plist file when you make this change.

   - If you're creating a CFM (Code Fragment Manager) application or library, you should switch to creating a Mach-o target by changing the Linker setting to Apple Mach-O PowerPC in the Target Settings window's Target pane.

   - Remove any targets that you don't want imported from your CodeWarrior project (or duplicate the project and remove the unnecessary targets from the copy).

2. **Import the CodeWarrior project as follows:**

   a. **Invoke Xcode's project importer by choosing File → Import Project.** The Import Project Assistant (see Figure B-1) appears.

Figure B-1
The Xcode Import Project Assistant

   b. **Select Import CodeWarrior Project and click Next.** The Import CodeWarrior Project pane (see Figure B-2) appears.

   c. **Type the full path to the CodeWarrior project or click the Choose button and navigate to the project.** Xcode will offer the same project name, but with an .xcode extension, as the default name — feel free to specify a different name.

   - The **Import "Global Source Trees" from CodeWarrior** option tells the importer whether to add global source trees identified in your CodeWarrior preferences to Xcode's Source Trees list.

- The **Import referenced projects** option tells the importer to import external referenced projects, renaming them with the same name they had, but with an .xcode extension.

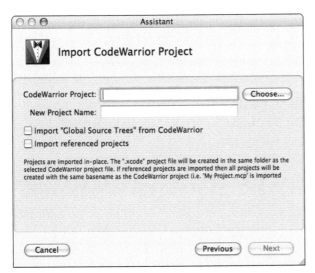

Figure B-2
The Import CodeWarrior Project pane

d. **Click Finish and let the importer start to work.**

The Import Status window keeps you informed of the import's progress and the new project window opens when the import is complete. And what is that process? The importer sends CodeWarrior a series of AppleEvents that tell CodeWarrior to duplicate the project; these events include specifying various settings and performing sundry other operations needed to prepare the duplicate. Next, CodeWarrior is told to export the copy to XML, which the importer will use to create the new Xcode project. *This series of steps can take quite a while, even on a fast Mac!* (You might be asked to choose a language encoding.)

▼ Note

Just because the import was successful doesn't mean that your new Xcode project will build successfully. For example, you might have converted to Mach-o and not switched to 4-byte bools. Check out step 3 for some things you might have to do after the import succeeds.

If CodeWarrior presents an alert at launch in response to the AppleEvent (for example, if it can't find the last project it had open), the import will fail. The old adage, "Try, and try again," holds sway here.

Canceling an import requires quitting and relaunching Xcode before attempting to perform that import, or a different import, again.

3. **Now, the real work begins!** The importer does an excellent job of replicating a CodeWarrior project's structure in the Xcode project, but you're going to have to check (and probably adjust) the project's build settings, in particular its compiler optimization settings. You should now try building your project. Some of the common roadblocks follow:

- You're probably using a different gcc version now — check your compiler settings.

- You might need to add or rename libraries if you're performing a static link, or you might need to specify a prefix file to replace whatever CodeWarrior prefix file you were employing.

- You might need to add some source files or frameworks. Make sure you specify the target(s) requiring the files or frameworks.

- Make any source code changes required by the change in compiler or by the standard libraries that are now in play. This will always be necessary when your CodeWarrior project is PowerPlant-based.

- Make sure you have an `info.plist` file, either by converting the `CodeWarrior.plc` file (if you had one) or creating it from scratch.

The preceding looks like a lot of work — and it can be — but if you programmed "cleanly" in CodeWarrior, you'll usually have a pretty easy go of things.

MIGRATING OTHER KINDS OF PROJECTS

From a user perspective, one of the most satisfying aspects of OS X is the abundance of Unix tools and open source programs that are now available to us (particularly for one of our favorite timesinks — digital video).

We aren't going to deal with building X11 applications and the like, because those aren't Xcode-based efforts and, while you can build command-line tools with Xcode, that really doesn't merit any discussion here — just pick one of the command-line tool templates (like Standard Tool), add your source, and go. However, if you want to add a Mac GUI to your command-line tool, choose a template (the AppleScript Studio template is a really quick way to put an interface on a command-line tool), give your new project a name, and then save it. Now, proceed as follows:

1. **Choose Project ➔ New Target.**

2. **Select either External Target or GNU Make Target from the list that appears, and name the new target.**

3. **Select the new target in your Groups & Files list. The Inspector window displays the target's build information.**

4. **Modify the build settings to include your existing makefile and any other options you might need, such as which build tool to use.**

5. **Create your interface's** `.nib` **file(s).**

6. **Build your project.**

Not much to it, was there?

Index

C

0-7645-7957-6

0-7645-6796-9

There's only one Andy Ihnatko...

0-7645-6797-7

0-7645-7322-5

. . . but fortunately, there's more than one book!
Each loaded with valuable information, color, anecdotes, tidbits, and Andy's distinctive style.

WILEY
Now you know.

wiley.com